THE NEW CHRISTIAN RIGHT

Mobilization and Legitimation

CONTRIBUTORS TO THIS VOLUME

JAMES L. GUTH, *Associate Professor of Political Science, Furman University*

PHILLIP E. HAMMOND, *Professor of Religious Studies and Sociology, University of California, Santa Barbara*

DONALD HEINZ, *Associate Professor and Chair of Religious Studies, California State University, Chico, California*

JEROME L. HIMMELSTEIN, *Assistant Professor of Sociology, Amherst College*

JAMES DAVISON HUNTER, *Assistant Professor of Sociology, University of Virginia*

MARGARET LATUS, *Doctoral Candidate, Princeton University*

ANSON SHUPE, *Associate Director of the Center for Social Research and Associate Professor of Sociology, University of Texas at Arlington*

JOHN H. SIMPSON, *Associate Professor of Sociology, Adjunct Associate Professor of Religious Studies, and Director of the Graduate Centre for Religious Studies, University of Toronto*

WILLIAM STACEY, *Director of the Center for Social Research and Associate Professor of Sociology, University of Texas at Arlington*

THE NEW CHRISTIAN RIGHT

Mobilization and Legitimation

Edited by

ROBERT C. LIEBMAN
ROBERT WUTHNOW

With Contributions by:

James L. Guth
Phillip E. Hammond
Donald Heinz
Jerome L. Himmelstein
James Davison Hunter
Margaret Latus
Anson Shupe
John H. Simpson
William Stacey

 Aldine Publishing Company
New York

ABOUT THE AUTHORS

ROBERT C. LIEBMAN *is Assistant Professor of Sociology at Princeton University. In addition to his work on social movements, he is currently writing a book on labor markets and political protest in 19th century France.*

ROBERT WUTHNOW *is Associate Professor of Sociology at Princeton University. He is author/co-author/editor of* The Conscious Reformation, Experimentation in American Religion, Adolescent Prejudice, *and* The Religious Dimension.

Aldine Publishing Company
200 Saw Mill River Road
Hawthorne, New York 10532

Library of Congress Cataloging in Publication Data

The New Christian right.
  Bibliography: p.
  Includes index.
    1. Evangelicalism—United States—Addresses, essays,
lectures. 2. Moral Majority, Inc.—Addresses, essays,
lectures. 3. Christianity and politics—Addresses,
essays, lectures. I. Liebman, Robert C. II. Wuthnow,
Robert
BR1642.U5N48   1983   322'.1'0973   83–13443
ISBN 0–202–30307–1

Printed in the United States of America

CONTENTS

v

VI/CONCLUSION

INTRODUCTION

Scarcely anyone expected it. For more than 50 years evangelicals kept studiously aloof from American politics. They sang hymns and tended to souls, but left the burdens of legislation and social policy to their more worldly counterparts in the Protestant mainstream. From time to time an occasional voice broke the self-imposed silence—Carl McIntire striking out at the liberal establishment or Billy James Hargis stirring up anti-Communist fears. But these were the exceptions and even fellow fundamentalists tended to regard them with suspicion. Politics was an evil of the flesh, an exercise in futility. Only repentance and salvation could bring genuine renewal. That evangelicals might emerge as a political force seemed dubious at best. They were, by all indications, a declining remnant, destined to survive only by withdrawing from active confrontation with the secular age. Like Prohibition and creationism, evangelicals appeared to be more a vestige of the past than a vital dimension of the present. That their own pastors would lead a political movement seemed out of the question.

The forces which brought about the New Christian Right, as it was dubbed by the media, were an unlikely combination of circumstance and ingenuity. Some of those who were to emerge as its leaders cut their political teeth defending Christian schools they had helped to organize. When local courts and the Internal Revenue Service threatened to undo the tax-exempt status of these schools, fundamentalists began to realize their political vulnerability. Others mobilized in reaction to abortion laws, gay rights bills, and Equal Rights Amendment efforts. For the most part, these were local battles fought out at the county or district levels with little coordination from one battle to the next and virtually no centralized organization. Still others, on a more national scale, found themselves courting power in order to protect and expand vast media empires created with the assistance of television and computer technology. The conjuncture of these developments was largely coincidental. The ingenuity (which came from organizers like Richard Viguerie and Paul Weyrich, who have strong credentials in the secular conservative realm, or Jerry Falwell of the huge Thomas Road Baptist Church in Lynchburg, Virginia) was applied in welding these disparate elements and interests into a coherent national movement.

By far the most successful of these ventures was the Moral Majority, Inc., headed by fundamentalist pastor and television evangelist Jerry Falwell. Combining yellow journalism and firey preaching with the latest in computerized direct mail and video programming, Moral Majority managed to add hundreds of thousands of names to its roll during the first 2 years of its existence, register thousands of potential voters, support lobbying and mass petition campaigns against abortion and pornography, and capture the skeptical fascination of most of the nation's journalists. Moral Majority, however, was but one of several closely interconnected groups that comprised the national nucleus of the New Christian Right. Christian Voice and Religious Roundtable each created effective organizations at the national level and joined with Moral Majority and a variety of secular New Right groups to coordinate legislative battles and to air political issues from a conservative perspective. Behind the scenes, less visible organizations, like the National Christian Action Coalition and Intercessors for America, also waged sustained campaigns on behalf of such issues as freedom for Christian schools, prayer and Bible reading in the public schools, anti-Communism, a constitutional ban on abortions, and tighter restrictions on pornography and homosexuality. Together, these organizations coalesced into a loosely structured movement representing common issues and, for the first time in many decades, provided a political voice that many evangelicals could claim as their own.

Social movements come and go. If the historical record is any indication, the long-range viability of the New Christian Right is highly uncertain. Movements that only a few years ago attracted widespread attention, such as the Black Panther Party, the Weather Underground, or the Symbionese Liberation Army, are now virtually forgotten; while earlier movements, like Moral Rearmament or the Know-Nothing Party, seem distant and unimportant. From sheer indifference and the onslaught of ever-changing political climates, or from success in attaining goals and loss of their *raison d'etre,* most political movements have been little more than a glimmer in the long sweep of history.

The significance of a social movement cannot be captured in either the size of its membership or the longevity of its existence, however. Despite their ephemerality, social and political movements have had a decisive impact on the ways contemporaries in every period have understood the conditions of their existence, and on the memories with which later generations form impressions of these periods. It is not without importance that social movements have been called the stuff of which history is made. In this, the New Christian Right is no exception. Its significance goes well beyond whatever measurable effect it may have had, or may yet have, in influencing legislation and social programs.

Any political movement that attracts a broad national constituency raises profound questions about the underlying cultural and political tensions that have combined to produce its attractiveness. When the McCarthy movement erupted in the early 1950's, questions immediately arose concerning the international tensions that had inspired it. Some of the best social commentaries on the period, including analyses of the Cold War, of the fears spawned by the nuclear age, and of the changing fortunes in the American economy, were written with an eye toward understanding that movement. Similarly, the youth movement of the late 1960's and early 1970's (the "counterculture") provoked troubling questions about the sources of alienation among America's young people and the broader social strains contributing to this unrest. So, too, with the New Christian Right. Beyond whatever impact it may have had in the political arena, it is a symbol of change, a symbol that expresses something deeper about American culture. To some, it represents the last gasp of a dying age, an age when small businessmen and farmers from the towns and villages dotting the American South and Midwest were predominant in national politics. To others, it indicates that traditional values of decency and morality cannot be neglected in national life, and that the strength of America can be revitalized only by reincorporating them into the public sphere. In both of these views the New Christian Right is significant not so much because it may itself shape the future of America, but because it demonstrates the presence of unrest in the populace at large. What this unrest consists of and in what parts of the society it resides constitute significant questions.

Any movement utilizing organizational tactics with the apparent effectiveness of the New Christian Right also provides an important model for observing the secrets of political mobilization. The Christian Right did not appear simply because there were masses of individuals with fears and political ambitions. It emerged because there was an effective leadership, a network of dedicated persons with organizational talents and financial resources at their disposal. These leaders had organizational models firmly in mind from previous encounters with state and local politics and, perhaps more importantly, from politics within their own churches and denominations. In addition, they relied on up-to-date methods of computerized direct mail solicitation, fund raising, mass media publicity, political organization, and targeted lobbying. These technologies were deployed in the context of campaign laws and lobbying regulations virtually new to American politics. How these technologies worked, what tactics were used by various groups, why they adopted particular organizational forms, and the manner in which these forms were influenced by broader conditions represent a second set of important questions raised by the emergence of the New Christian Right.

Third, movements that come largely without warning or anticipation inevitably challenge conventional wisdom about the groups involved. The New Christian Right's appearance in American politics was particularly significant because it challenged many of the prevailing assumptions about American evangelicals and, indeed, about American politics in general. Had it been organized by groups with a long history of political involvement, only the timing of its occurrence might have been notable. But the fact that evangelicals had refrained from politics for so long meant that its appearance was something truly exceptional. Many of the most respected theories about the relations between religious convictions and politics, such as the assumption that fundamentalist convictions were too otherworldly to countenance political involvement, had been supported by evangelicals' political abstinence. When abstinence yielded to political action, at least for a substantial segment of evangelicals, the theories themselves required reexamination. Similarly, many of the most widely accepted theories of political movements relied on a rather selective examination of conservative movements before and immediately following World War II to argue that conservatism was a temporary aberration in American politics, brought on by discontents arising from American internationalism and its new economic order. The liberal movements of the 1960's appeared to demonstrate a return to the mainstream of American political culture and lent support to the argument. That the New Christian

Right could have wide appeal in a dramatically different cultural and economic context called these theories into question. Therefore, whether the conventional wisdom on these issues remains satisfactory or whether it needs serious rethinking is a third question of considerable importance.

Finally, whenever political movements are inspired by broad-based religious sentiment, the possibility of serious long-run social transformation cannot be ruled out. Such has been the case repeatedly in American history. Before the War of Independence, the Great Awakening and the influence of the Scottish Enlightenment combined to produce what historians have described as a decisive coalition between the seaboard elite and rural frontier, a coalition without which the movement for independence itself would likely have failed. During the nineteenth century, too, the influence of an evangelical revival contributed significantly to the solidification of the Jacksonian reforms, the birth and success of the abolition movement, and vast efforts to reform the morality of industrializing America. Whether religion can again inspire political transformation of this magnitude must be assessed in light of the greater secularity of the culture at large in the twentieth century and against the high degree of bureaucratization characteristic of both government and the private sector. Nevertheless, the second half of the twentieth century has not been without examples of religiously inspired political movements in other industrial and industrializing countries, as events in Northern Ireland, Poland, Iran, and Latin America have illustrated. Nor have such movements been entirely absent from the American context itself, as evidenced by the civil-rights movement and even by the frequent links between political protest and nontraditional religious groups of the late 1960's. Specific groups, such as Moral Majority or Christian Voice, may be as ephemeral as SNCC, SDS, or the movements symbolized by a variety of other half-forgotten acronyms; yet, the larger ferment, the debate, and the grassroots activity inspired by these groups may have consequences of wide-ranging importance.

These are the questions with which the essays in this volume are concerned. While much has been written in a journalistic vein about the New Christian Right, scholarly analysis based on systematic and, to the extent that impartiality is possible, unbiased examination of evidence has been virtually absent. These essays, collectively and often singly, attempt to describe the main dimensions of the New Christian Right and to provide explanations for its emergence and the forms it has taken by relating evidence to bodies of theoretical literature in the social sciences.

As is the case in most areas of scholarly debate, there are a variety of competing perspectives in which the New Christian Right can be interpreted. As editors, we have not sought to weed out perspectives which differed from our own or which have been at odds with one another in the published literature. Upon close examination many of these debates turn on subtle points of style and preference, and together they illuminate a variety of different issues. The reader will discover, therefore, that several of the authors argue strongly that ideology, for example, played a critical role in the formation of the New Christian Right, while others largely deny the importance of ideology. Or for another example, several of the chapters draw on theories from the 1950's to argue that the Christian Right stems from declining social status and threatened life styles among its adherents, while other chapters argue against this interpretation in order to highlight the importance of organizational resources. This, we believe, is how it should be, since the various perspectives cast light on different aspects of the movement.

All of the chapters in this volume are previously unpublished. Our criteria for selecting chapters were essentially two: first, to include only the finest while omitting ones of less substantial quality; and second, to represent the main aspects of the New Christian Right that our own research and that of our colleagues indicated were important. To this end, chapters were solicited from scholars in a number of different disciplines, including sociology, political science, and religious studies, all of who were engaged in research projects of their own concerning various facets of the New Christian Right.

The chapters are grouped into five sections which examine the organization of the New Christian Right and the broader set of circumstances which served as the movement's environment. Two introductory chapters present an overview of the New Christian Right. The following three sections explore the forms of its mobilization, the character of its constituency, and the major tenets of its ideology. The final section evaluates the cultural environment in which the movement emerged.

The New Christian Right appeared in the context of a larger conservative movement known as the New Right. The structure and ideology of the New Right is the subject of Jerome Himmelstein's chapter which charts the intellectual currents that characterize contemporary American conservatism. He finds their source in the conservative reaction to statism and social intervention which dates to the New Deal. By combining the ideological themes of economic libertarianism, social traditionalism, and militant anti-Communism with an organizational strategy featuring extensive networking, independent political initiatives such as political action committees, and an aggressive direct mail campaign, the New Right courts a growing constituency of corporate conservatives and Americans worried about the nation's perceived economic and moral decline. The analysis suggests that what is new about the New Right is not its ideology, but its strategy of establishing linkages among a variety of conservative constituencies. The New Christian Right is an important member of the alliance.

While the New Christian Right made common cause with the secular New Right on many issues, its roots lay elsewhere. In his examination of the three major organizations of the New Christian Right—Christian Voice, Religious Roundtable, and Moral Majority—James Guth demonstrates their mobilization around religious institutions. While these groups adopted different tactics and targeted different constituencies, they shared a common concern with the penetration of civil authorities into the lives of believers and their institutions, especially Christian schools and the electronic church. Guth suggests that regardless of its impact on secular politics, the New Christian Right promises to influence the politics and policies of major Protestant denominations.

The chapters in Section II examine the mobilization of the New Christian Right. Of the major evangelical groups, none has been more successful in mobilizing conservative Christians than Moral Majority. Robert Liebman's chapter compares the careers of four major movement organizations in order to discern the factors responsible for Moral Majority's success. What distinguished Moral Majority was its access to a national network of fundamentalists united by a common fellowship, a commitment to building great churches and Christian schools, and prior experience in fundamentalist political crusades. By incorporating this group, Moral Majority inherited the strong traditions of local autonomy and pastoral authority characteristic of fundamentalist churches.

The interplay of strategy and ideology is the theme of Margaret Latus' analysis of political action committees. Ideological and issue-oriented PACs have sparked a wave of criticism from political observers alarmed by their use of independent expenditures and negative campaigning. While some observers saw a close connection between issues and tactics, Latus' study of nine ideological PACs suggests that multiple and single issue groups differ more sharply in strategy than groups on opposing sides of the liberal/conservative divide. More than its ideology, the influence of sponsoring organizations and the character of its constituency determine the choice of tactics by PACs.

The constituency of the New Christian Right has been the subject of considerable speculation. The movement's leadership made bold claims about the size and diversity of their following and the strength of their mandate from conservative Americans. Drawing on original surveys, the chapters in Section III evaluate support for Moral Majority among laypersons and clergy.

A survey of the Dallas-Fort Worth Metroplex conducted by Anson

Shupe and William Stacey confirms the results of several national polls that find limited support for Moral Majority. Their analysis reveals that its strongest supporters came from the ranks of fundamentalists, especially those who were regular viewers of the Electronic church. Not surprisingly, Moral Majority supporters were also much more likely than nonsupporters to believe that religion should play a role in politics.

James Guth's national survey of Southern Baptist clergy provides parallels with the character of Moral Majority support among the laity. Members of the nation's largest Protestant denomination, Southern Baptists are evangelical and largely Southern, two factors which would appear to make them prime candidates for recruitment by the Moral Majority. However, only a handful identify themselves as members. The proportion of opponents is roughly equal to the proportion of sympathizers and adherents. Guth finds that support for Moral Majority is strongest among ministers at the margins of the Southern Baptist Convention: those with farm backgrounds, modest educational accomplishments, and the least involvement in the activities of the Convention.

Social movements are known as much by their choice of foes as by the friends they keep. Their rhetoric is often two-pronged, at one and the same time, railing against their enemies and rallying their supporters. The chapters in Section IV examine the ideology of the New Christian Right through the perspective of countermovements. Both emphasize the central role of symbols in the program of social movements.

Donald Heinz interprets the New Christian Right as a countermovement locked in battle with secular humanists and liberal Christians for the control of major symbols. Television, schools, and the family are the major sources of conflict. Each represents an important symbol and provides the means of access to symbol production for which the New Christian Right is contending.

James Hunter examines the liberal reaction to the New Christian Right. Grounded in different values, assumptions, and interests, the liberal counterattack portrays the New Christian Right as absolutist, intolerant, and antidemocratic. But as Hunter shows, the liberal complaint is fraught with irony. In its efforts to countermobilize the liberal community, it employs the same formula of simplification, distortion, and manipulation for which it faults the New Christian Right. Each side attempts to monopolize the symbols of legitimacy at the expense of its opponent.

While they stand worlds apart in inspiration and ideology, both the New Christian Right and the liberal reaction reflect the contradictory imperatives of American society. Social movements are shaped by the cultural environment from which they emerge. The three essays in Section V examine the roles of religion, morality, and politics in the rise of the New Christian Right.

Robert Wuthnow's chapter addresses the forces responsible for the politicization of American evangelicals. For decades, evangelicals preferred the duties of personal piety and proselytizing to the uncertainties of political life. In the 1970's a number of symbolic events brought a decisive shift in the priorities of public life for evangelicals and other Americans. The Carter presidency increased public recognition of evangelicals and provided a strong sense of legitimacy. At the same time, episodes such as Watergate and the Supreme Court decision on abortion, rearranged the symbolic boundaries among religion, morality, and politics within the larger society. The politicizing of evangelicals suggests that religious ideologies are dynamic systems responsive to changes in the cultural climate.

Using national survey data, John Simpson assesses the attitudes of Americans toward the socio-moral program of the Moral Majority. While there is no "moral majority" in America, a substantial proportion of Americans oppose abortion and homosexuality and favor school prayer and traditional women's roles. Simpson suggests that support for the Moral Majority platform is strongest among devalued groups seeking to enhance their sociopolitical position. Threatened by the secularization of American society, evangelicals and fundamentalists turned to political action in their strivings for power and prestige.

Like a fire spotter, Phillip Hammond sets his sights on the New Christian Right as a sign of a possible religious revival in American life. To estimate the size of the conflagration, he draws a parallel with Tocqueville's description of the Great Awakening in nineteenth century America. While the current fervor signals deep shifts in American religious life, Hammond concludes that the appearance of the New Christian Right does not bode another Great Awakening.

What can be learned from studying the New Christian Right? Each of the essays draws on original research to suggest much that is new about the New Christian Right. As a group, however, the essays speak to old questions about the character of social movements and the nature of American life. It is the concern with these larger questions that makes the study of any particular social movement valuable to scholars and general readers. The concluding chapter examines the forces that were responsible for forming the New Christian Right and considers their implications for the study of social movements.

I The Movement

1 THE NEW RIGHT

Jerome L. Himmelstein

The New Christian Right has appeared in the context of a broader conservative political movement that calls itself the "New Right." Our study of evangelical Christians in politics, therefore, appropriately begins by examining that broader movement.

As a first approximation, the New Right consists of the network of activists, organizations, and constituencies that have been the most militant opponents of the Equal Rights Amendment, the Panama Canal Treaty, SALT II, affirmative action, federal social programs, and government regulation of business; the most vocal critics of liberalism and "secular humanism"; and the most ardent proponents of the Human Life Amendment, the Family Protection Act, increased defense spending, prayer in public schools, and the teaching of "scientific creationism."

This network of right-wing activity can be divided into three levels: (1) the core activists and their coordinating organizations, who are responsible for welding the New Right into a coherent coalition; (2) the various single-issue and religious groups that constitute the various parts of that coalition; and (3) the constituency that the core activists of the New Right have sought to mobilize.

The most important among the core activists and their respective organizations as of early 1982 were: Richard Viguerie and his direct mail company, Senator Jesse Helms and the Congressional Club, Paul Weyrich and the Committee for the Survival of a Free Congress, Howard Phillips and The Conservative Caucus, and John T. Dolan and the National Conservative Political Action Committee. Other figures on the New Right, such as antifeminist leader Phyllis Schlafly or Moral Majority head Jerry Falwell, perhaps were better known; but these five core activists were central to building and maintaining the network that embraces Schlafly, Falwell, and many others in a broader coalition.

The single-issue groups the core activists have sought to tie together include such antiabortion groups as the National Right to Life Committee, the National Pro-Life Political Action Committee, the Life Amendment Political Action Committee, and the American Life Lobby; such antigun control groups as the Citizen's Committee for the Right to Keep and Bear Arms and Gun Owners of America; such antifeminist groups as Stop ERA and the Eagle Forum; such anti-pornography groups as the National Federation for Decency and the Coalition for Better Television; and the antiunion National Right to Work Committee. The major New Right religious groups include the Moral Majority, the Christian Voice, and the Religious Roundtable.[1]

Through these single-issue and religious groups, the core activists of the New Right have tried to appeal to a broad constituency—virtually

---

[1] The list of groups embraced by the New Right seems endless. One can add to those already mentioned: Accuracy in Media, Allied Educational Foundation, American Association of Christian Schools, American Legislative Exchange Council, American Christian Cause, American Security Council, Americans for Life, Americans United for Life, American Conservative Union, Black Silent Majority, Concerned Women for America, Council for a Competitive Economy, Christian Women's National Concerns, Council for National Policy, Christian Family Renewal, Conservatives Against Liberal Legislation, Christian Coalition for Legislative Action, Citizens for Constructive Education, Committee for Responsible Youth Politics, Coalitions for America, Center on National Labor Policy, Citizens for Educational Freedom, Citizens for the Republic, Coalition for Freedom, Coalition for Peace Through Strength, Council on Inter-American Security, Conservative Victory Foundation, Consumer Alert Foundation, Education Research Institute, Family, Life, America Under God, Family Life Seminars, Family Protection Lobby, Family America, Heritage Foundation, Intercollegiate Studies Institute, Intercessors for America, Leadership Action, Life Advocates, Leadership Institute, March for Life, National Association of Pro-America, National Christian Action Coalition, National Defeat Legal Services Committee, National Journalism Center, National Pro-family Coalition, National Rifle Association, National Tax Limitation Committee, National Taxpayers Union, Pacific Legal Foundation, Project Prayer, Public Service Research Council, Pro-family Forum, Pro-family United, Second Amendment Foundation, U.S. Coalition for Life, United Council on Welfare Fraud, United Families of America, Washington Legal Foundation, Young Americans for Freedom.

anyone who agrees with them on any of a wide range of "social" issues (antiabortion, anti-ERA, antigun control, pro-school prayer, etc.) or who is generally concerned about social breakdown and moral decay in American society. They have focused especially on evangelical Christians.

The literal newness of the New Right in a historical sense is best indicated by the fact that its core activists were largely unknown until a few years ago. Jesse Helms, long a right-wing radio and television commentator in North Carolina, won election to the Senate in 1972 and in 1973 founded the Congressional Club with the help of Richard Viguerie. Viguerie himself had been doing mail fund raising for conservatives since 1965, and hit the big time in 1973 when he was hired to retire George Wallace's 1972 campaign debts. He raised $7 million for Wallace in the next 3 years and came away with several million new names for his mailing list. Weyrich, Dolan, and Phillips founded their respective organizations in 1974 and 1975 (Viguerie, 1980; Drew, 1981; Range, 1981a and 1981b; Clymer, 1981b). Indeed, the New Right is such a recent development that of the 23 United States Senators identified as allies in the November 1980 *Conservative Digest,* only three had been in the Senate before 1972—Barry Goldwater, Strom Thurmond, and John Tower.

IDEOLOGY

The New Right does not speak one consistent language; its *ideology* is not one uniform body of principles and concepts applied evenly to all issues, but rather a conjunction of three distinct sets of themes invoked with regard to three different areas of concern. We may call these sets of themes *economic libertarianism, social traditionalism,* and *militant anticommunism.* Their combination is neither historically inevitable nor logically necessary. They do not "obviously" belong together, but are a historically specific combination that is fraught with potential contradictions.

Economic Libertarianism is concerned with the economic problems of contemporary American society: inflation, unemployment, a sagging economy, lagging productivity, and high taxes and interest rates. These problems are approached with the assumption that left to itself economic interaction between rationally self-interested individuals in the market will spontaneously yield broad prosperity, social harmony, and all other manner of public and private good. Accordingly, blame for economic problems is placed on such interferences with the natural working of the market as government spending on social problems, government regulation of business, and unions. The liberalism that is perceived to be at the root of these interferences is also condemned.

The central themes in the New Right's economic libertarianism are specific notions of *freedom* and *individualism*. "What unites most conservatives," Richard Viguerie wrote, "is a desire for less government and more freedom for every American" and a belief in the "American Dream" of "each person reaching as high and going as far as his ability and ambition will take him" (1980, pp. 131, 132). A March 1981 *Conservative Digest* article on the National Right to Work Committee put the case against the union shop ("compulsory unionism") in terms of its restriction of "freedom of choice for millions of American workers." Another article in the same issue publicized the work of the Council for a Competitive Economy, an organization "determined to put the 'free' back into a free economy."

The New Right, then, conceptualizes freedom and individualism largely in terms of the right to pursue one's interests in a market context unhampered by external interference. Underlying this is an image of society as simply an aggregate of self-contained individuals held together by the natural meshing of their respective interests. From this perspective, the individual pursuit of self-interest is not a threat to the social bond, but its very basis.

The *Social Traditionalism* of the New Right is generally concerned with what is seen as the breakdown of family, community, religion, and traditional morality in American life. Abortion, the Equal Rights Amendment, busing, affirmative action, sexual permissiveness, drugs, prohibitions on school prayer, the secular curriculum in public schools, and many similar things are opposed on the grounds that they contribute to this process of social breakdown and moral decay. The spread of secular, materialist, and humanist values ("secular humanism") that deny the existence of God and the importance of nonmaterial goals is also resisted. Blame for much of this is placed on liberals operating through the federal government. In this view, the government has undermined family, religion, and morality through such diverse actions (and inactions) as Internal Revenue Service cases against Christian private schools, the failure to crack down on pornography, support for abortion and ERA, advocacy of lenient drug laws, opposition to prayer in public school, and by generally encouraging a secular humanist outlook. What characterizes the New Right's social traditionalism, in short, is the belief that America is in the midst of a spiritual crisis coupled with the conviction that the cause of this crisis is simply the application by the federal government of liberal ideas and policies.

Among the themes of social traditionalism are *community* and *restraint*.

Society is pictured as a web of shared values and integrating institutions that bind individuals together and restrain their otherwise selfish, destructive drives. It appears, in other words, to be more than a mere collection of rationally self-interested individuals.

The final component of New Right ideology is *Militant Anticommunism*, which focuses on the issue of national security. According to this view, the United States and Western civilization itself are in a life-or-death struggle with the menacing aggressive forces of the Soviet Union and world communism. Success in this struggle, however, has been hampered by insufficient defense spending and "foreign policies of appeasement, retreat, and accommodation" (Viguerie 1980, p. 5). Blame is thus placed on liberal defense and foreign policies (in some cases reaching back to the late 1940's), that appear to be the only things keeping communism in power.

In other words, underlying the New Right's anticommunism are three assumptions of McCarthyite vintage: first, that the conflict between the West and communism is one between unalloyed good and unalloyed evil; second, that communism establishes and maintains itself only by force of arms; and third, that only a liberal lack of will has prevented the United States from using its superior resources to utterly defeat communism. Accordingly, the New Right advocates greatly stepped up military spending and the abandonment of détente in favor of a major ideological and political mobilization aimed at containing and rolling back the forces of communism. The theme of *total mobilization* against a deadly enemy is central to the New Right's militant anticommunism.

The New Right, then, invokes different themes in regard to its different areas of concern, speaking of freedom and individualism on economic matters, restraint and community on social matters, and total mobilization on national security matters. Nonetheless, a clear unity underlies these differences. The New Right identifies the same enemy within each area of concern; economic, social, and national security problems equally are blamed on liberals operating through the federal government. The economy would be fine if liberals hadn't enacted social welfare and regulatory programs; the family would be sound if liberals had not promoted alternative lifestyles; and the USSR would pose no threat to American security if liberals hadn't hobbled defense spending. The New Right also believes that its economic, social, and national security concerns are causally related; economic stagnation, moral decline, and military weakness reinforce each other and equally reflect a loss of national greatness.

Despite the underlying unity, however, New Right ideology remains fraught with tensions and contradictions. Its economic libertarianism and social traditionalism, for example, are based on some apparently inconsistent assumptions. The libertarian notions of individualism and freedom picture society as nothing more than an aggregate of individuals that will work admirably well if these individuals are left free to pursue their own interests. Libertarianism takes an optimistic view of human drives and a dim view of any effort to restrain those drives. Social traditionalism, in contrast, regards society as a web of values and institutions that transcends individuals and binds them together. It fears untrammeled human drives and stresses the importance of societal restraints. If economic libertarianism stresses the dangers of too much restraint on the individual, social traditionalism stresses the danger of too little. Similarly, while economic libertarianism is comfortable with self-oriented, materialist values, social traditionalism regards such values as dangerous and corrosive of the social bond.

HISTORICAL ROOTS

The New Right's ideological combination of economic libertarianism, social traditionalism, and militant anticommunism has clearly historical roots; it is the characteristic mode of thought of American conservativism that has developed since 1945. As George Nash notes in his comprehensive history of the "conservative intellectual movement in America," as of 1945 "no articulate, coordinated, self-consciously conservative intellectual force existed in the United States" (1979, p. xvi). The movement that subsequently emerged was the intellectual component of the delayed right-wing Republican reaction to the New Deal, which surfaced in the early 1950s and found political expression in McCarthyism (Rossiter, 1962; Miles, 1980).[2]

The cornerstone of this emerging conservatism was the conviction that the United States and Western civilization were threatened by a growing tide of what was termed statism, collectivism, or rationalism—the trend toward centralization of power in the state and the use of that power to reorganize and plan social life in a systematic, self-conscious way. In the conservative view, fascism, communism, social democracy, and the New Deal were merely different versions of this same trend—some more benign than others (Meyer, 1970).

[2] The right of this intellectual reaction to the New Deal to call itself conservative has been challenged by an unending line of critics (Rossiter, 1962; Viereck, 1962; Guttman, 1967; Lora, 1971; Wills, 1979), who have provoked an unending line of defenders of that right (see Nash, 1979). I should like to sidestep that debate. In referring to this intellectual movement as conservative, I am merely following a more or less widely accepted usage. I am not passing judgment on whether or not it is conservative in some transcendent sense, or whether or not it is in keeping with the tradition of Edmund Burke and other exemplars of past conservatisms.

American conservatism developed from this core belief as an often unsteady synthesis of three intellectual tendencies: a libertarianism "apprehensive about the threat of the state to private enterprise and individualism"; a traditionalism (or new conservatism) "appalled by the erosion of values and the emergence of a secular, rootless, mass society"; and a militant anticommunism rooted in the "profound conviction that the West was engaged in a titanic struggle with an implacable adversary—Communism—which sought nothing less than the conquest of the world" (Nash, 1979, pp. xvi, 131).

This synthesis has been uneasy, and differences between the three tendencies have often erupted in acrimonious debate in the pages of conservative journals. Some libertarians have regarded the traditionalist emphasis on restraint and its suspicion of individualism as one more kind of collectivism; others have mistrusted the militarist mentality of anticommunism. Traditionalists have sometimes viewed libertarianism as one more example of corrosive materialist, secular thought. Discussion of the relationship between libertarianism and traditionalism continues.[3]

Despite the continuing intellectual contention, American conservatism slowly consolidated itself in the 1950's and early 1960's into a distinct intellectual world. Conservatives developed or adopted common forums for ideas (*National Review, Human Events, Modern Age*), political action groups (the American Conservative Union), and organizations to educate a new generation (the Intercollegiate Studies Institute, the Young Americans for Freedom). Although they did not reach an intellectual consensus, they developed a common focus of disagreement and debate—a position called "fusionism," developed by Frank Meyer (1970) in an effort to synthesize libertarianism and traditionalism. When all common intellectual ground seemed to slip away, moreover, conservatives could at least point to agreement on practical issues and to shared enemies (Buckley, 1970, pp. xv–liv; Hart, 1966). Finally the conservative world developed relatively clear boundaries separating those who belonged from those who did not. The precise intellectual justification may not have been always clear or unanimously accepted, but libertarians who were too militantly secular (e.g., Ayn Rand) or antimilitarist (e.g., those who opposed American involvement in Vietnam and left the Young Americans for Freedom to form the Libertarian Party) and traditionalists who found the New Deal quite consistent with conservative principles (e.g., Peter Viereck) found themselves unambiguously beyond the pale.

During the past 20 years, the conservative intellectual movement has grown slowly, developing an expanding cadre of intellectuals and a grow-

[3] See Nash, 1979, pp. 154–185, 308–319; *Intercollegiate Studies Institute Campus Report*, Spring 1981, pp. 5, 11; and *Modern Age*, Fall 1980, **24**(1).

ing network of journals, research institutes, and political organizations. It allied itself closely with the Goldwater campaign of 1964, and while standing aloof from both Wallace and Nixon, it fed on the same mass of political reaction to civil rights, the antiwar movement and the counterculture, feminism, environmentalism, and other progressive movements of the late 1960's and the 1970's. Its research institutes have been underwritten by contributions from the more conservative capitalist foundations, including the J. Howard Pew Freedom Trust, the John M. Olin Foundation, the Adolph Coors Foundation, the Smith Richardson Foundation, and the various Scaife family trusts (Rothmyer, 1981; Weinraub, 1981). It has been strengthened by partial alliances with "neo-conservatives" like Irving Kristol and Norman Podhoretz (Steinfels, 1980; Tonsor, 1977).

The New Right is simply one effort to bring elements of this growing conservative movement together into an effective, autonomous political organization. Its debt to previous American conservatism is quite explicit. In his semiofficial history of the New Right, Richard Viguerie (1980, pp. 39, 11) clearly rooted the movement in American conservatism: he credited William F. Buckley, Jr. (editor of *National Review*) and Barry Goldwater as the "two men more responsible than any other for the strength and vitality of conservatism in America today"; for a definition of conservatism, he turned to the fusionism of Frank Meyer; he also invoked such other conservative luminaries as traditionalist Russell Kirk, libertarian Frank Chodorov, and anticommunist Whittaker Chambers. Buckley and Goldwater, moreover, received high ratings from the readers of *Conservative Digest* in that journal's August 1981 poll of the most admired conservative leaders. Buckley returned the compliment, praising the New Right as the "front-line troops of the conservative movement" and as "brilliant technicians" who had created "the kind of lobbying pressure we haven't seen in years" (*Human Events,* March 7, 1981).[4]

These continuities between the New Right of today and the American conservatism of the 1950's and 1960's call into question the claim of Crawford (1980), Lemann (1981), and others that the New Right repre-

----

[4] Goldwater, however, has been less friendly. Especially since the New Right opposed the nomination of fellow Arizonan Sandra Day O'Connor to the United States Supreme Court, Goldwater has thundered against his conservative fellows. (See *New York Times,* September 16, 1981.) Goldwater's antagonism to the New Right, moreover, goes back to some angry exchanges in 1976, during which the New Right accused Goldwater of being an ineffective leader for the conservative cause (*Conservative Digest,* August and September 1976). There is less here than meets the eye, however; none of the nastiness betokens any major ideological split within American conservatism. If anything, Goldwater seems to have separated himself from the conservative community over the O'Connor nomination, which drew almost universal criticism from conservatives. His broadside drew sharp condemnation from the conservative journal *Human Events* (August 15, 1981).

sents a sharp break with an older Right or that American conservatism has undergone some major transformation in recent years that has all but turned it inside out. According to this argument, the ideology and program of the New Right have been distinctly *un*conservative. The New Right has been too eager to reject established elites and institutions, too neglectful of historical continuity, too enthusiastic about the free market, and too immersed in an individualistic frontier psychology. Far from being conservative, Crawford argues, it has been "neo-populist," an inverted continuation of the tradition of American agrarian radicalism. The recurrent tensions between New Right organizations and older conservative groups in the mid-1970's simply reflected these deeper differences.

This argument is fundamentally flawed. The worldview of American conservatism as represented by the New Right today has not changed in three decades, and the one-time organizational conflicts between the New Right and older conservative groups were largely over tactics and turf, not ideology and goals. In other words, the New Right differs from the Old Right largely on matters of organizational strategy, not ideology. The ideological disparity described by Crawford exists not between the New Right and previous American conservatism, but between post-1945 American conservatism as a whole (New and Old Right) and an ideal image of conservatism that has not been realized in the United States for a long time, if at all. Indeed, Crawford's characterization of the New Right as "neo-populist" merely echoes the similar charge made 20 years ago that the New Right's conservative forebears also were not true conservatives, but a species of "right-wing radicalism" (see Bell, 1963).[5]

THE NEW RIGHT, CONSERVATISM, AND AMERICAN CULTURE

The New Right's combination of economic libertarianism and social traditionalism, its worship of the market, economic growth, and limitless individual striving in the economic sphere coupled with its emphasis on spiritual values, restraints on individual drives, and the evils of material-

---

[5] Conservatives themselves have not been receptive to the "transformation thesis" with its implicit denial of the New Right's conservative credentials. Consider the response to Alan Crawford's *Thunder on the Right*, the main statement of the thesis. Crawford, who once worked for both Young Americans for Freedom and *Conservative Digest*, expounded his ideas not in conservative journals, but left-liberal ones like *The Nation* ("Fission on the Right," January 29, 1977) and *Social Policy* ("Right-wing Populism," May/June, 1980). His condemnation of the New Right as unconservative, moreover, drew no agreement from conservatives. Even the staid, traditionalist *Modern Age* rejected Crawford's analysis and ratified the conservative credentials of the New Right. [See George W. Carey, "Thunder on the Right, Lightning on the Left," Spring 1981, **25**(2), 132–142.]

ism in the social sphere represents what Clinton Rossiter once called "the paradox known as American conservatism" (1962, p. 206). Indeed, this paradoxical combination is the central feature of contemporary New Right ideology as much as of American conservatism as a whole. We can see this paradox clearly in the speeches of Ronald Reagan, who partakes of American conservative ideology although his relationship to the New Right is ambiguous: the deft combination of an appeal to a stable social world of established community, shared values, and moral restraints with an evocation of a wide-open, ever-growing economic world where the possibilities for individual expression and fulfillment are endless.

We might well expect that such a paradox would limit the political appeal of American conservatism. In fact, however, the opposite is more nearly true. The irony of the New Right (and of American conservatism) is that its paradoxical combination of libertarianism and traditionalism is precisely the key to its ideological appeal. Neither pure traditionalism nor pure libertarianism carries much weight on its own in American culture, while a combination of the two, however paradoxical, speaks to some deeply rooted cultural themes.

Pure traditionalism, which emphasizes the dangers of material progress, the limits of human nature, and the corrosiveness of individualism, materialism, and secularism, does not have much appeal, because it conflicts too clearly with the general orientation of American culture to economic growth and material success as well as with that culture's fundamental optimism about progress and human perfectability. Such traditionalism flourished in Europe in the aftermath of the industrial and French revolutions, but as Louis Hartz (1955) and others have noted, never established itself on these shores. Any history of traditionalist conservatism in America, whether sympathetic [Kirk, (1953) 1978], mildly standoffish (Rossiter, 1962), or downright critical (Guttmann, 1967; Lora, 1971), reveals not an ongoing tradition of thought and sentiment, but isolated, disconnected pockets of resistance to and alienation from the mainstream of American culture.

At the same time, pure libertarianism, stressing materialism, secularism, and pure individual self-interest, also has limited success, although it is a recurrent strand in American culture. The current embodiment of this ideology, the Libertarian Party, failed to get 1% of the vote in the 1980 elections despite a well-financed campaign. The problem with libertarianism is that although it validates worldly individualism, it does so in terms that are too secular and too atomistic. The most potent justifications for the orientation to economic growth and material success within American culture have been those that imbue this orientation with broader religious meaning—something in keeping with Max Weber's analysis of the Protestant Ethic, of course—and that embued it within a world of stable social relationships and community.

In contrast, if American conservatism has flourished it is because its combination of traditionalism and libertarianism overcomes the problems of each standing alone. American conservative ideology captures the libertarian emphasis on material progress and individual success, but envelopes these within an appeal to divine providence, transcendent values, and collective social bonds. At the same time, it adopts the traditionalist concern with social stability and spiritual values without the otherworldliness and the pessimism about progress and human nature.

In this way, contemporary American conservatism affirms both God and capitalism, both social stability and economic ferment. Each combination speaks strongly to important abiding cultural themes. The first resonates with the strong residue of the Protestant Ethic in American culture, which sees the pursuit of economic growth and worldly success as divinely inspired and sanctioned. The preference of American conservatism for a religious, rather than a secular, justification of capitalism is reflected most clearly in George Gilder's *Wealth and Poverty* (1981), a book much favored by the New Right and treated as a veritable bible by the Reagan Administration. Gilder's work eschews the standard arguments that justify capitalism merely as technically efficient and materially productive in favor of a broader argument that capitalism is also built upon transcendent moral values and divine inspiration.

The second combination, social stability and economic ferment, fits with American culture's optimistic belief that economic growth, technological innovation, the expansion of capitalist enterprise, and the ever-widening individual search for success can somehow proceed without any unsettling of or change in social institutions or culture; in other words, one can combine unbridled economic growth with unqualified social stability. We can see this belief at work in American culture as early as the 1830's in attitudes toward rural life, industry, technology, and capitalism. Thus, Americans of the middle nineteenth century could idealize the agrarian republic and the self-sufficient yeoman while actively promoting the market and production for profit. They could laud the idea of pastoral happiness, yet be remarkably open to all manner of new technology and industry. They saw no contradiction between the values and institutions of small-scale rural life and the advance of technology, industry, and capitalism—a paradox that haunts historians of the period (e.g., Hofstadter, 1955; Marx, 1964; Meyers, 1957). The happy innocence that allowed for this no doubt has been chastened with the passage of time, but the paradoxical love of economic growth and social stability still persists within the archives of American culture.

ORGANIZATIONAL STRATEGY

Since the 1950's, American conservatives have hoped that deep in the hearts of most Americans lurked conservative beliefs that were being betrayed by moderate and liberal leaders. However, for the generation of conservatives that constitutes the core activists of the New Right, this hope blossomed into certainty during the early 1970's. The successful appeal of Richard Nixon and George Wallace to the "silent majority" and the polarization of American society over the Vietnam War, student radicalism, Black militancy, feminism, and other issues convinced them that a conservative majority was not just a quiet possibility, but an angry reality waiting to be mobilized. The late 1960's and the 1970's saw the publication of a series of books advertising the existence of this majority and suggesting ways of hastening its emergence: *The Emerging Republican Majority* by Kevin Phillips (1969), *Taking Sides* by Richard J. Whalen (1974), *The Making of a New Majority Party* by William A. Rusher (1975), and *Conservative Votes, Liberal Victories* by Patrick J. Buchanan (1975).

Conservatives came to believe that all that was lacking, and perhaps what had been lacking all along, were leaders willing and able to organize this majority into a political movement. The New Right's often-voiced criticism of previous conservatives, and a cause of friction between the two groups, was that the latter had failed to develop a coordinated political strategy for pushing conservative causes. Both Richard Viguerie and Paul Weyrich remarked on the lack of leadership and organization they found in conservative ranks in the late 1960's and early 1970's (Viguerie, 1980; Edwards, 1981). Older conservative leaders, Viguerie opined, "didn't understand how to lead"; they "had no stomach for a hard-nosed fight"; they were "defensive and defeatist" (1980, pp. 32, 52, 53). They were "spokesman," who were good at articulating positions and taking stands, but not "leaders" capable of organizing a political force. As a result, conservatives had "no organized, continuing effort to exert a political influence on elections, on Capitol Hill, on the news media, and on the nation at large" (Viguerie, 1980, p. 49). The core activists of the New Right set out to become those leaders and to build that organized, continuing effort. Their writings are replete with pep-talk rhetoric about the importance of aggressive, tough optimistic leadership and organization.

The goal of these core activists has been not to inject a conservative presence into political debate, but to reorient the major political parties and political discourse as a whole around conservative principles. To do so, they have sought to build a conservative coalition capable of influencing every element of political life. To their minds, such a coalition must have three characteristics. First, it must be *autonomous:* independent from both political parties, self-sustaining, and capable of setting its own agenda. Second, it must be *broad* enough to bring together the various kinds of conservatives concerned about any of a large number of issues into a coherent movement. Third, it must support a *comprehensive* set of political organizations: think tanks (e.g., the Heritage Foundation), media watchdog groups (e.g., Accuracy in Media), organizations to recruit and train political candidates and future leaders (e.g., Committee for the Survival of a Free Congress), and other organizations to do political advertising, fund raising, and to mobilize public opinion.

The core activists of the New Right accordingly have sought to develop an organizational basis for coordinating the actions of diverse conservative and single-issue groups. Weyrich founded Coalitions for America, which serves as a central forum for some 120 independent conservative organizations and helps to coordinate and organize their actions "to have a collective impact on key issues of the day" (Edwards, 1981). Under the Coalition's auspices, conservatives meet regularly to discuss economic issues (the Kingston Group), education and social issues (the Library Court Group), and national defense and foreign policy (the Stanton Group).

The result of these coordinating efforts has been to create a dense network of conservative activists, whose intensity of interaction can be gauged by the interlocking of various New Right groups and by the diverse audiences at ceremonial gatherings. In February 1981, for example, Donald Wildmon, head of the National Federation for Decency and a regular columnist in *Conservative Digest,* announced the formation of the Coalition for Better Television (CBTV) to pressure the major networks to reduce the sex and violence in their programs. CBTV's board of directors reads like a *Who's Who* of the New Right, including Ronald S. Godwin, chief operations officer of the Moral Majority; Phyllis Schlafly of Stop ERA and the Eagle Forum; and Judie Brown of American Life Lobby. For his efforts, Wildmon made the cover of the April 1981 *Conservative Digest.* Two months later, the magazine's cover was graced by Budget Director David Stockman, on the occasion of his receiving the Council for National Policy's first annual Thomas Jefferson Award For Leadership. The Council, whose president is religious writer and Moral Majority cofounder Tim LaHaye, had been established as (in Viguerie's words) a "broad, all-inclusive organization of conservative-thinking people." The award ceremony, which took place at Viguerie's home, was attended by over 160 conservative leaders, including Howard Phillips, Weyrich, Schlafly, industrialist and conservative fund-raiser Joseph Coors, Ed Feulner of the Heritage Foundation, Reed Larson of the National Right to Work Committee, Ed McAteer of the Religious Roundtable, Bill Saracino of Gun Owners of America, and Robert Billings, former executive director of Moral Majority (Clymer, 1981a; *Conservative Digest,* April 1981). In both cases, one sees a wide array of conservatives coming together on quite different issues.

In the course of building this conservative coalition, the core activists of the New Right played a central role in mobilizing evangelical Christians. Several years ago, Howard Phillips recruited Edward McAteer to be a field director for The Conservative Caucus, and then in 1980 helped him found the Religious Roundtable. Paul Weyrich helped Robert J. Billings, long active in the Christian Schools movement, to found the National Christian Action Coalition to lobby for legislation relevant to these schools. Billings in turn brought Weyrich together with television evangelist Jerry Falwell, who they finally convinced in 1979 to found the Moral Majority (with Falwell as president and Billings as the first executive director). These New Right-based organizations have attempted to build upon bases of mobilization indigenous to the evangelical world, especially the network of Christian schools, local churches, and television evangelism. Summing up his role in developing the religious right, Weyrich remarked, "We are sort of the operations people. It has been our job to tell them, 'Okay, here is what to do'." (Herbers *et al.,* 1980) Or as Hadden and Swann (1981, p. 142) put it, "The New Christian Right . . . obviously owes its genesis to the master plan of the New Right."

The overall effort to build an autonomous, broad, comprehensive coalition belies the claims of some critics that the New Right has focused exclusively on single-issue politics. The single-issue emphasis has simply been a means to build a wider coalition around a broader conservative program.

The key to the New Right's strategy for creating this conservative coalition has been to stress the social, rather than the economic or national security, issues. The core activists seek to appeal to such traditionally Democratic constituencies as blue-collar workers and Southern whites on the basis of their concern about abortion, ERA, pornography, permissiveness, and the general decline of morality, family, and religion. These social issues are the substance of the New Right's effort to mobilize evangelical Christians and to encourage a proliferation of single-issue groups.

> For the past 50 years, conservatives have stressed almost exclusively eco-
> nomic and foreign policy. The New Right shares the same basic beliefs of
> other conservatives in economic and foreign policy matters, but we feel that
> conservatives cannot become the dominant political force in America until
> we stress the issues of concern to ethnic and blue-collar Americans, born-
> again Christians, pro-life Catholics and Jews. Some of these issues are busing,
> abortion, pornography, education, traditional Biblical moral values and quo-
> tas.
>
> Paul Weyrich, a leader of the New Right and of the new pro-family coalition,
> believes that family issues in the 1980's could be what Vietnam was in the
> 1960's and environmental and consumer issues were in the 1970's for the
> Left. [*Conservative Digest*, October, 1980, pp. 11, 17]

The New Right's emphasis on social issues is consistent with, though
not always consciously based on, two interrelated theories familiar to
social scientists. The first holds that right-wing movements must effect a
marriage of social classes by combining an economic conservatism (i.e.,
libertarianism) that appeals to the higher strata with a social conservatism
(i.e., traditionalism) that appeals to the lower strata (Lipset and Raab,
1978). The second argues that as the United States has evolved into a
"post-industrial" society with growing affluence and an increasing number
of jobs requiring high levels of education, social issues come to the fore
in the place of (or along with) economic issues, and the relative political
positions of the social classes becomes reversed. The upper-middle class,
as it becomes more and more educated, tends to take liberal, permissive
positions on social issues, while the lower-middle and working classes,
having gained a foothold on economic security, tend to take conservative
positions (Ladd, 1979). Together these theories imply that a large mass
of economically liberal lower-strata voters can be appealed to by conservatives on social issues.

Following the 1980 election, the New Right was quick to claim success
for its strategy by arguing that the social issues were the key to Reagan's
victory and the Republican Party resurgence. The January 1981 *Conservative Digest*, for example, contained no less than three articles on this
theme: "Religious Right Played Key Role in Many Races for U.S. Senate";
"Shift of Religious Voters Defeated Carter"; and "The Conservative Pro-
family Movement Nominated, Elected Ronald Reagan." In the last of these
three articles, anti-ERA leader Phyllis Schlafly proclaimed that "Ronald
Reagan won both the nomination and the election because he rode the
rising tides of the pro-family movement." In response to the pollsters'
claim that economic, not social, issues were crucial, she argued that while
the economy may have been the "main" issue, the social issues were
the "motivating" ones:

It was the moral issues that moved millions of Americans into the political process in the first place. After they got to the polls, most would indeed say that inflation is the biggest national issue; but inflation was not why they went to the polls. [p. 21]

In line with this conviction, the New Right was strident in its insistence that the Reagan Administration and the Congress act quickly on the social issues. The April 1981 *Conservative Digest* received enthusiastically Reagan's proclamation to a meeting of the Conservative Political Action Conference in March that conservatives "do not have a separate social agenda, a separate economic agenda, and a separate foreign policy agenda. We have one agenda" (p. 25). The May 1981 issue ridiculed Senate Majority Leader Howard Baker's reluctance to pursue the social issues by picturing on its cover a very small Baker about to be inundated by a very large tide of "social issues." The failure of the Reagan Administration to get serious about these issues in its first year was one of the New Right's main sources of dissatisfaction with Reagan.

The strategic importance that the New Right has given to social conservatism has directly reflected the immediate historical moment. Such core social issues as abortion, ERA, busing, affirmative action, the role of women, and gay rights were simply not of major importance before the 1970's. Social conservatism was made politically salient only as a result of the Supreme Court's ruling on abortion, Congress' passage of ERA, the emergence of the women's movement, the establishment of busing and affirmative action as federal government policy, and so on. The liberal and radical social changes of the early 1970's, in short, determined the emphasis of the conservatism of the late 1970's.

The 1970's witnessed two sets of changes in the process of campaigning for national political office that have had important implications for the strategy of the New Right. First, the role of the established political parties in candidate selection and voter education have been reduced by growing public disaffection, the expanding role of primary elections in choosing presidential candidates, the increased use of the mass media, and other factors (Wicker 1980). Second, the Federal Election Campaign Act of 1974 has reduced the role of large contributors in funding a candidate for national office by limiting individual contributions to any particular campaign to $1,000. These developments have created a partial political vacuum, which has been filled by a proliferating number of political action committees (PACs) and by the increasing use of direct mail. One result of these changes has been increased operating room for political movements independent of either major party. Capitalizing on tactical opportunities not available to previous generations of conservatives, the New Right has made better use of PACs and direct mail than any other contemporary political force in the United States.

The 1974 campaign reform law gave PACs considerably more leeway than individuals. While individuals were limited to giving $1,000 per campaign, PAC's could spend $5,000. The limits on large contributions, moreover, favored organizations like PACs that could raise small amounts of money from numerous contributors and then systematically use that money to support a number of candidates. Most importantly, subsequent judicial interpretations limited the 1974 law to contributions to the actual campaigns of political candidates, thus putting no limits on expenditures by PACs formally "independent" of a candidate (Sorauf, 1980; Weinraub, 1980). The result was the growth of PACs by 1980 to the point where they raised more money than either political party. This proliferation of PACs, moreover, has generally favored the more conservative forces in society; by 1980, New Right groups headed the list of the biggest spending PACs (Dionne, 1980; Clymer, 1981b and 1981c).

Political action committees, however, would scarcely have flourished without the capacity for direct mail solicitation of small contributions from a large number of persons. This mode of fund raising for political campaigns has recently become especially important, not only because of campaign reform laws but also because of advances in computer technology. These advances allow fund raisers to store information on large numbers of contributors, pinpoint those persons most likely to respond to a particular fund-raising appeal, and produce large numbers of personalized letters. The systematic use of such technology transforms direct mail from a mere fundraising technique into a way of building, maintaining, and mobilizing a political constituency.

The New Right has all but monopolized this broader use of direct mail. When Richard Viguerie, the New Right's main fund raiser, says that "direct mail is the life blood of the New Right," (*Conservative Digest*, October 1980, 5–9) he means precisely that it has served as a way not only of raising money but also of propagating ideas, recruiting activists, and mobilizing supporters. Use of direct mail has allowed conservatives to circumvent the mass media, which they regard as too liberal and too hostile to their ideas. It has, in short, become a major means of communication and cohesion for conservatives and is thus a key to the New Right network.

The New Right is both old and new. On the one hand, it has adopted a combination of themes well-established in previous American conservatism and deeply embedded in American culture. If its ideology appears paradoxical at points, these paradoxes nonetheless have solid historical roots. On the other hand, the New Right's organizational strategy for the most part has reflected the immediate contingencies and opportunities of contemporary American politics. This particular union of ideology and organizational strategy gives the New Right its distinctiveness, and thus provides a point of departure for further inquiry.

2 | THE NEW CHRISTIAN RIGHT

James L. Guth

By November 1980, the New Christian Right was a loose and poorly articulated collection of approximately a dozen TV evangelists, renegade main-line clergymen, nascent lobbies, an ill-defined constituency, and numerous coordinating committees. Nevertheless, a clear organizational structure had become apparent, as Christian Voice, the Roundtable, and especially Moral Majority, emerged into national prominence and drew religious activists from local and smaller organizations.

ORGANIZATIONS

Christian Voice was the first to appear, launched in January 1979 by California ministers Robert Grant and Richard Zone. The Voice was, in effect, a merger of several preexisting anti-gay, anti-pornography, pro-family groups on the West Coast. Several well-known fundamentalist ministers were recruited for the policy board of Voice, which at times also included author-lecturer Hal Lindsey (*The Late Great Planet Earth*) and actor-singer-theologian Pat Boone. By mid-1980, the group boasted of a mailing list of 150,000 laymen and 37,000 ministers, including 3000 Catholic priests and some Mormon clergymen. Although far short of an original goal of one million, the membership was still quite impressive. Voice claimed membership of adherents from 37 denominations, but most activists seemed to come from independent Baptist, Bible, and Assembly of God churches. Membership is strong in the West and Southwest, although local chapters have appeared in Virginia, South Carolina, and Florida as well (Lindsey, 1979; Plowman, 1979).

When organizing, Christian Voice depended heavily on TV evangelists, especially Pat Robertson, head of the massive Christian Broadcasting Network, who featured Voice on his "700 Club" and provided access to the hundred or more stations directly tied to his network. Some observers have surmised that his assiduous support was calculated to undercut fundamentalist support for Moral Majority, founded by Virginia TV rival Jerry Falwell. In addition to seeking membership and money through TV and radio appeals, the Voice also raised funds through direct mail solicitation, directed by Jerry Hunsinger, a former United Methodist minister, who also handled accounts for Falwell, Robert Schuller ("Hour of Power"), and for Moral Majority. Indeed, Voice used many of the same mailing lists as Moral Majority in 1979–80 (Plowman, 1979; *U.S. News,* 1979).

Moral Majority, founded by Falwell in July 1979, had a much heavier *Southern* flavor, although many of its greatest political triumphs occurred outside the South. In addition to Falwell, its board consisted of a shifting collage of independent Baptists and a few well-known conservatives from the main-line Southern Baptist and Presbyterian denominations. Robert Billings, a graduate of fundamentalist Bob Jones University, acted as executive director and Washington lobbyist before joining the Reagan campaign. Billings also sat for a time on the policy committee of Christian Voice, serving with money man Hunsinger as a link between the two organizations during their early months. Moral Majority actually kicked off fundraising in November 1979, using Falwell's computer lists of 250,000 prime "Old Time Gospel Hour" donors. Within a month, a third of the projected $3 million first year budget was in hand (Plowman, 1979; Clendinen, 1980; Jorstad, 1981).

In the meantime, Falwell continued his travels to all fifty states to hold "I Love America" rallies (usually on the State House steps with prominent local politicos as guests of honor) and continued to set up local chapters of Moral Majority. He soon announced that 47 states had units, but in reality, most consisted primarily of Falwell's mailing lists. By the 1980 election, only about 18 states had real organizations, concentrated in the South and Southwest (Perry, 1981). By all accounts, these groups were pastor-dominated, with few laymen in leadership roles (Vecsey, 1980; Zwier, 1981). The national organization claimed a membership of 300,000 by mid-1980, including 70,000 ministers; a year later the total hit 4 million by Falwell's count (Covert, 1981a). Like Christian Voice, Moral Majority appeals especially to ministers and some laymen from independent Baptist churches (Falwell seems to have drawn heavily from ministers in the Baptist Bible Fellowship and the Southwide Baptist Fellowship), small fundamentalist sects, and a few conservative militants in mainline Southern groups.

The third major Christian Right organization was created especially to attract conservative clergymen not comfortable with either Christian Voice or Moral Majority. Ed McAteer, a Southern Baptist and field organizer for the Conservative Caucus, sensed that neither did well with mainline Southern Baptist, Presbyterian, and Methodist ministers. To enlist their energies, he set up Religious Roundtable (later simply "Roundtable") as a forum for political discussion and education, conducted by such New Right luminaries as Paul Weyrich, Howard Phillips, Terry Dolan, and Phyllis Schlafly (Clendinen, 1980; *Conservative Digest*, 1981). After a series of "get acquainted" sessions, McAteer turned his attention to political organization, sponsoring workshops around the country which instructed ministers in the political arts of mobilizing their congregations on behalf of conservative candidates and causes. The best-publicized of these meetings was the August 1980 Dallas extravaganza, where thousands of clergymen and laymen heard from every leading New Right figure, most of the TV evangelists, Southern Baptist President Bailey Smith, and, of course, candidate Ronald Reagan, who endorsed the Roundtable's efforts (Briggs, 1980a; Raines, 1980). After the election, McAteer sought to extend his work by organizing local units of the organization (Clymer, 1981).

Roundtable's membership overlapped substantially with the Coalition for the First Amendment, sparked by Roundtable vice president, Southern Baptist TV evangelist James Robison. The Coalition's chief goal was to coordinate lobbying for Jesse Helms' bill to put prayer back into the public schools. Almost every TV minister was a member, including Oral Roberts and Rex Humbard, who were hesitant to throw their full weight into politics. The Coalition, like its parent organization, served as a useful meeting place for the TV evangelists and some of the main-line Southern Baptists such as Adrian Rogers, past president of the Southern Baptist Convention (Baptist Press, 1980).

LOBBYING: ISSUES AND STRATEGIES

Although these organizations generally agreed on policy and their activities overlapped, in the early months they put varying degrees of emphasis on different issues. But they did share a common lobbying strategy: to focus press and public attention on individual "Christian" or "moral" issues, activate local fundamentalist and evangelical ministers, and count on them to mobilize their congregations.

Many of the Christian Right's earliest efforts to influence Congress took the form of "grassroots" lobbying through the mail, with Christian Voice and Moral Majority stimulating their supporters to contact legislators *en masse* on several issues. Voice brought a mountain of anti–SALT II letters into Hill offices in late 1979, elicited some 115,000 to the IRS (with Majority's help) protesting further interference with Christian schools, and also prompted some anti-abortion mail. Moral Majority focused on leading the charge for Helms' school prayer proposal. All in all, early experience with the pioneer efforts of the Christian Right led many legislators to conclude (perhaps prematurely) as did one Midwestern Republican, that "if their ability to generate mail is at all indicative of their political power, we are in trouble" (Myers, 1980a).

The direct lobbying activities of Moral Majority and Christian Voice were much less impressive, due in part to the political inexperience of the fundamentalists and, sometimes, their considerable naiveté. At first, Moral Majority misdirected much of its energy behind Senator Paul Laxalt's catchall "Family Protection Act"—a sort of programmatic statement of every conceivable social goal held by any element of the New and Christian Rights. Whether because of increasing sophistication or greater public interest, Majority soon shifted to the school prayer proposal. Majority lobbyists sought to persuade enough House members to discharge the bill from the hostile House Judiciary Committee, but failed. This frustration resulted in part from a massive countercampaign by the main-line and traditionalist conservative churches, which united as seldom before to fight what they perceived as a violation of the First Amendment separation doctrine (Hunter 1980a, 1980b). Moral Majority did receive some consolation at session's end by the failure of "domestic violence" legislation, against which it had expended considerable lobbying resources (*Congressional Quarterly*, 1980).

Christian Voice devoted more attention to seemingly "secular" issues. The group's now famous "Morality Rating" of congressmen included not only votes on prayers in schools, IRS rulings on Christian schools, and abortion; but on restoration of the United States defense treaty with Taiwan, the establishment of the Department of Education, economic sanctions against Rhodesia, busing, "parental rights," and behavioral research funding. Most of these morality issues were also on the rating lists of the American Conservative Union and Americans for Constitutional Action. The release of the findings created quite a stir on Capitol Hill and in the press, as a number of evangelical legislators (including several clergymen) flunked the morality exam, while Representative Richard Kelly of Abscam fame hit 100%. Gary Jarmin's subsequent effort to explain that the ratings were not intended to convey any judgement about the legislators' personal moral standards did little to ease the embarrassment. Nevertheless, Voice delivered an updated version to its members just before the 1980 elections (Moser, 1980; United Press, 1980).

ELECTORAL STRATEGIES

The point of the Voice's rating system (which was also used by Moral Majority for a time) was not only to generate pressure from the "folks back home" on recalcitrant legislators, but also to single them out for punishment by evangelical voters. Although all three groups anticipated electoral involvement from the start, the disappointments of their maiden lobbying efforts during 1979 and 1980 probably solidified that resolve.

Although the Christian Right made some early efforts to recruit Congressional candidates who were, in the words of Robert Billings, "pro-life, pro-American—free enterprise, etcetera—pro-Bible morality and pro-family," the major goal was to defeat opponents, rather than electing friends. This strategy no doubt derived from the lack of success in recruiting attractive candidates, and from the 1978 experience of the New Right in defeating several outspoken liberals. The names on the Christian Right "hit lists" for 1980 were also on the New Right's: Packwood, Church, Bayh, McGovern, Culver, and several House members from marginal, conservative districts. During the primaries, Moral Majority was credited with mobilizing enough voters to help defeat Senator Stewart of Alabama and, more surprisingly, Alabama Congressman John Buchanan, a Southern Baptist minister, who failed to support the Right's position on school prayer with enough enthusiasm (Myers, 1980b; McFadden, 1980). Such early victories provided a fillip to the fundamentalist forces, leading them to expect even greater things in November.

While the Christian Right was gearing up its congressional campaigns, it was also testing the presidential waters. By late 1979, the electronic ministers and their allies were already negotiating with Republican hopefuls (Glen, 1979). Few, if any, were willing to exercise the Christian virtue of forgiveness toward their brother evangelical in the White House, despite strenuous efforts by Southern Baptist minister Robert Maddox, Carter's religious liaison. Although Carter was out of the question, the Christian Right leaders were divided on their favorite. Some preachers, like their mentor Richard Viguerie, inclined toward a true-blue conservative Christian like Phillip Crane. But when Crane's rocket failed to ignite, most shifted their gaze to John Connally and Ronald Reagan. Reagan was viewed as too liberal and not enough of a leader by some of the clergymen, but he was all that was left after Connally withdrew from the race. "Reagan was not the best Christian who ever walked the face of the earth," said fellow Californian Richard Zone of Christian Voice, "but we really didn't have a choice." Falwell was more hopeful: "the only thing we're waiting for is in our hearts to believe he's a real leader." Reagan apparently convinced Falwell; by the time of the Republican Convention, Falwell was claiming that Moral Majority would mobilize for Reagan, "even if he has the devil running with him." Among the devils listed by Falwell were Howard Baker and George Bush (Sawyer and Kaiser, 1980).

In fact, the decision to support Reagan was helped not only by the elimination of the alternatives, but by the evident enthusiasm of local fundamentalists for Reagan. Christian Voice had reacted more quickly than Majority, setting up a Christians for Reagan subsidiary of the Moral Government Fund (Voice's PAC) to aid him in the primaries, sending endorsement letters to all New Hampshire clergymen on the eve of that primary and buying newspaper advertisements throughout the state. Local Moral Majority chapters actively backed Reagan in caucuses and primaries, soon forcing Falwell to switch directions to get back in front of his troops (Turner, 1980; Clymer, 1980).

The Religious Right's efforts paid off. Not only did their favored candidate win the Republican nomination, but many of the activists embedded themselves deep in the party organization. Although members of Moral Majority, Christian Voice, and Roundtable worked within both major parties (Majority infiltrated the Democratic party in parts of Alabama and Florida), their greatest success came within the GOP, as might be expected from that party's growing conservatism. Just as important was the Republicans' minority status. "When you are as distinct a minority as we are, you welcome anything short of the National Order of Child Molesters," observed one party official. Indeed, in some strong Democratic areas, the Christian Right did not so much infiltrate the Republican organization as create it from scratch. In any case, the Rightists were a much-noticed presence at the 1980 Republican Convention. The Alaska delegation was comprised almost entirely of Moral Majority activists, and evangelicals were a vocal and visible minority in other states, especially

Virginia. And they had their say. As one enthusiastic delegate confided to the *Washington Post*, if the GOP platform were not etched in stone "it ought to be. It's right down the line an evangelical platform" (Barringer, 1980; Sawyer and Kaiser, 1980).

After the convention, Reagan strategists met with Christian Right leaders to determine what contribution they could make to the "community of shared values" that the candidate hoped to make the basis of the first partisan realignment in 50 years. Not only did the Republicans anticipate a larger portion of the normal evangelical vote, but they hoped to attract a substantial number of previously uninvolved citizens into the electorate on their side. Both GOP strategists and Christian Right leaders were impressed by poll data which suggested (perhaps wrongly) that only 55% of all evangelicals were registered to vote, compared with 72% of nonevangelicals (Sawyer and Kaiser, 1980). Even more disturbing—and tantalizing—was Robert Teeter's poll result which showed that 30% of all nonvoters attended church services at least three times a week (Moser, 1980). To mobilize such voters, Moral Majority and Roundtable geared up registration drives, urging ministers to get their congregants on the rolls. The typical device was to deputize a member of the congregation as a registrar, who then enrolled voters at the church on Sunday morning. Moral Majority alone claimed to have registered between four and eight million new voters. Such claims are clearly exaggerated, but some close observers have suggested that two million would be a realistic estimate for the combined efforts of Majority, Voice, and Roundtable (Sawyer, 1980; Lipset and Raab, 1981).

Of course, novice voters need direction. And this is where the minister was crucial to the Right's strategy. As Robert Billings said, "People want leadership. They don't want to think for themselves. They want to be told what to think by some of us here close to the front." Throughout the election year, Falwell, Christian Voice leaders, and McAteer were urging pastors to make clear political pronouncements. As Falwell explained: "What can you do from the pulpit? You can register people to vote. You can explain the issues to them. And you can endorse candidates, right there in church on Sunday morning." All the minister had to avoid was the temptation to have his church endorse candidates, an action which might threaten its tax exemption. Falwell, for one, was convinced this strategy would work: "I'm not saying that Jerry Ford was the perfect candidate in 1976 but he was better than the other guy. I told my people in church how I was going to vote. We held a straw poll two weeks before the election and it turned out 97% for Ford, and you know, that's how they voted in the election, too" (Vecsey, 1980).

To what extent did such activities of the Christian Right fulfill the hopes of its secular allies? Victory has a hundred fathers, as John Kennedy reminded us, and immediately after the election Falwell and other Right leaders claimed at least some credit for the election of Reagan, the defeat of several prominent Congressional liberals, and the election of many new conservative legislators. Pollster Louis Harris seemingly agreed, arguing that Reagan's margin among evangelicals put him in the White House (Harris, 1980). Subsequent analyses of the often conflicting mass of evidence from polls, academic surveys, and the politicians themselves suggest that Seymour Martin Lipset and Earl Raab (1981) have a point: evangelical voters did switch to Reagan in large numbers, but for the same economic and foreign policy reasons other voters were switching. Nor did they change their usual patterns with greater frequency than other voters. The studies also demonstrate that a central strategy of the Religious Right failed to catch on: very few Americans were asked by a minister to vote for a candidate, and even fewer were inclined to honor the request. (In fact, a larger number said such pressure would lead them to vote for the other candidate.) Turnout did increase in the evangelical South, alone of all regions, perhaps reflecting the Right's registration drive, but more likely as the result of a spirited contest between a regional conservative favorite and a native son.

Perhaps the fairest assessment of the Right's impact lies somewhere between Falwell's and Lipset's. In the 1980 elections, the Christian Right demonstrated the same political capacities as some other narrowly gauged interest groups: it mobilized enough activists to influence some state and local races, especially in low-visibility, low-turnout primaries and caucuses; it raised some money to assist favored candidates—Christian Voice gathered in over $200,000 while Moral Majority added a mere $25,000 (Mintz, 1980); and it may have changed a few old votes and added a few new ones to the conservative total. These real, but limited, accomplishments are consistent with the interpretation suggested above: across-the-board political conservatism is characteristic of a relatively narrow range of evangelical opinion, located primarily among fundamentalist clergy and a few committed laymen. There is little evidence of a massive new commitment of evangelicals to the ranks of Republicans or ideological conservatives.

The experience of 1981 buttresses this conclusion. The Right remained much in evidence, but fulfilled neither the hopes of its friends nor the fears of its foes. The three major groups underwent rather different organizational transformations. Christian Voice lost much of its leadership when its two founders moved on to other endeavors and several of the legislators on its "advisory board" resigned in protest over the "Morality Rating," leaving the organization without much of its early vigor. The Roundtable popped up occasionally, primarily as a platform for Edward McAteer's political pronouncements, but vice-president James Robison resigned and other leading figures lost interest, supporting some observers' contention that Roundtable had always been primarily a vehicle for mobilizing ministerial support for Reagan's election (Elder, 1981). Moral Majority, on the other hand, became almost a household word, at least among ministers (Guth, 1981) and politicians, if not among the general public (Peterson and Sussman, 1981). The organization enjoyed continued public attention, growing revenues, increasing membership, and proliferating state and local units.

Despite these achievements, Moral Majority and its allies logged few legislative successes in 1981, at least at the national level, despite the accession of a friendly Administration and a conservative Congress. The Christian Right claimed some victories: defeating a District of Columbia ordinance liberalizing sex laws; pressuring TV sponsors and the networks to reduce sex and violence in programming; influencing some family-related provisions in the Federal criminal code revision; and getting the Senate to endorse "voluntary" school prayers. On the other hand, the Right failed to get more than a few token Federal appointments; to win Reagan Administration or Republican leadership approval for "top priority" status for abortion, school prayer, tuition tax credit, and other important measures in Congress; and, in a most embarrassing episode, failed to muster any Senate opposition to Sandra Day O'Connor's nomination to the Supreme Court. Local successes on issues such as gay rights, textbook and library censorship, pornography, and creationism in some areas were offset by defeats in other parts of the country.

POTENTIAL AND LIMITATIONS

Thus far, then, the New Christian Right has had some success in building organizations, affecting legislation, penetrating one political party, and mobilizing and perhaps influencing new voters. Whether the Right's current legislative drives will come to fruition and its electoral influence grow remains to be seen. What are the long-range prospects for the Christian Right?

To begin with, the developments which resulted in the appearance of the movement are likely to persist, or even intensify. The continuing rise in education, income, and occupational status of evangelical Christians may provide an even larger corps of activists for the Right. This is especially true among the clergy, given the increasing self-selection of religious conservatives to the ministry. The organizational infrastructure is also likely to remain. At the local level, the Christian school movement is still burgeoning, and may receive a fillip if a tuition tax credit bill is enacted by the Reagan Administration (Maeroff, 1981). Christian colleges are also growing at a rapid rate, providing an evangelical higher education for the products of both private and public schools (Briggs, 1980c). It is not clear whether other efforts to establish among evangelicals "alternative institutions," such as business networks, will succeed. At the top, the electronic evangelists will probably remain, although considerable evidence suggests they have exhausted the potential market for their product (Martin, 1981). Despite this, many of their commercial ventures are profitable enough to survive, given the technological possibilities of "narrow-casting" (Stone and Bagamery, 1980).

Nor will the "trigger issues" go away. Surveys reveal continuing divergence in moral values between conservative religious identifiers and proponents of "new" or "contemporary" moral standards (Connecticut Mutual Life, 1981). Public controversy over abortion, pornography, gay rights, and similar issues will not abate soon; nor will government decisions settle conflicting claims. And it is not only the battle over the "secularization of morals" which continues. Government increasingly intrudes into areas traditionally left to the family, locality, or religious institutions. The last of these incursions may be especially significant. As John M. Swomley, Jr. (1981) has pointed out, "government regulations that impinge on the free exercise of religion seem to be expanding." Even many of the traditional and main-line conservative churches are disquieted by this trend (Briggs, 1981b).

All of this raises crucial strategic choices for the Christian Right. Its leaders can choose to focus on the moral and institutional interests that concern a wide spectrum of conservative religionists, thereby broadening their present appeal. Alternatively, they can cast their lot with the secular New Right, with its economic and foreign policy priorities, thus gaining political allies outside the "fold," but making the formation of pragmatic religious alliances more difficult. Which choice the Christian Right will make is yet unclear. Christian Voice leaned toward the secular Right option (and apparently lost), while Moral Majority seems at times to be narrowing its preoccupations to the more widely held social and moral values of conservative churchmen, down-playing, but not repudiating, positions on other questions. Assuming that the Right chooses this latter strategy, what are the primary obstacles to success?

One difficulty will certainly be the continuing antipolitical residues of evangelical and fundamentalist religion. Although much of that traditional bias has been eroded by the "trigger issues" of recent years, there are bound to be persistent effects of generations of indoctrination that "you can't get the church mixed up in politics." As Hendricks (1977) pointed out, fundamentalist religion still puts great stress on the futility (or even sinfulness) of trying to reform society rather than "save" individuals. And although the press focused in 1980 and 1981 on the political mobilization of the TV evangelists and local fundamentalist ministers, there is ample evidence that many conservative Christians at both levels stuck with the old verities. The stridency and overt Reaganism of Falwell, Robison, and McAteer overshadowed the quieter decisions by Robertson, Bakker, Humbard, and Roberts to pull back from electoral involvement. These decisions, like countless similar ones by local ministers (Nickerson, 1981), reflected organizational as well as theological concerns. As Rex Humbard put it, "If I backed a Republican for President, what about all the Democrats in my audience? (Burnet, 1981). Even Jerry Falwell felt the effects of tradition; thousands of viewers asked to have their names removed from his mailing lists and, according to Nielsen, he lost part of his audience (Martin, 1981). Even now, a devotee of electronic evangelists can sense temptation to take competitive advantage; one radio evangelist signs off by asserting that he is "just preaching the Gospel of Jesus Christ and is not involved in any politics whatsoever" (Bible Broadcasting Network, 1980).

A second danger for the Christian Right is rivalry and discord among its various elements. Few journalists have captured all the personal, organizational, and ideological divisions present. There is considerable enmity between the electronic evangelists, especially Falwell and Robertson, neither canonized as yet for humility. Similarly, Robertson and Jim Bakker have never overcome the animosity resulting from their early partnership and subsequent split. The organizational rivalries are just as severe and, in the long run, more important. The recent financial difficulties of several of the TV evangelists and some survey evidence (Martin, 1981) suggest that the leaders of the Christian Right are drawing from the same pool of support—a pool that may be drying up. Not only do the TV audiences for the various evangelists overlap, but so do the mailing lists for the political organizations. One might anticipate considerable interorganizational competition as the religious entrepreneurs seek a stable and secure resource base, a struggle which would not enhance political cooperation.

Already these personal and organizational rivalries have set off a revealing feud between Falwell and Bob Jones, II, one of the most political of the old fundamentalists. During the summer of 1980, Jones attacked Falwell as "the most dangerous man in America so far as Biblical Christianity is concerned." Falwell replied that he was "dangerous to liberals, feminists, abortionists and homosexuals, but certainly not to Bible-believing Christians." Here were all the elements of intra-Right factionalism.

Jones not only accused Falwell of wanting to run for President in 1984, thereby "straying from preaching the Gospel," but attacked Falwell's pragmatic political design to "rally Jews, Catholics, Protestants, and nothings" for conservative causes—alliances which did not set well with Jones' historic fundamentalist separatism. Nor did it help that Falwell has made deep inroads into the large national network of Bob Jones—trained fundamentalist ministers, who have kept the money and students flowing back to their alma mater for thirty years (Associated Press, 1980).

Ultimately, of course, the evangelists and their political arms may follow the example of interest groups in other sectors by developing a clear division of labor, which might avoid conflicts and facilitate joint action. Even if a certain amount of rivalry remained, this would not necessarily be counterproductive for the movement as a whole; competing organizations within a constituency may serve to mobilize that community more completely than a single organization could, simply by appealing to different portions of it. For example, Falwell might be more successful in attracting blue-collar workers and marginal white-collar employees, while the smoother Robertson might draw a somewhat more upscale evangelical (Wilson, 1973).

If the present Christian Right does hold together, will it be able to forge a larger alliance with other conservative religious identifiers distressed with the direction of American society, such as black evangelicals, Catholics, and other conservative denominations? Already the Christian Right has made extensive overtures to Catholics: Robertson and Bakker frequently feature Catholic conservatives (especially charismatics) on their TV programs; both Christian Voice and Moral Majority have made much of the number of Catholic adherents. And, by 1981, Christian Right activists were joining the "pro-life" movement in large numbers, vocally encouraged to do so by their leaders. In 1981 Moral Majority and Catholic leaders both supported tuition tax credits for private school parents. It is not clear whether such commonality of moral and institutional interests can overcome the latent anti-Catholicism characteristic of some Protestant fundamentalism. The economic conservatism and foreign policy militarism of the Christian Right has also encouraged the Catholic hierarchy to maintain an "arms-length" relationship (Briggs, 1980b).

Attracting black evangelicals will be even more problematic, despite shared positions on many moral questions. Although Falwell and Robertson have made appeals to blacks, the conservative economic posture of the Christian Right (and, no doubt, lingering racism) are likely to put off this potential ally. Although Falwell features black conservatives such as the Reverend E. V. Hill and economist Walter Williams in the *Moral*

Majority Report, there is no evidence of favorable response from individual blacks even comparable to that received from Catholics.

Most crucial for the Christian Right will be its ability to activate the larger, main-line evangelical denominations. To this point, the Right has essentially been a "parachurch" movement, attracting supporters from independent churches, minor denominations, and from within the main-line groups (Marty, 1980). No major denomination has aligned itself with the Right. The National Association of Evangelicals (NAE), an alliance of smaller denominations and individual evangelical churches, has cautiously cooperated with some of the Right's lobbying, but has held aloof from the electoral activities and urged more moderate policies and less stridency on the TV preachers. The NAE has established its own permanent Washington lobbying office to serve member churches and instituted a "legislative alert" system like those used by Moral Majority and Christian Voice. Despite the widespread membership support for conservative politics, the NAE also harbors political moderates (and even a few "evangelical leftists") who would prefer more action on world hunger, racial reconciliation, poverty, and human rights (Maust, 1979; Pierard, 1981). These minority forces have been bolstered recently by Billy Graham, who urged evangelicals to work for social justice, nuclear disarmament and the spread of a simpler "Christian lifestyle" (Briggs, 1981a). A battle for the soul of the NAE is in the offing.

If the Christian Right is unable to capture existing denominational machinery, the problem of institutionalization becomes even more pressing. During its first 2 years, the Christian Right depended not only on the electronic church, but on considerable attention from the national press (Ravenel, 1980). Falwell himself was in many ways the "Ralph Nader of the Christian Right," shifting the spotlight from issue to issue, attempting to bring grassroots pressure to bear. But by the spring of 1981 Moral Majority's Ronald Godwin noted that "one of our top priorities is to move from what I call the media period to the organizational period" (Clymer, 1981). And, given the propensity for great fundamentalist leaders to run afoul of the law, morality, good taste, or public opinion, the Christian Right's survival would seem to depend upon the growth of independent institutions and leaders, cut off from direct association with, or dependence on, the charismatic "founders." A possible model here might be Americans United for Separation of Church and State (AU), founded in the 1940's by leading fundamentalist clergy, with some support from humanists, agnostics, and a few liberal clerics. AU drew much of its early strength from alliances with the SBC, Methodist Church, and other conservative denominations, but eventually built its own (modest) cadre of state and national leaders, supporting churches, and individual members. A similar structure of Christian Right organizations across the country might be able to derive similar strength from the associations of its members, without finding it necessary to control denominational bureaucracies (Morgan, 1968).

The most likely candidate for success in such an effort is the Moral Majority, assuming it can put some distance between itself and Falwell before his financial house of cards collapses. But creating a disciplined political organization of this sort is not easy. Moral Majority has already been seriously embarrassed by the zealotry of its own local activists: the drive by a Maryland official to outlaw anatomically-explicit gingerbread men; anti-Semitic statements by local officials; a proposal by California activists to make homosexuality a capital offense; and the resignation of the New York chapter's head in protest against the refusal of the national office to take on an issue "more important than abortion, homosexuality, or the arms race"—the *Reader's Digest* condensation of the Bible (Perry, 1981; Dart, 1981). The irony may well be that recruitment and retention of local fundamentalist true-believers may require rhetoric and actions which preclude the kind of alliance with more moderate religious forces necessary for political efficacy. But that, at least for a time, was also the price AU paid (Sorauf, 1976).

Of course, the Right's impact will depend upon more than its ability to survive. The opposition of other religious interest groups (such as the "liberal" National Council of Churches), of secular organizations, and of liberal political activists seems likely to mount in direct proportion to the Right's "threat." Over the past 2 years, the wire services have literally teemed with stories of counterorganization, full of familiar names such as Norman Lear, Common Cause, the NAACP, the ACLU, and many others (Data Center, 1981, pp. 546–604). And politicians, even friendly ones, sometimes react adversely to the superior moral claims of the Christian Right, as Senator Goldwater has reminded us (Miller, 1981). Whether this resistance swells or diminishes may depend upon the Right's ability to compromise at times and see some moral ambiguity in all political questions.

The most likely prospect, then, is that the Christian Right will survive, enjoying a modest degree of organizational success. The increasing penetration of government into the lives of believers and their institutions will provide both the motive and the incentive for activism. Increasing levels of education and income will provide the personal skills and financial resources for such involvement; modern organizational technology will continue to provide the machinery. If, however, changes in government policy relieve some of these pressures, or if existing religious institutions are able to incorporate and speak for the more legitimate concerns of the Right, these parachurch organizations might wither away, leaving but a small mark on the history of the 1980's.

II Mobilization

3 | MOBILIZING THE MORAL MAJORITY

Robert C. Liebman

The 1970's brought the formation of many conservative evangelical groups which sought to influence national politics. Most were single-issue groups which waged campaigns on behalf of freedoms for Christian schools, prayer and Bible reading in public schools, a constitutional ban on abortion, and tighter restrictions on pornography and homosexuality. With names like American Christian Cause and the National Christian Action Coalition, these organizations mobilized modest numbers of evangelicals and largely escaped national attention.

A handful of groups differed in goals and strategy from the great majority. Eschewing single-issue campaigns, they sought to address a wide range of moral, economic, and foreign policy issues from a distinctively Christian perspective. Favoring an ecumenical strategy, they sought to mobilize large numbers of conservative Americans from a variety of denominations.

Four of these groups—Third Century Publishers, Christian Voice, Religious Roundtable, and Moral Majority—received considerable national attention. Although they shared similar goals and pursued similar strate-

49

gies, each had varying success in mobilizing conservative Americans. Of the four, Moral Majority attracted the largest following. The social movements literature provides a number of alternative explanations for the success of social movement organizations. How well do these account for differences in the mobilization of conservative evangelical groups?

MOBILIZING THE MORAL MAJORITY

The first major effort to build a national movement of conservative evangelicals came in 1974. Arizona Congressman John Conlan and Bill Bright, president and founder of Campus Crusade for Christ, devised a plan to politicize and educate people in every Congressional district who would become part of a national grassroots effort to elect evangelical Christians sharing a conservative political agenda. At the center of their plan was Third Century Publishers, organized in 1974 to publish books and other materials promoting a conservative political and economic philosophy based on scriptural principles. Its chief publication was *One Nation Under God* by Rus Walton, intended for use in the study of "Christian economics." In addition to his post as editor-in-chief of Third Century, Walton was a director of the National Association of Manufacturers and the American Conservative Union.

In the summer of 1974, Conlan and Bright obtained substantial pledges of financial support for Third Century from a group of wealthy evangelical businessmen such as Richard DeVos, president of the home products company, Amway, and Art DeMoss, chairman of the board of the National Liberty Corporation, an insurance firm. Third Century used the funds to hire a number of regional directors responsible for recruiting representatives from each congressional district who would develop a program of home study groups to motivate evangelical Christians to get involved in politics and to train them in methods of political organizing. The approach was used because evangelical Christians were familiar with home Bible studies. Central to the local effort was a Good Government kit consisting of three Third Century publications: *The Spirit of '76* which provided instructions on how to run a successful political campaign, a supplement for each state titled *"The Nature of Government and Politics in . . . ,"* and of course, *One Nation Under God*. In addition to these publications, the home study kit included the "Third Century Index" which rated Congressional voting records according to how well they measured up to the principles of individual freedom, fiscal responsibility, and free competitive enterprise.

At the national level, additional outreach was accomplished through

Intercessors for America, a tax-exempt lobby which used telephone prayer chains to encourage participants to write their congressmen. In June 1976, Intercessors sent letters to 120,000 pastors urging them to buy large quantities of Bill Bright's pamphlet, *Your Five Duties as a Christian Citizen.* The pamphlet was a guidebook for political action which instructed voters on how to take over their local voting precincts.

The individuals who led the Third Century movement were also active in the establishment of the Christian Embassy. The Embassy was an impressively furnished building on Capitol Hill where Campus Crusaders were to evangelize members of Congress, the military, the judiciary, and the diplomatic service. Twenty businessmen contributed $50,000 each to buy and refurbish the building. A number of the donors sat on the Embassy's board with religious leaders such as Billy Graham, W. A. Criswell, Norman Vincent Peale, and Harold Lindsell of *Christianity Today.*

Allied with Third Century Publishers was Bright's plan to save America, which centered on an organization called *Here's Life, America.* Here's Life was a city saturation evangelistic campaign which utilized the resources of local churches in cooperation with Campus Crusade staff. Its initial goal was to train five million Christians from 50,000 local churches to carry out intensive evangelistic efforts. Here's Life planned to organize a three week saturation campaign in each city using billboards, radio, and television advertising. A pilot program was launched in Atlanta in 1975. In 1976, Here's Life kicked off campaigns in eighteen major cities. Plans called for similar campaigns in each of the nation's metropolitan areas and 18,000 smaller communities.

After a 1976 exposé in *Sojourners* (Wallis and Michaelson, 1976), a publication of the evangelical left, the political elements of Bright's plan to save America disappeared. The achievements of Third Century Publishers were mixed. While its literature was used in at least thirty 1976 congressional campaigns, Third Century failed to spawn the grassroots evangelical movement which was its major goal. After the election, it moved from Washington to the relative obscurity of Virginia. Rus Walton left Third Century to join the right-wing Plymouth Rock Foundation as editor and writer of church study packets. The Christian Embassy closed.

But Bill Bright persevered. He announced a $100 million dollar fundraising campaign with $35 million earmarked for Here's Life, America and the remainder destined for evangelical efforts abroad. By 1977, Bright upped the target to $1 billion. His efforts were helped by billionaire Nelson Bunker Hunt who donated $10 million of his personal fortune, and who is committed to raising the entire $1 billion budget of Here's Life. Hunt serves as chairman of the organization's International Executive Committee and was able to raise over $20 million from several hundred businessmen during a spring 1980 Dallas weekend retreat. By mid-1980, Here's Life collected over $170 million, much of it from large donors such as Pepsico, Mobil Oil, Coca-Cola, and the Adolph Coors family.

While there is no direct evidence of political activity on the part of Here's Life, America, many of its organizers played important roles in the political wing of the New Christian Right. Bill Bright served as co-organizer of the 1980 Washington for Jesus rally which brought over 200,000 conservative Christians to the nation's capital. Here's Life donor Hunt contributed $5,500,000 for the film "Jesus," produced by Campus Crusade and used as a promotion for the rally. Taking a page from Third Century's book, Washington for Jesus attempted to organize conservative Christians by political district (Huntington and Kaplan, 1980; *Interchange*, Spring, 1980: pp. 1–2). It appears to have had little success in creating local chapters.

Perhaps more important than their electoral impact, the political activities of Bill Bright and Third Century Publishers provided a model for a later generation of conservative evangelical groups. Christian Voice was formed in late 1978 by California ministers Robert Grant and Richard Zone. Grant was the founding dean of the California Graduate School of Theology and later organized American Christian Cause to fight the gay activist movement. Voice was formed through the merger of several California anti-gay, anti-pornography, and pro-family groups. Two New Right political operatives, Gary Jarmin and David Troxler, held important posts in the organization. Several well-known evangelicals were recruited for its policy board, including singer Pat Boone and Hal Lindsey, author of *The Late, Great Planet Earth* (Plowman, 1979). Christian Voice's early promotional literature reported that if Christ were to return today, he would find ample evidence of moral decay, including legalized abortions, limitations on school prayer, rampant homosexuality, and "Secular Humanism and evolution taught to our young in school as opposed to creation." In addition, he would discover "a government so immoral that it thinks nothing of betraying Christian allies, whether in Taiwan or Rhodesia, while catering in every way possible to Godless forces of anti-Christ Communism" and "a National Council of Churches, which calls for . . . national redistribution of wealth (à la Karl Marx) and actively supports Marxist guerrillas in Africa, whose preoccupation seems to be the slaughter of Christian missionaries."

To counter these trends, Voice distributed a "Congressional Report Card" which rated the morality of congressmen by examining their votes on fourteen key moral issues. Moral positions included voting for the lifting of sanctions on trade with Rhodesia and the Taiwan defense treaty; and voting against the unionization of teachers, school busing, racial and sexual quotas in school hiring, and appropriations to the National Science Foundation, since "most of these funds are used to stack the ideological deck in favor of Godless behavioral humanist research which contradicts the Christian viewpoint of mankind's nature." Voice sent these ratings to the 37,000 pastors and 150,000 lay people on its mailing list (Huntington and Kaplan, 1980).

Voice depended heavily on television evangelists for organizing. Pat Robertson, head of the Christian Broadcasting Network, featured Christian Voice on his "700 Club" and provided access to the more than one-hundred stations affiliated with CBN. In addition to its television appeals, Voice initiated a direct mail fundraising campaign, directed by Jerry Hunsinger, a former United Methodist minister, whose accounts included the television ministries of Jerry Falwell and Robert Schuller, Anita Bryant's anti-gay campaign, and Citizens for Decency Through Law which had merged with Christian Voice. In 1979, Voice claimed 130,000 members from 37 denominations. Most however, were members of independent Baptist, Bible, and Assembly of God churches. Voice's strongest support came from the West and Southwest, although local chapters appeared in Virginia, South Carolina, and Florida (Guth, 1981a; Plowman, 1979).

Formed in late 1979, the Religious Roundtable charted a different course. Modeled after industry's Business Roundtable, it was more a trade association for the leadership of the secular and Christian New Right than a mass membership organization. Its board of directors represented a wide range of groups and personalities on the right, including the Christian Broadcasting Network, National Religious Broadcasters, Christian Voice, Moral Majority, Campus Crusade, the Plymouth Rock Foundation, the National Association of Evangelicals; and such individuals as Rus Walton, Richard Viguerie, Phyllis Schlafly, Paul Weyrich, and Adrian Rogers, former president of the Southern Baptist Convention (Huntington and Kaplan, 1980). With the help of secular conservatives such as Viguerie and Weyrich, Roundtable was "to coordinate Christian leaders from around the nation who are willing to fight in the political arena for pro-God, pro-family, pro-America causes" (*Conservative Digest,* November 1979, quoted in Huntington and Kaplan, 1980, p. 3).

Roundtable's founder, Ed McAteer, a Southern Baptist and National Field Director for the Conservative Caucus, targeted as potential recruits conservative clergymen who were not comfortable with either Christian Voice or Moral Majority. McAteer sensed that neither did well with mainline Southern Baptist, Presbyterian, and Methodist ministers. The Roundtable initially organized a series of national seminars for political discussion and education led by New Right luminaries such as Paul Weyrich, Howard Phillips, Terry Dolan, and Senator Jesse Helms. Later seminars included workshops to teach participants how to mobilize their congregations on behalf of conservative causes and candidates. The most successful of these events was the August 1980 Dallas National Affairs Briefing, where thousands of clergy and laymen heard from leading New Right figures, many of the nation's prominent televangelists, Southern Baptist Convention president Bailey Smith, and presidential candidate Ronald Reagan.

After the election, Roundtable shifted its efforts to the formation of local affiliates (Clymer, 1981). Although its leadership claimed a membership of 160,000 ministers, the figure represented the size of its vast mailing list. Its turn to local mobilization provided indirect evidence of its failure to reach the grassroots.

Founded in June 1979, Moral Majority is by far the largest conservative evangelical group. Majority is in fact four separate organizations. Moral Majority, Inc. is a tax-exempt, but not tax-deductible, lobbying arm organized for the purpose of influencing legislation at the national, state, and local levels. With tax-deductible status, the Moral Majority Foundation was established to educate ministers and lay people on important issues and to conduct voter registration drives. Also tax-deductible, the Moral Majority Legal Defense Fund was organized to combat the American Civil Liberties Union and to battle the forces of humanism through the courts. A Moral Majority Political Action Committee was set up to support political campaigns by morally conservative candidates (Shriver, 1981).

Moral Majority initially emphasized name recognition and voter registration. The organization received extensive national exposure. A December 1980 Gallup poll reported that 40% of its national sample had heard or read of the Moral Majority. In May 1981, a Washington Post–ABC News poll repeated the question and reported that the figure had risen to 49% (Peterson and Sussman, 1981). Surveys conducted in the nation's Bible Belt showed that its visibility was even greater. An October 1980 survey of potential voters in Alabama's Sixth Congressional District (including Birmingham) reported that 75% of respondents were aware of Moral Majority (Penfield and Davis, 1981). Nearly identical results were obtained in a summer 1981 survey of residents of the Dallas–Fort Worth Metroplex (Shupe and Stacey, 1982). The successes of Moral Majority's voter registration campaign are harder to measure. While the organization boasted of registering over four million voters, some observers set the figure at two million for the combined efforts of Moral Majority, Christian Voice, and the Roundtable (Lipset and Raab, 1981).

From its inception, Moral Majority worked aggressively to build ties to the grassroots. At the time of its second anniversary, Moral Majority was able to claim chapters in all fifty states, numerous local affiliates, and an active Washington office which spent over $6 million during the fiscal year ending in August 1981. Much of the money went to Moral Majority's extensive media campaign. The organization published full-page replies to its critics in major national papers such as *The New York Times* and *The Wall Street Journal.* Its *Moral Majority Report* reached over 840,000 homes with an estimated readership of three million. Over 300 radio stations broadcast the daily Moral Majority commentary. With an initial goal of two million members, its organizational efforts bore fruit at the grassroots. By its count, over four million Americans, including over 72,000 ministers, priests, and rabbis, were Moral Majority members (Covert, 1981a; Associated Press, 1981). Outsiders greatly diminish the figure, arguing that the organization included anyone on its extensive mailing lists as a member. Conservative estimates set Moral Majority membership at about 400,000.

Regardless of the exact figure, the number should give pause. Moral Majority's membership was orders of magnitude larger than that of its competitors. To be sure, all four groups had similar goals and sought the support of roughly the same constituency. However, none achieved the success of Moral Majority in attracting members, raising funds, creating affiliates, and obtaining public recognition. In time, Moral Majority became the byword for the entire New Christian Right. With his frequent appearances on television talk shows, Jerry Falwell came to personify the movement in the eyes of millions of Americans. But perhaps the best statement of its success came from its most fervent opponents. When the ACLU, Planned Parenthood, and other liberal organizations lashed out at the New Christian Right, they attacked Moral Majority by name.

THE DETERMINANTS OF SUCCESS

What accounts for Moral Majority's greater success in mobilizing conservative Americans? Four possible explanations stand forth in many journalistic accounts. All have firm roots in the literature on social movements. Each speaks to a different ingredient of organizational success.

One common explanation holds that movement success depends on access to financial resources. Large-scale mobilization campaigns require massive amounts of money. Organizations which begin with strong financial backing have substantial advantages. Of the four groups, Bill Bright's Third Century Publishers and Here's Life, America began with the greatest financial patronage. With help from well-heeled evangelical contributors, Bright's enterprises raised tens of millions of dollars. None of the 1979 groups shared its financial success. Moral Majority spent over $2 million during its first year and about $6 million during its second year. Christian

Voice spent about half as much in each year. While exact figures are not available, Religious Roundtable's budget was probably smaller. If the size of a group's war chest is a predictor of its success, we would expect that Bill Bright's ventures would have resulted in extensive mobilization. Yet with a considerably smaller budget, Moral Majority mobilized much larger numbers. Financial patronage was not responsible for its success.

A second explanation contends that movement success depends on an extensive network of communications between organizers and constituents. Many journalistic accounts suggested that the electronic church was the key to the mobilization of the New Christian Right. At first glance, the explanation is compelling. The electronic church grew rapidly during the 1970's and provided an available channel of communication between leaders and followers of the New Christian Right. But the evidence on the role of the electronic church is inconclusive. The failure of Here's Life, America and its predecessor, Third Century Publishers, to develop durable links with the electronic church may have hurt their mobilization. In contrast, all three of the 1979 organizations were allied with televangelists: Pat Robertson with Christian Voice, James Robison with the Religious Roundtable, and Jerry Falwell with Moral Majority. Televangelism may have given Moral Majority an edge. Falwell broadcasts on more television stations than any of the ten most popular evangelists. But the link with the electronic church is only part of the reason for Moral Majority's success. Falwell reaches fewer than a million homes and, as many evangelists who stayed aloof from politics had feared, his audience share declined during the early months of Moral Majority mobilization (Martin, 1981).

A third explanation characterized the reports of journalists who kept one eye on the secular New Right and the other on the New Christian Right. Fascinated by the New Right's skillful use of direct mail technologies and its extensive networking, many came to believe that its superior organizational expertise was the key to its apparent success. Their suspicions had echoes in theories which credit the success of movement organizations to the talents of professional social movement entrepreneurs (McCarthy and Zald, 1973). When they confronted the New Christian Right, many assumed that the contributions of New Right political operatives were substantial. While such New Right figures as Paul Weyrich and Howard Phillips were instrumental in the formation of Christian Voice, Religious Roundtable, and Moral Majority, the relationship between their efforts and the eventual success of these organizations is tenuous. Accumulated through extensive experience in building local churches and evangelical organizations, the talents of their indigenous leadership were more decisive. There is no reason to suspect that Moral Majority's greater success was due to its disproportionate share of outside expertise.

Another journalistic explanation identifies movement success with a favorable conjunction of issues. Social movement organizations which tailor their programs to suit the ground swell of public opinion stand to mobilize extensive numbers. If the argument holds, we should expect that groups formed at different points in time face different opportunities for mobilizing their constituency. The limited success of Third Century Publishers might have been due to its appearance at the wrong time. There is strong evidence to suggest that circumstances at the end of the seventies may have been more propitious for the politicization of evangelicals than the political atmosphere of 1976. The 1979 groups had greater success in mobilizing conservative Americans. However, all three groups differed little in goals and programs and each should have shared equally the good fortune of a conservative mood among evangelical Christians. The argument loses its bite when confronted with the different fates of similar organizations formed at roughly the same time.

While all four of the explanations are suggestive, none of them is completely satisfactory. Factors shared by the four organizations cannot account for differences in the extent of their mobilization. All of the factors contributed to the Moral Majority's mobilization, but none of them provides compelling evidence for its relative success.

Are we to conclude that Moral Majority was specially blessed? Before crediting higher powers, most sociologists will want to take a second look at the ground on which Moral Majority was formed. Social movement organizations do not appear spontaneously. They are nurtured by shifts in the cultural environment which provoke changes in the mood of potential participants and by alterations in the political environment which provide opportunities for collective action. They develop through deliberate efforts to organize participants and accumulate resources. They take shape through the sustained effort of movement activists to effect programs of change.

These considerations provide the starting point for resource mobilization theories of social movements (Tilly, 1978; McCarthy and Zald, 1977). The theories give pride of place to the role of resources and structure in mobilization. They hold that mobilization depends on the ability to increase control over valued resources. They suggest that rapid mobilization is most likely in groups characterized by extensive internal organization and high participation (Oberschall, 1973). When mobilizing groups are able to incorporate members of pre-existing collectivities, the costs of mobilization decrease. Recruitment into mobilizing groups is facilitated by an existing structure of ties. Recent research on recruitment into social movement organizations suggests that the key factors were links to movement members through interpersonal ties and the relative weakness of countervailing networks (Snow, Zurcher, and Ekland-Olson, 1980).

MAJORITY'S NATIONAL NETWORK

Can Moral Majority's more rapid mobilization be explained by its access to pre-existing networks which were unavailable to other conservative Christian groups? Pre-existing associations played an important role in the two phases of Moral Majority's mobilization program. In its formative period, Moral Majority capitalized on ties among evangelical leaders and drew on their previous political experience. In its organizational phase, Moral Majority forged strong links with a national network of fundamentalist clergy.

Moral Majority's founders were a group of prominent conservative clergymen. The original triad consisted of Jerry Falwell, Tim LaHaye, and Greg Dixon. Urged on by such New Right figures as Howard Phillips, Paul Weyrich, Robert Billings, and Ed McAteer, Falwell was the prime mover in the effort. Charles Stanley and D. James Kennedy were added to the original board of directors (LaHaye, 1980: 201; Mayer, 1980: 31). The five men ministered to five of America's hundred largest churches (Towns, Vaughan, and Seifert, 1981). Each held a special place in the fundamentalist pantheon.

Jerry Falwell built the Thomas Road Baptist Church into one of the nation's largest, and perhaps its most visible, church. Starting with 35 worshippers who met in the former plant of the Donald Duck Bottling Company, Falwell now oversees a congregation of 17,000. He was one of the first pastors to recognize the importance of media preaching, and began radio broadcasts one week after opening his church in 1956. Falwell later turned the bulk of his efforts to television. His "Old Time Gospel Hour," constructed around the eleven o'clock service of the Thomas Road Baptist Church, is seen weekly on 373 television stations. In fiscal 1979, the program raised $35 million from the two and a half million people on its mailing lists. In 1980, contributions from his fundraising operations approached $1 million a week. Much of the money was earmarked for Falwell's many enterprises, including Liberty Baptist College, Liberty Baptist Seminary, and the Liberty Home Bible Institute. (Fitzgerald, 1981; *Broadcasting*, October 13, 1980, p. 46; Mayer, 1980).

Falwell's broadcast was partly responsible for his involvement in politics. He soon realized that he could gain greater attention by talking about social issues than theological topics. In 1976, Falwell began a series of "I Love America" rallies on the steps of state capitols throughout the nation. The rallies followed the model of religious revivals. Local pastors met with Falwell during a fellowship hour before the event. The rallies were large spectacles which featured singing groups from Liberty Baptist College, appearances by local politicians, and Falwell's call for a moral America. In 1977, Falwell associated himself with campaigns led by Anita Bryant and Phyllis Schlafly, and the following year launched his Clean Up America campaign. At the end of 1978, Falwell took credit for the defeat of a gay-rights ordinance and a state version of the ERA in Florida, and the defeat of a proposal to legalize pari-mutuel betting in Virginia (Fitzgerald, 1981).

While Falwell spanned the airwaves, Tim LaHaye's reputation stretched across the shelves of Christian bookstores nationwide. One of the nation's leading fundamentalist writers, LaHaye is the author of at least sixteen books which sell more than 300,000 copies a year. While most of his books describe his philosophy of spiritual control over the human tempera-ment, a few became primers for political action by conservative Christians. *The Battle for the Mind,* for example, became the key tract in the attack on secular humanism. LaHaye is probably best known for his Family Life seminars, presentations with his wife Beverly which teach the joys of Christian marriage. Beverly was one of a small number of female evan-gelical activists. After her involvement with the pro-life movement, she founded Concerned Women for America, a national prayer chain with more than 94,000 members. LaHaye himself was no stranger to organiz-ing or politics. He was founder of the San Diego Christian Unified School System and of Christian Heritage College. LaHaye claimed that he first became aware of the importance of politics during a fight over a zoning variance for his church. He later played a role in the campaign to defeat Proposition 6, the California gay-rights measure. In 1979, he and his wife became co-chairpeople of Family America, a clearing house for pro-family groups (LaHaye, 1980).

Founder of the 8000–member Indianapolis Baptist Temple, Greg Dixon was a veteran of fundamentalist political battles in the 1970's. A strong opponent of state interference in church affairs, Dixon pushed for passage of the Church Freedom Legislative Package in the Indiana legislature. In Indianapolis, his attacks on Marion County prosecutor James Kelly for his support of gay rights contributed to Kelly's decision not to seek re-election. Dixon came to national attention when he led 400 ministers who formed a human chain around Reverend Lester Roloff's home for children to prevent its closing by Texas welfare officials. During the 1970's, Dixon also organized large rallies in support of Anita Bryant's anti-homosexuality campaign, the Church Freedom Legislative Package, and strict controls on pornography (*Conservative Digest,* August 1979).

By inviting Charles Stanley and D. James Kennedy to join its board of directors, Moral Majority built bridges to other denominations. A South-ern Baptist, Stanley is a leader in the campaign to get Christians involved in politics. His cassette sermon, "Stand Up America!," circulated widely among churches. The morning service of his 8,000–member First Baptist Church in Atlanta is telecast across the nation by satellite. Stanley is the author of *Is There a Man in the House?* which teaches fathers their God-given place of leadership and love in the home (*Conservative Digest,* May/June, 1980, p. 21; *Voice of Liberty,* Fall, 1979, p. 13).

Dr. D. James Kennedy is pastor of the Coral Ridge Presbyterian Church in Fort Lauderdale, Florida, reportedly the fastest-growing Presbyterian church in America with more than 4,800 members and peak attendance in excess of 9000 at its three morning services. Kennedy is the author of several books including *Evangelism Explosion,* which has been trans-lated into almost a dozen languages (Towns, Vaughan, and Seifert, 1981, p. 320). In addition to his role in the Moral Majority, Kennedy serves as a board member of the Religious Roundtable. His July 1980 letter inviting pastors to attend the Dallas National Affairs Briefing sponsored by the Roundtable included a legal opinion on legislative and political activities by clergymen and religious organizations permitted under the Internal Revenue Code (Kennedy, 1980).

Reverend Bob Billings was selected as Moral Majority's first executive director. His post marked a temporary stopping place in his long odyssey with the New Christian Right. Originally a high school principal, Billings left when he became disenchanted with governmental red tape and hu-manist philosophy. With his wife, he set out across the nation to found a series of Christian schools. Working with church groups, he set up schools in Ohio, Pennsylvania, Maryland, New York, Michigan, and Indi-ana. Billings later became affiliated with Reverend Jack Hyles, pastor of the First Baptist Church of Hammond, Indiana. With a fleet of buses and a commitment to aggressive evangelism, Hyles had built the largest Sunday School enrollment in the nation. Drawing on his national reputa-tion, Hyles organized a series of pastors' conferences to teach the techni-ques of church growth to clergy throughout the nation. Billings played a role in these conferences and later served as president of the church-affiliated Hyles-Anderson College. In 1976, after a meeting with Ed Mc-Ateer, Billings ran unsuccessfully for Congress. During his campaign he came into contact with Paul Weyrich, who helped him found the National Christian Action Coalition after Billings left his college presidency. The Coalition's chief goal was to fight government interference in Christian education. Billings was widely credited with organizing the 1978 cam-paign against IRS efforts to withdraw the tax-exemption of racially im-balanced Christian schools. When more than 120,000 letters of protest reached Washington, the IRS shelved its plan (Clendinen, 1980; Towns, Vaughan, and Seifert, 1981; Skerry, 1980, p. 19). After leaving Majority in 1980, Billings served as religious advisor to the Reagan campaign and became special assistant for nonpublic schools in Reagan's Department of Education.

In its early months, Moral Majority capitalized on the organizational resources of its founders. Falwell's "Old Time Gospel Hour" provided a communications link to a large national audience. Its major resource was its 2.5 million–member mailing list. Moral Majority used the list of 250,000 prime donors to initiate a fund-raising campaign, which brought in over 2.2 million dollars during its first fiscal year. By incorporating *Journal Champion*, a publication distributed to the Old Time Gospel Hour's many contributors, *Moral Majority Report* began life with a circulation base that many publishers work a lifetime to achieve. At about the same time, Tim and Beverly LaHaye brought Family America into the Moral Majority fold (Plowman, 1979; Associated Press 1981; *Conservative Digest*, May/June, 1980, p. 19).

The resources developed by its leadership gave Moral Majority a running start. The organization was rapidly able to reach a national constituency through contacts established by its leadership. These contacts proved even more important as Moral Majority shifted its efforts to the creation of state chapters.

Moral Majority's genius lay in linking with a national network of conservative clergymen. Table 3.1 presents the list of Moral Majority state chairmen. All but two are identifiable as clergymen. While the national office made frequent claims that it presented a broad spectrum of conservative Protestants, Catholics, and Jews, the list of state chairmen suggests otherwise. All of the forty-five whose denominational affiliations were identified through an extensive survey of church directories, telephone books, and newspaper articles are Baptist ministers. The great majority pastor to independent Baptist churches. Twenty-eight are affiliated with the Baptist Bible Fellowship, a loose confederation of more than 2500 independent fundamentalist churches and nearly 2500 pastors (Baptist Bible Fellowship, 1981). Its most prominent members include the trio of Moral Majority founders—Jerry Falwell, Tim LaHaye, and Greg Dixon.

The Baptist Bible Fellowship represents a small slice of the nation's large number of Baptist churches, estimated at 95,000 in 1971 (Mead, 1980, p. 34). Doctrinally, the Bible Baptist Fellowship is in the main line of traditional Baptist beliefs. While strongly fundamentalist, its members are not separatists. The main way in which Bible Baptists differ from most Baptists is in their ecclesiasticism. They emphasize the autonomy of the local church and the placing of strong authority in the pastor as the shepherd of his flock (Mead, 1980, p. 44).

It was not doctrine which placed the Baptist Bible Fellowship in the vanguard of the Moral Majority. Assembly of God and Nazarene

TABLE 3.1. Moral Majority State Chairmen

			Conservative Evangelical
Alabama	Rev. Dick Vignuelle	Shades Mt. Independent Church Birmingham (School)	BBF[a]
Alaska	Dr. Jerry Prevo	Anchorage Baptist Temple (School)	BBF
Arizona	Dr. J. C. Joiner	New Testament Baptist Church Tucson (School)	BBF
Arkansas	Rev. Roy McLoughlin	First Baptist Church Vilonia	Baptist
California	Dr. Tim LaHaye	Scott Memorial Baptist San Diego	BBF
Colorado	Mr. Ed McKenna	(Not available) Parker	NA[b]
Connecticut	Rev. Robert Crichton	Colonial Hills Baptist Danbury	Independent Baptist
Delaware	Dr. R. H. Hayden	Pine Creek Baptist Temple Newark (School)	BBF
Florida	Dr. Bob Gray	Trinity Baptist Church Jacksonville (School)	BBF
Georgia	Dr. Bill Pennell	Forest Hills Baptist Church Decatur	Baptist
Georgia	Dr. Charles Stanley	First Baptist Church Atlanta	Southern Baptist
Hawaii	Dr. Don Stone	Lanakila Baptist Church Waipahu (School)	BBF
Idaho	Rev. Buddy Hoffman	Treasure Valley Baptist Church Boise	Independent-Baptist

State	Name	Church / City	Affiliation
Illinois	Dr. George A. Zarris	Fox River Valley Baptist Church, Aurora	Independent-Fundamentalist
Indiana	Dr. Greg Dixon	Indianapolis Baptist Temple, Aurora	BBF
Iowa	Dr. Olin R. Adams	Quint City Baptist Temple, Davenport (School)	BBF
Kansas	Rev. Ray Melugin	Wichita Baptist Tabernacle (School)	BBF
Kentucky	Dr. W. Robert Parker	Kosmosdale Baptist Church, Louisville	Baptist
Louisiana	Rev. Bob Buchanan	Central Baptist Church, Baton Rouge	Baptist
Maine	Dr. Harry Boyle	Grace Baptist Church, Portland	BBF
Maryland	Dr. Herbert Fitzpatrick	Riverdale Baptist Church, Upper Marlboro	BBF
Massachusetts	Dr. Thomas B. Ward	(Not available), Boston	NA
Michigan	Dr. David Wood	Heritage Baptist Church, Grand Rapids	Independent Baptist
Minnesota	Rev. Rich Angwin	Temple Baptist Church, St. Paul (School)	BBF
Mississippi	Dr. James Johnson	Capitol City Baptist Church, Jackson (School)	BBF
Missouri	Dr. W. E. Dowell	Springfield Baptist Temple (School)	BBF
Montana	Don Jones	(Not available), Billings	NA

TABLE 3.1. Cont.

Nebraska	Rev. Gene Hutton	Marshall Drive Baptist Church Omaha (School)	BBF
Nevada	Rev. Duane Pettipiece	Gateway Baptist Church Las Vegas (School)	BBF
New Hampshire	Dr. Arlo Elam	Tabernacle Baptist Church Hudson (School)	BBF
New Jersey	Dr. Harry Vickery	Heritage Baptist Temple Saddle Brook (School)	BBF
New Mexico	Dr. Curtis Goldman	Temple Baptist Church Albuquerque (School)	BBF
New York	Dr. Dan Fore	Staten Island Baptist Church New York City	Independent Baptist
North Carolina	Rev. Lamar Mooneyham	Tri-City Baptist Church Durham	BBF
North Dakota	Rev. Ken Schaeffer	New Testament Baptist Church Larimore	Independent Baptist
Ohio	Rev. Thomas Trammell	Deer Park Baptist Church Cincinnati (School)	BBF
Oklahoma	Rev. Jim Vineyard	Windsor Hill Baptist Church Oklahoma City (School)	BBF
Oregon	Rev. Mike Gass	Harvest Baptist Temple Medford	Independent Baptist
Pennsylvania	Dr. Dino Pedrone	Open Door Baptist Church Chambersburg	Baptist
Rhode Island	Rev. Tom Crichton	Greater Rhode Island Baptist Temple Johnston	BBF

South Carolina	Dr. Bill Monroe	Florence Baptist Temple (School)	BBF
South Dakota	Rev. R. L. Tottingham	Bible Baptist Church Sioux Falls (School)	BBF
Tennessee	Dr. Bobby Moore	Broadway Baptist Church Memphis	Baptist
Texas	Dr. Gary Coleman	Lavon Drive Baptist Church Garland (School)	BBF
Utah	Rev. Robert Smith	(Not available) Salt Lake City	NA
Vermont	Rev. David Buhman	(Not available) Milton	NA
Virginia	Rev. Danny Cantwell	Open Door Baptist Church Richmond (School)	BBF
Washington	Rev. Tom Starr	Valley Forth Memorial Spokane	Community
West Virginia	Dr. Fred V. Brewer	Fellowship Baptist Church Huntington	BBF
Wisconsin	Dr. Harley Keck	First Bible Baptist Church Green Bay	Independent Baptist
Wyoming	Dr. Morgan Thompson	First Baptist Church Cheyenne	Baptist

SOURCE: *Moral Majority Report*, January 13, 1981. Denominational identifications from Baptist Bible Fellowship *Directory* and local telephone books.

[a] Baptist Bible Fellowship (BBF).

[b] NA, Not available.

churches, for example, share similar theology and many of their ministers served as members of state executive committees. Rather, it was the distinctive organizational character of the Fellowship which made possible Moral Majority's mobilization and gave it a reputation as "perhaps the largest and fastest-growing body of independent Baptists in the United States" (Mead, 1980, p. 44).

At the heart of its success is its strong commitment to church-planting. This is the mission of the Fellowship's Baptist Bible College, which bills itself as the world's largest Bible college. The college catalogue bears the slogan: "Building people to build churches." A statement from W. E. Dowell, college president and Missouri state chairman of Moral Majority, epitomizes the mandate set forth by its founders: "It was their purpose to make Baptist Bible College a real Baptist college, and not only turn out great Christians, but solid Baptists that would go out to build Baptist churches" (Baptist Bible College, 1981). Its most famous alumnus, Jerry Falwell, was the featured speaker at the college's thirtieth anniversary celebration (*Alumni Advocate of Baptist Bible College*, Spring, 1981, p. 1).

Fundamentalist colleges provided a link in the chain that bound Moral Majority state chairmen. Baptist Bible College alumni serve as state chairmen in at least three states. Many other state chairmen completed their college or seminary training at a small number of fundamentalist institutions including the Tennessee Temple Schools, Billings' Hyles-Anderson College, and Falwell's Liberty Baptist College and Liberty Baptist Seminary.

From its start, Moral Majority was a movement of superchurches. Falwell, Dixon, LaHaye, Stanley, and Kennedy were builders of great churches. Many state chairmen followed their example, having started their own churches and worked aggressively to build them into great churches. Several stood at the forefront of the church growth movement. State chairmen from Alaska, California, Hawaii, Michigan, Oregon, Rhode Island, and South Carolina pastor to churches with the fastest growing Sunday schools in their states according to 1979 and 1980 lists. Of the 100 churches with the nation's largest Sunday school attendance for 1979–80, six are led by Moral Majority state chairmen (Towns, Vaughan, and Seifert, 1981, pp. 356–365).

The work of church-planting strengthened ties among independent Baptists. While ministers in mainstream Protestant churches can count on financial assistance from national bodies when they start churches, independent fundamentalists must rely on a combination of personal resources, support from friends and family, and the sponsorship of established fundamentalist churches.

The great majority of pastors interviewed in studies of growing independent fundamentalist churches reported that outside assistance was crucial in the early months of their churches (Towns, 1972). Moral Majority's national leaders played important roles in starting several churches whose pastors later joined the organization. For example, South Carolina Moral Majority chairman Bill Monroe had served as music director at the Indianapolis Baptist Temple prior to returning to his home state to found his own church. Greg Dixon provided help to the young congregation and drove down from Indianapolis to preach the organizational sermon on the night that the church was chartered as the first Baptist Bible Fellowship church in the area. Jerry Falwell makes a practice of preaching at churches started by graduates of Liberty Baptist College and Liberty Baptist Seminary.

While the work of church-building took place throughout the country, much of its impetus came from national pastors' conferences where ministers learned the fundamentals of church growth. Falwell was a leader in the movement. A number of state chairmen made their first contacts with national Moral Majority leaders at conferences sponsored by the Thomas Road Baptist Church and Jack Hyles' First Baptist Church in Hammond, Indiana.

The Christian schools movement provided another set of ties among Moral Majority leaders. Of the twenty-eight state chairmen affiliated with the Baptist Bible Fellowship, at least twenty-five sponsor Christian schools. As a group, they are nearly four times as likely to sponsor schools than the general membership of the Fellowship (Baptist Bible Fellowship, 1981). While the statistic suggests that state chairmen probably represent the larger churches in the Fellowship, it also emphasizes the importance of Christian education among fundamentalists. Falwell had worked with other members of the Baptist Bible Fellowship to develop Sunday School curricula for fundamentalist churches. The designers hoped to encourage unity within the decentralized fundamentalist community. In their statement of purpose, they wrote: "The members of the editorial committee are seeking to encourage fundamentalists, by their own experience, to cooperate with one another in the task of reaching the world for Christ. Their aim is to create a spirit of agreement so that there can be a united front in the fight against wickedness" (Strober and Tomczak, 1979, pp. 172–173).

Like the national leadership, many state chairmen were not strangers to politics. Several played important roles in local moral campaigns. South Carolina's Bill Monroe was the only Protestant member of the state pro-life organization (*Moral Majority Report,* May 1, 1980, p. 13). Former New Jersey co-chairman George Riddell led the members of his congregation in the burning of rock and roll records, magazines, and televisions which he claimed were poor influences on Christians. In 1979, members of his church forced the cancellation of three adult education classes which they considered harmful [(Washington Department Township, New Jersey) *News Report*, November 26, 1980]. Alaska's Jerry Prevo claimed that he was drawn into politics in 1977 when the Anchorage municipal assembly passed an ordinance protecting homosexuals against job discrimination. When the mayor vetoed the measure, Prevo helped organize a campaign that led to the upholding of the veto and the re-election of the mayor (Turner, 1980). Ohio Moral Majority grew out of an organization called God Bless America, Inc., formed in early 1980 to warn the public about America's declining morals and military power. God Bless America founder Thomas Trammel became Moral Majority state chairman and brought his organization into the fold (Beach, 1981). All four state chairmen mentioned above are members of the Baptist Bible Fellowship.

Moral Majority's preference for recruiting clergy should come as no surprise. With large amounts of discretionary time and influence over enduring local groups, clergymen have substantial opportunities for political work. But the special appeal of independent Baptists must be addressed. Three organizational factors made them attractive and available to Moral Majority. Unlike their counterparts in mainstream denominations, independent Baptists do not have claims on resources held by national bodies. The fates of their churches depend largely on their success in local evangelism. For fundamentalist pastors, aggressive soul-winning is more than a matter of conviction; it is an organizational imperative. Their work in recruiting congregants through telephone chains and door-to-door visits sharpened the skills of grassroots mobilization. Local autonomy contributed to a second organizational feature of fundamentalist clergy—an emphasis on strong pastoral authority. Men who start their own churches and recruit their membership are more likely to exert control over their congregations. Most church builders report that they keep a close eye on the activities of their church and a firm hand on its budget. Finally, independent Baptists are not beholden to the dictates of national decision-making bodies. While mainstream clergy generally follow policy set in national conferences and administered by church hierarchy, fundamentalist clergy are free to follow the calls of conscience. Without countervailing pressure from denominational organizations, they were available for mobilization. With a strong local resource base and extensive organizational experience, they were especially attractive to conservative Christian groups. Ties with the national leadership of Moral Majority made their mobilization possible.

Thus, the leadership of Moral Majority recruited men most like themselves. Their success in starting state chapters depended on the conjunction of shared identity and common organization. The presence of a national network of fundamentalist clergy united by a common fellowship, attendance at a small number of Bible colleges, a commitment to building churches and Christian schools, and prior experience in fundamentalist political crusades made rapid mobilization possible.

THE FUNDAMENTALIST CONNECTION

Given its strong traditions of local autonomy and pastoral authority, it is ironic that the fundamentalist connection is strong. These features have contributed to the fragmentation of American fundamentalism, a movement characterized by a large number of small denominations led by strong leaders (Marsden, 1980; Gasper, 1963). The structure of Moral Majority suggests its accomodation to fundamentalist ecclesiasticism.

The tradition of local autonomy is reflected in the charter of Moral Majority affiliates (for a discussion of an organization's charter, see Meyer, 1970). Jerry Falwell writes, *"We encourage our Moral Majority state organizations to be autonomous and indigenous.* Moral Majority state organizations may, from time to time, hold positions that are not held by the Moral Majority, Inc. national organization" (Falwell, ed. 1981, p. 190). The structure of Moral Majority resembles the fundamentalist fellowship organizations from which it draws its leadership.

Moral Majority's charter of autonomy sets the relationship between the national organization and its affiliates. State chapters receive no financial support from the national organization. Each must operate like an independent church, developing its own resource base at the local level.

Despite its reluctance to provide funds, the national organization does not turn its back on state chapters. In dispensing aid, it functions like a mission office. The national headquarters maintains a full-time staff to assist its affiliates. Jerry Falwell devotes a portion of his extensive travelling schedule to forming state chapters. During 1980, Falwell served as a magnet for the state capitol rallies that marked the birth of most state chapters. The rallies closely followed the revivalist script designed for Falwell's "I Love America" campaign. Clergymen throughout the state were invited to a prayer breakfast featuring appearances by Falwell and Moral Majority state leaders. The audience for the rallies included hundreds of children bussed from Christian schools who watched the pageantry provided by the Liberty Baptist choir and the stars of the Old Time Gospel Hour. Friendly politicians were invited to appear on the podium, and after the rally influential local clergy were treated to personal meetings with Falwell. Press conferences surrounding the events received extensive media coverage (Carpenter, 1980).

Apart from its involvement in forming state chapters, the national office seems willing to let state chairmen run their own show. The chartering of autonomous chapters encourages the maintenance of strong local leadership. State chairmen have substantial control over the program of their chapters. As a result, they are able to select issues with broad appeal to local clergy. Churches are the main targets of mobilization for most Moral Majority chapters and the support of local clergy is crucial. Under current IRS regulations, churches are able to contribute up to five percent of their income to lobbying groups. The sum represents the difference between survival and success for many state chapters.

Local issues also provide the opportunity to build coalitions with other moral action groups. Coalitions are the best means for broadening the constituency beyond the boundaries of the narrow fundamentalist universe. In the spirit of most New Right organizations (Crawford, 1980), the national office strongly encourages coalition-building. A recent issue of the Moral Majority Report praised the Arizona state chairman for his "outstanding job in putting together a strong coalition to advance pro-life and pro-moral objectives" (*Moral Majority Report,* November 23, 1981, p. 8). At times, the national office takes the initiative, forging coalitions at the top and calling on state chapters to ally with local units of another national organization. In 1981, the national office arranged cooperation between Moral Majority chapters in Virginia and Florida and affiliates of the Eagle Forum to stall the passage of ERA legislation (*Moral Majority Report,* November 23, 1981, p. 3).

While the national office encourages cooperation with its programs, it exerts little influence over the activities of local chapters. A remark by the Ohio state chairman characterizes the position of many state chairmen toward the national office. He reported that while his chapter is concerned with many of the same issues as the national organization, it operates autonomously (Beach, 1981). True to their fundamentalist creed, most state chairmen reserve the right to write the script for the political activities of their chapters.

At the start, most chapters marched in step with the national organization. The 1980 Presidential election and the large number of congressional races provided a common focus for chapters throughout the nation. Majority's massive voter registration campaign supplied a common agenda. Through most of 1980, state chapters put aside their special projects and poured themselves into the work of registering and influencing voters. Some did a great deal more. Chapters in Alaska and Indiana made efforts to capture the delegate selection process for the GOP convention (Turner, 1980; Gelarden, 1980). State chapters in Alabama, California, Georgia, Iowa, and Oklahoma worked on behalf of Congressional candidates in their states. Chapters in California, Ohio, North Carolina, and Oregon rated candidates on morality scales or questioned candidates on their moral stances. At the local level, Moral Majority affiliates played a role in county and district politics. The Lee County, Florida chapter saw sixteen of its members elected to the executive committee of the local Republican party. Two of its members ran for seats on the Lee County School Board (*Moral Majority Report,* September 15, 1980, p. 13).

To many observers, its activities during the election provided convincing proof of Moral Majority's ability to orchestrate a national chorus of fundamentalist political action. In fact, the elections only masked the different concerns of state leaders. When November passed, their diverse programs reemerged in full flower.

Several common themes distinguished the activities of state chapters. Many worked for the passage of pro-family legislation. Chapters in California and Minnesota opposed gay-rights bills, while their counterparts in Arizona, Connecticut, Idaho, Maryland, New Jersey, New York, Ohio, and Washington fought for pro-life legislation. The California chapter organized a well-attended Pro-Family Conference in Long Beach. The Kentucky chapter sponsored marches against pornography, while the New York chapter organized the picketing of a theatre showing X-rated films. The Washington chapter lobbied for the passage of a bill imposing severe penalties on vendors of pornographic material. Educational issues provided a second major focus. Chapters in Louisiana, Mississippi, Tennessee, and Virginia sought to limit government interference with Christian schools. State leaders in California, Kansas, Maryland, New Jersey, Oregon, and Washington sought to increase parental control over the teaching of sex education in public schools. The North Carolina chapter reviewed school textbooks and developed lists of questionable materials for parents concerned about the education of their children, while in Arkansas, Illinois, Louisiana, Oregon, and Washington, chapters worked for the passage of legislation for the teaching of scientific creationism.

In time, a rough division of labor developed between the national office and its state chapters. As might be expected, the Washington office trained its eyes on Congress, taking positions on national issues ranging from abortion to Zimbawe. The national office was a multiple-issue organization, while most of its affiliates came to look like single-issue groups which devoted their energies to one or two items from the full list presented by the national leadership. Were Moral Majority a more centralized organization, one might expect that its affiliates would follow its dictates. Instead, the decentralized structure compelled the national office to devise programs which provided a common focus for its chapters. For example, in the spring of 1981, the national office encouraged state chapters to take part in a national campaign to monitor the content of prime-time TV. Only a handful of chapters appear to have taken part. Many state leaders joined with the belief that as long as it could pay its pipers, each state chapter could call its tune. Faced with obstacles to centralized control by the national office, Majority's leadership was forced to rely on exhortatory rhetoric to get state chapters to march in step on issues of national concern. In its structure, Moral Majority resembles a fellowship rather than a denomination. By incorporating a national network of funda-mentalists, it inherited an organizational model which set limits on its action.

CONCLUSION

Let us return to our original question. Why was Moral Majority more successful in mobilizing conservative Christians? All four conservative evangelical groups—Bill Bright's crusade, Christian Voice, Religious Roundtable, and Moral Majority—shared similar goals and targeted roughly the same constituency. Standard journalistic explanations which credit financial patronage, the electronic church, outside expertise, and propitious circumstances fail to fully account for their differential success in mobilizing moral Americans. While all of these factors contributed to the different fates of the groups, Moral Majority's greater success de-pended on features which its competitors lacked.

Moral Majority's successful strategy lay in welding disparate local activi-ties and activists into a national movement. It was more able than its competitors to mobilize groups already active at the grassroots. To be sure, the distribution of these groups was not uniform and Moral Majority's national mobilization was highly uneven. But it was able to establish a beachhead in all fifty states in a relatively short span. Its strong links to fellowshipped fundamentalists and its willingness to champion issues which were the major concerns of the group were crucial to its rapid mobilization.

The centerpiece of its mobilization campaign was the local church. While many accounts of the New Christian Right suggest that its mobiliza-tion depended on a steady diet of direct mail, the career of Moral Majority suggests otherwise. Direct mail fund raising nurtured the national office, but its link with local churches was the crucial ingredient of its mobilization at the grassroots. Its founders were champions of the local church. Falwell had transformed Thomas Road Baptist Church into the nation's leading media church. Largely independent Baptists, Moral Majority's state lead-ers were church planters and builders of great churches.

While its allegiance to the primacy of the local church had wide appeal, it created potential problems for the organization. In the tradition of independent Baptists, the national organization renounced centralization and hierarchy. Recent events suggest that Moral Majority may be vulnerable to the factional splits which have long plagued American fundamentalism.

The mobilization of the New Christian Right suggests two lessons for students of social movements. The first is largely a recitation of familiar theories and recent research. While alternative explanations proliferate, there is strong evidence that successful movement organizations build on existing networks. Moral Majority outdistanced its competitors by riding on the back of a large and growing body of fellowshipped fundamentalists. The second lesson suggests a possible next assignment for research on social movements. When movements incorporate members of preexisting associations, they are likely to inherit organizational models which may be hard to put aside. Moral Majority's charter for state chapters reflected the priorities of local autonomy and pastoral authority within American fundamentalism. For sociologists, the moral of Moral Majority's mobilization is simply put: While the availability of pre-existing networks lowers the cost of mobilization, social movement organizations may have to pay a stiff price when they incorporate previously organized constituencies.

4 IDEOLOGICAL PACs AND POLITICAL ACTION

Margaret Ann Latus

This chapter focuses on the resource mobilization and expenditure tactics of selected liberal and conservative Political Action Committees (PACs), including one case of a religiously based group. Political Action Committees are interest groups that seek to accomplish their objectives through influencing the electoral process. Unlike lobbying organizations, PACs are authorized to engage in a range of electoral activities and to attempt to influence legislation by electing sympathetic legislators.

PACs EXAMINED

Eight liberal and conservative PACs and the Christian Voice Moral Government Fund were examined as representative of the most successful ideological and religious PACs in the 1978 and 1980 elections. The committees were selected in pairs to facilitate comparison of the tactics of both the conservative and liberal groups. Four multi-issue PACs were selected, as well as pairs of PACs focused on the abortion issue and the gun control issue.

The liberal National Committee for an Effective Congress (NCEC) is contrasted with the conservative Committee for the Survival of a Free Congress (CSFC). The National Committee for an Effective Congress is the sample PAC which has been in existence the longest, providing extraparty campaign expertise to progressive candidates for over 30 years. In addition, NCEC retains a wide range of consultants to assist in individual campaigns as requested by the PAC. Patterned after the NCEC, the CSFC is perhaps the center for strategy planning in the conservative movement. Founded by Paul Weyrich in 1974, the Committee provides campaign services to conservative candidates and gathers election information for use by many other conservative PACs.

The other pair of multi-issue PACs appears at first to be a mismatch: the National Conservative Political Action Committee (NCPAC) is the best-financed group in our sample, while the Americans for Democratic Action (ADA/PAC) has the fewest resources. Nonetheless, at the time of the 1980 election, ADA/PAC was the closest nonlabor organization to study as a liberal alternative to NCPAC. NCPAC has existed since 1975, when it was formed by John (Terry) Dolan, Roger Stone, and Charles Black to give conservatives expertise and support in campaigns. In contrast, ADA/PAC was founded in 1978 at the urging of a major leader in the original Americans for Democratic Action organization, but it did not become electorally active until 1979.

After examining the above four multi-issue PACs, contrasts are then drawn to two pairs of single-issue groups—those concerning the gun control and abortion issues. Gun Owners, the California based PAC that fights gun control along with the National Rifle Association, has both a state and a national committee founded in 1975 by Senator H. L. Richardson. The national committee, Gun Owners of America (GOA), concentrates primarily on making contributions to congressional races, according to Executive Director Bill Saracino. In contrast, Handgun Control, Inc. PAC, founded in the fall of 1979 to counter the political activities of the NRA and Gun Owners of America, attempts to influence campaigns by the use of negative expenditures and local political activity.

Responding to the Supreme Court's abortion decision of *Roe* v. *Wade,* 410 U.S. 113 (1973), numerous pro-life organizations have sprung up along with liberal counterparts to oppose them. Life Amendment Political Action Committee (LAPAC) was founded by its present director, Paul Brown, in 1977 with a mere $1,000 contribution. Mr. Brown claims that the PAC's greatest potential strength is in mobilizing abortion opponents to become involved at the grassroots level.

Representing the women's pro-choice side of the abortion issue is NOW/PAC, although contrasting NOW/PAC with LAPAC is a less than ideal comparison for several reasons. Technically speaking, abortion is only one of a series of issues which concern NOW/PAC; although what is perhaps its primary issue—passage of the ERA—is promoted separately by NOW/ERA/PAC. NOW/PAC concerns itself with a combination of issues of interest to women, not the least of which is abortion. Thus, the study of NOW/PAC's involvement in national races may show some interesting differences in tactics between this more broadly based women's group and the more narrowly focused pro-life PAC.

The eight PACs have been selected as representative of successful PACs based upon their financial accomplishments in the 1980 elections. Six were among the top 50 PACs in receipts and expenditures in 1980, according to Federal Election Commission reports. Handgun Control, Inc. PAC ranked 136 and ADA/PAC ranked 491. In general, the resource mobilization and expenditure tactics of these PACs ought to shed insight into how successful conservative and liberal PACs conduct their business. Only after drawing conclusions about the behavior of these ideological PACs will the one religious PAC in the sample, Christian Voice Moral Government Fund, be examined.

According to Gary Jarmin, National Director of Christian Voice Moral Government Fund, this PAC was an offshoot of the Christian Voice lobby, which was an outgrowth of American Christian Cause, an educational group founded by Dr. Roger Grant in 1975. American Christian Cause was a religious, tax-exempt organization which sought to inform and mobilize citizens to oppose gay rights and pornography. Because of its tax-exempt status, however, the group was limited in the extent to which it could become politically involved. Thus, in 1977, the Christian Voice lobby was formed to educate Christians in the country about political issues, to direct them in political action, and to engage in lobbying. Three years later, Mr. Jarmin and others at Christian Voice decided that the formation of a PAC was the next logical step in order to increase the political impact of Christian citizens.

Although the PAC could have been formed as an affiliate of Christian Voice and thus have the lobby organization to underwrite its fund-raising and operating expenses, this would have prevented the PAC from soliciting beyond the membership rolls of the lobby. Sections 114.5 and 114.7 of 11 Code of Federal Regulations–Federal Elections, require that PACs affiliated with parent corporations must limit their solicitations to the established membership rolls, although affiliation also means that the parent group may provide the fund-raising and administrative expenditures for the PAC. (This same provision applies to the affiliated, segregated funds discussed in this chapter, including ADA/PAC, Handgun Control, Inc. PAC, and NOW/PAC.) In order to permit broader solicitation efforts, however, the Christian Voice Moral Government Fund was established as a separate and independent PAC in February 1980. Despite this late founding and the need to cover its own operating expenses through its solicitations, Christian Voice Moral Government Fund was an important New Christian Right force in the 1980 elections.

The purpose of examining these nine liberal, conservative, or religious PACs is to determine whether ideology results in characteristic resource mobilization and expenditure tactics. Are the tactics used by conservative organizations different from those used by liberal counterparts? If so, is ideology the key to explaining these distinct approaches? Are differences in the tactics and successes of PACs tied to the type of group (multi-issue or single-issue) or the type of issue with which the focused groups are concerned? Does the expertise of the PAC leadership, the extent of the group's financial resources, and its previous experience in electoral politics also affect the approaches taken to solicit funds and members and to achieve campaign successes?

Table 4.1 lists the receipts of selected liberal and conservative PACs from 1977 to 1981. Conservatives are five to six times as successful as liberals in raising substantial sums of money, a proportion which did not change significantly with the emergence of two of the liberal PACs in the sample in 1979. In the 1978 election cycle, the four selected conservative groups raised $6.4 million to the $1.2 million raised by NCEC and NOW/PAC. In the 1980 election, with two new liberal PACs,

TABLE 4.1. Receipts ($) of Liberal and Conservative PACs 1977–1981

	1977–1978	1979–1980	Through June 1981
Multi-issue PACs			
NCEC	1,051,616	1,570,899	505,457
CSFC	2,023,133	1,647,567	407,439
ADA/PAC	—	49,382	8,170
NCPAC	2,842,865	7,609,973	2,031,779
Single-issue PACs			
Handgun Control	—	170,591	3,432
Gun Owners of			
America	1,452,148	1,416,061	339,206
NOW/PAC	117,691	265,518	—
LAPAC	110,896	625,756	111,561
TOTAL receipts for			
Liberal PACs	1,169,307	2,056,390	517,059
Conservative PACs	6,429,042	11,296,357	2,889,985

Source: All figures based on official Federal Election Commission summary reports.

the liberals raised only $2.1 million to the conservatives' $11.3 million. After the first quarter of the 1982 election cycle, conservatives were ahead in receipts by $2.9 million compared to the liberals' $520,000.

Examination of pairs of committees indicates that only NCEC and CSFC are anywhere near comparable in their fund raising for liberals and conservatives, respectively. In fact, NCEC narrowed the gap in 1980 and began to surge ahead in 1981. Still, none of the liberal PACs come close to the financial power of NCPAC, which raised almost as much in the first half of 1981 as it did in the entire 1978 election cycle. The liberal counterpart selected for NCPAC, ADA/PAC, is, in fact, the weakest of the liberals in fund-raising, with only about $50,000 raised in the 1980 election. Nonetheless, prior to the 1980 elections, ADA/PAC was the best known and closest liberal analog to NCPAC. Since the election, however, several serious challengers to NCPAC have emerged on the liberal side, including Victor Kamber's Progressive PAC and Senator Kennedy's Fund for a Democratic Majority.

Table 4.1 also shows that, in this sample, multi-issue committees tend to have a larger financial base than single-issue groups. Perhaps because multi-issue groups can contact a range of constituencies on different issues, they are able to build broader coalitions of support than single-issue groups. However, Morton C. Blackwell, New Right leader and Special Assistant to President Reagan as a liaison with PACs, disagrees; he argues that, in principle, focused-issue groups have a much greater potential for building a broad base of support. *Focused-issue* groups, a term Blackwell argues is more accurate than *single issue,* must only retain the support of members within a relatively narrow set of issues. Multi-issue groups, however, must retain the support of members as the PAC takes positions on a range of issues—from defense spending to abortion, from gun control to prayer in the schools. Rather than building a broader constituency by attracting members interested in any one of these issues, multi-issue groups risk alienating members who disagree with certain positions while supporting others, Blackwell argues. The more issues a PAC considers, the more potential areas of disagreement there are that might cause supporters to quit. In truth, however, certain multi-issue PACs have been able to educate members to become interested in new issues, setting the stage not only for expanding the PAC's base of support, but also the range of electoral concerns it can have. At least in this sample, the multi-issue PACs are financially stronger than single issue PACs. Whether this relationship holds for ideological PACs in general is open to debate and further research.

Table 4.2 indicates interesting differences in resource expenditures among these groups in the 1980 election. Although the expenditures

TABLE 4.2. 1980 Expenditures of Liberal and Conservative PACs

PAC	Expenditures[a]	Contributions	Independent expenditures[b]	Number of contributions	Average contrib.[c]	Percentage of expenditures which were contributed[d]
NCEC	$1,416,595 [$1,420,238]	$422,785 [$426,725]	None	138	$3,092	30 [30]
CSFC	$1,623,812 [$1,827,517]	$125,265 [$136,588]	None	94	$1,453	8 [7]
ADA/PAC	$48,252 [$48,252]	$48,250 [$46,750]	None	36	$1,299	100 [97]
NCPAC	$7,470,770 [$9,740,522]	$253,327 [$234,271]	$3,343,322 [$1,939,252]	143	$1,638	3 [2] Indep. 45 [20]
Handgun Control	$164,022 [$164,997]	$6,400 [$6,300]	$42,782 [0]	45	$140	4 [4] Indep. [26]
Gun Owners of America	$1,411,255 [$1,398,670]	$181,494 [$183,480]	$8,795 [$114,213] (for Reagan)	96	$1,911	13 [13] Indep. 1 [9]
NOW/PAC	$271,977 [$535,717]	$172,139 [$165,400]	$1,200 [0]	156	$1,060	63 [31]
LAPAC	$623,988 [$623,977]	$11,395 [$22,371]	$66,698 [$58,653]	51	$438	2 [4] Indep. 11 [9]
Christian Voice	$458,717 [$458,714]	$850 [$1,450]	$382,718 [$339,381]	7	$207	0.2 [0.3] Indep. 83 [74]

[a] Top figures derived from official FEC summary reports filed by PACs. Bracketed figures derived from FEC printout which itemizes contributions to candidates and independent expenditures *on behalf of* candidates.

[b] Figures have same origin as those above. Note: the bracketed figures only include positive independent expenditures.

[c] Because contribution amounts are itemized on the printout, this source is the basis for the average contribution calculations.

[d] These statistics represent the ratio of contributions to expenditures, showing what proportion of expenditures was from direct contributions to candidates. Figures preceded by "Indep." show the percentage of total expenditures that was due to independent expenditures.

column shows disparities similar to those of the receipt figures, the rest of the data point to significant differences in the electoral tactics of these PACs. There is a spread of almost $7.5 million in the amount of expenditures by different groups; the amount given in direct contributions ranges within about $425,000—from NCEC's $422,785 to Christian Voice's $850. With the exception of the gun control case, the liberal groups spent a substantially higher proportion of their funds in direct contributions. In fact, while the four conservative groups combined outspent the liberals by $11.1 million to $1.9 million, the liberals gave more in direct contributions, $645,175 to the conservatives' $475,789. On the other hand, conservatives also spent at least $3.5 million in independent expenditures, a tactic not yet widely used among liberal groups.

There also appear to be great differences in the percent of funds spent on direct contributions when comparing ADA/PAC and NCPAC or NOW/PAC and LAPAC. Some PACs are independent groups with no financial ties to their "parent organizations," whereas others are "separate segregated funds," the FEC designation for PACs connected with membership corporations. Of the four PACs mentioned above, ADA/PAC and NOW/PAC are affiliated with their parent organizations and receive substantial financial support from them. By law, the sponsoring organizations may pay for the establishment, administration, and fundraising costs of the affiliated PAC. Thus, funds raised by the PAC need not cover operating expenses, leaving a much larger proportion of the funds for campaign related activities.

In contrast, NCPAC and LAPAC spend between 50 and 75 percent of their resources on fund-raising and administrative costs. A large part of this is due to the tremendous costs of maintaining a direct mail solicitation program. Groups that rely totally on direct mail fund raising are bound to have at least half their spending power consumed by overhead. This fact must be borne in mind whenever PACs are compared on the basis of the proportion of funds actually used for political purposes.

RESOURCE MOBILIZATION: MONEY AND MEMBERSHIP

These selected PACs can first be compared on the basis of the most common and significant mobilization tactic: direct mail. Used especially for fund raising, direct mail technology is perhaps the political tactic most characteristic of the New Right and of national politics in the 1980's. Mail solicitation involves designing effective "packages" that are then carefully targeted (by use of demographics or other techniques) to potential audiences. The first stage, *prospecting*, attempts to locate new members and contributors from selected lists. The second stage uses this carefully constructed *house file* to resolicit past contributors and to cement their loyalty. The success of mailings is measured not only by the amount of money raised, but also by the size of the average return and response rate—the percentage of people contributing to a given appeal. While only 1.5–2% is considered an acceptable return on a prospect mailing, mailings to the house list should bring about 12 to 16%. Typical prospect mailings and house lists have average donations of between $15 and $20.

Because it can be directed to a more carefully controlled audience than other mass appeals, direct mail is the most cost effective way to raise large numbers of small contributions. This is important for PACs, since the 1974 amendments to the Federal Election Campaign Act limit the size of contributions individuals can make and impose strict reporting requirements. Direct mail is a multifaceted tactic which can achieve multiple objectives at once. A complete direct mail package can educate individuals on political issues, advertise the merits of the soliciting agency, promote feelings of identification and membership with the cause, and encourage other grassroots political activities, as well as request contributions. In sum, direct mail is an extremely effective resource mobilization tactic which has come of age in the late 1970s partly because of technical advances, partly because of election law requirements, and partly because of the increase of political entrepreneurs skilled in its use.

Table 4.3 shows that direct mail solicitation is the major fund-raising tactic used by the PACs selected. All information provided is based on interviews conducted in 1981 with representatives of the PACs. Although NCEC and CSFC have similar average contributions, the CSFC has a much higher response rate—40% compared to NCEC's 10%. Yet CSFC receives this high response from a list of only about 25,000 donors, while NCEC solicits a house list of 86,000. The major differences between the other multi-issue PACs, NCPAC and ADA/PAC, are not their response rates but their house list size and degree of reliance on direct mail. While ADA/PAC relies completely on direct mail for raising funds from its 20,000 contributors, NCPAC taps its 350,000 donors by mail to raise only 60% of its funds. The remainder comes from phone solicitations and special events.

Turning to the focused issue PACs, only LAPAC does not raise all of its funds through mail solicitations. The liberals seem to have the edge on list size, however, for Handgun Control has 450,000 donors to GOA's 125,000 and NOW/PAC solicits 140,000 members while LAPAC has a house list of only 30,000. The average contributions are significantly smaller for focused issue rather than multi-issue PACs, with LAPAC the

TABLE 4.3. Direct Mail Fund Raising by PACs

PAC	Percentage of funds raised by direct mail	Size of house list	Average response rate (%)[a]	Average contribution ($)
NCEC	75	86,000	10	28
CSFC	100	25,000 + 105,000 old donors	40	25
ADA/PAC	100	20,000	14	24
NCPAC	60	350,000	10	20
Handgun control	100	450,000	10	18
Gun Owners of America	100	125,000	—	14
NOW/PAC	100	140,000	—	—
LAPAC	80	30,000	10	7.50
Christian Voice	100	40,000	7–10	12–14

[a] Average response rate is the percentage of responses received from mailings to the house list. Prospecting response rate would range between 1 and 2%.

lowest at only about $7.50. Finally, in terms of direct mail, Christian Voice more closely resembles focused issue PACs than multi-issue groups. Its moderately sized house list of 40,000 has an average response rate of only 7–10% with a relatively small average contribution of between $12 and $14.

As the following analyses show, interviews with PAC officials also generated rich descriptive data about four aspects of resource mobilization: the use of direct mail and other media; the nature of the relationship with constituencies or members; the use of incentives to motivate participation; and the reliance on local organizations or chapters.

The National Committee for an Effective Congress has been active for over 30 years, providing progressive candidates with financial support, consultant services, and other professional political expertise. Over the years NCEC has come to rely more on direct mail for fund raising and building its membership. The PAC faced a potential crisis in 1979 because its lists were growing stale. Furthermore, most of the contributors were over 55 years old, an age when liberal idealism tends to give way to more conservative views.

The post–1980 election climate reinvigorated NCEC's direct mail program, however, and prompted Director Russell Hemenway to seek the services of the consultant firm Craver, Mathews, Smith and Co.—the liberals' best counterpart to Richard Viguerie. Since March 1981, CMS developed an aggressive prospecting campaign for NCEC, which located

16,000 new contributors by November 1981 by mailing about 2.5 million letters. Mr. Hemenway characterizes the NCEC's relationship with contributors as one of loyalty based on appreciation for the past performance of the PAC.

Although direct mail remains the cornerstone of NCEC's fund-raising efforts, the PAC has also relied on fund-raising events and personal appeals to large donors. For its own fund raising and to assist candidates, NCEC hosts parties to bring together contributors and potential beneficiaries, especially tapping "New York City's liberal community" (according to an NCEC pamphlet). NCEC has also initiated a celebrity program which uses music, television, theater, and movie stars to attract their constituencies and mobilize them to support NCEC's efforts and candidates. Mr. Hemenway hopes that this approach will enable NCEC to raise money, obtain publicity, and develop a pool of local volunteers by increasing the political consciousness of individuals initially attracted by the appeal of the celebrity.

If imitation is the sincerest form of flattery, then the NCEC should be deeply touched by the emergence of its conservative counterpart, the Committee for the Survival of a Free Congress. The CSFC quickly surged ahead of its liberal model by basing its resource mobilization on a highly personalized direct mail program. According to Finance Director Elaine Hartman, almost all of the CSFC's funds are raised by direct mail, most of which is handled from their office. Prior to 1978, much of the CSFC's fund raising was done by Richard Viguerie. In December 1978, the group began its own small direct mail program (list size of 1600), relying heavily on volunteers to reduce the proportion of the resources expended on fund raising. The list of the CSFC's largest donors is now handled completely within the PAC, whereas mailing to the house list of about 25,000 may be contracted to outside mailing houses.

Ms. Hartman characterizes the CSFC's relationship with contributors as strong, and characterized by a great deal of communication. About half the contributors include letters with their checks; others feel free to call her or Paul Weyrich when they have a concern. When CSFC began doing its own mailings, it aimed to be as personal as possible, including having all letters personally signed by Mr. Weyrich. These factors, plus the continuity of people at CSFC, help explain why the CSFC has a response rate of 40% for its house list, a figure unheard of among most direct mail programs.

Both Paul Weyrich and Ms. Hartman suggested reasons why the CSFC's supporters are so loyal. Questioned about whether the group relies on external incentives to motivate contributors, Weyrich insisted that: "The people give because they think their money is being well spent. Furthermore, everyone participates in a victory. Contributors are notified that their contribution made a difference in other races, even if they couldn't have influence in their own district."

The other two multi-issue PACs, ADA/PAC and NCPAC, can best be examined by contrasting their resource mobilization tactics. Many of the differences arise because ADA/PAC is a separate segregated fund which has its operating costs covered by the parent organization, whereas NCPAC must finance its substantial administrative costs as well as its campaign activities. NCPAC has a tremendous fund-raising potential, using direct mail (60%), telephone banks (20%) and special fund-raising appeals (20%) to tap its 350,000 donors for an average contribution of $20. On the other hand, ADA/PAC was restricted to soliciting its 20,000 members with only two mailings during its first year.

Because of ADA/PAC's affiliation with the parent group, it is impossible to consider its relationship with constituents as distinct from that of the parent organization. ADA itself must build the loyalty among its members which the PAC can later tap for its efforts. In comparison, NCPAC interacts frequently with contributors. Attempts are made to keep them informed and educated through periodic newsletters. Contributors are also encouraged to write letters, call their congressmen, or get others involved. Unlike the CSFC, NCPAC does not emphasize two-way communication with any but its largest donors.

While the first two multi-issue groups examined (NCEC and CSFC) do not use any local organizations, ADA/PAC and NCPAC rely on local groups for political mobilization. ADA/PAC counts on local chapters for information about races and to provide additional political assistance in campaigns, if they so choose. Furthermore, local chapters must request and approve all contributions the group decides to make in their locales. Although NCPAC does not rely on highly structured local chapters, it does establish committees in states and districts where it becomes involved. These groups, funded by NCPAC, are often not composed of contributors to NCPAC; rather, they consist of politicos who can connect the local efforts of NCPAC with those of other groups.

As opposed to multi-issue groups, focused-issue groups are often very particular about the type and timing of their resource mobilization. They must be quick to capitalize on changes in public sentiment and must also find innovative ways to identify their audience. Thus, the examination of focused-interest groups presents modifications on mobilization strategies and shows how the type of the issue influences which approaches can be used effectively.

Gun control as a focused issue pits the specific interests of the intensely motivated class of gun owners and sportsmen against the general interests of potential victims of gun crimes (virtually everyone). This distinction means that the Gun Owner's constituency, though small in comparison to those potentially benefited by gun control, is much easier to segment and motivate.

For its resources, Gun Owners of America relies entirely on direct mail fund raising by Richard Viguerie. Mr. Saracino claims that contributors to Gun Owners are basically apolitical. Prospect mailings to conservative candidate contributor lists are not as successful as those to outdoor and sportsmen magazine lists. Although members feel strongly about gun control, they are not perceived as broadly political or ideological. Thus, direct mail appeals concentrate on convincing members that Gun Owners of America will accomplish the political tasks individuals cannot ordinarily achieve through their small contribution.

Mr. Saracino characterizes the relationship with members as a consumer-producer one. The organization concentrates on its electoral objectives rather than on educating its members or promoting increased political participation by them. It occasionally attempts to boost support by the use of premiums in direct mail appeals. Curiously, while local organizations would be of little significance for grassroots political activity (since GOA does not feel its members are so inclined), the organization is considering the formation of local affiliates. Why? Partly because some amount of local organization is necessary to increase the effectiveness of GOA's efforts at state legislative levels, but primarily because local chapters may enhance the contributor's sense of loyalty and solidarity, increasing the likelihood of response to appeals.

In contrast, Handgun Control, Inc. must build its base of support on the foundation of handgun victims organized to raise the awareness of potential victims of handgun violence. While the parent corporation is a lobby with 600,000 supporters, only 150,000 of these are donors who can be solicited by the PAC. Although officials at Handgun Control estimate that their supporters are five to ten times more intense in their support for legislation than their opponents are against it, these supporters are much harder to identify and mobilize. The favorite tactic is to publicize the experiences of handgun victims to mobilize support in local areas, or to use such national events as the Lennon shooting and assassination attempts to raise the public's awareness of this issue. The Lennon shooting was particularly useful in mobilizing college students.

Handgun Control uses mass media to gain members it can then solicit through direct mail. After President Reagan was shot, for example, 250,000 people responded to the twenty-six newspaper ads that were run throughout the country. Curiously, Gun Owners of America also had an upsurge in support following the assassination attempt. This is attributed partly to heightened awareness of the gun control issue, and partly to the fact that contributors were warned that they needed to prepare to combat a new wave of gun control sentiment. Such gun control sentiments were championed by Handgun Control, Inc. PAC that presented itself as the forum through which individuals could act to halt handgun violence. Once interested parties are converted into gun control donors, they are then encouraged to gather more supporters. Handgun victims are encouraged to speak in local areas and to show a film on handgun violence.

Unlike the gun control issue, the abortion issue is not divided into constituencies with personal interests. Not all pro-choice opponents of the Human Life Amendment are active because the amendment may prohibit their having an abortion. Similarly, the victims or potential victims of abortions cannot represent themselves; thus, pro-life activists cannot entirely be acting out of a perceived personal threat. Instead, both sides are mobilizing individuals on the basis of their philosophical or religious beliefs; for example, personal freedom versus the sanctity of human life. The antiabortion forces have been particularly resourceful in locating and tapping potential supporters.

Life Amendment Political Action Committee decided early on to stress grassroots level activities. Identifying the pro-life constituency poses some difficulties for LAPAC, however, for as Mr. Brown explained, "Pro-life people are not necessarily conservative." Although LAPAC is part of a loosely knit coalition with groups of the New Right, one cannot simply tap into the other New Right lists to find pro-life people. Instead, Mr. Brown explained how LAPAC has a mobilization strategy built on public relations, newspaper campaigns, and contacts with churches. LAPAC issues "hit lists" to manipulate the press into providing attention for their cause and to educate potential supporters. Most of the active donor list of 30,000 has been built in response to inserts in religious periodicals, especially Catholic diocesan papers. Test mailings have been used for prospecting; direct mail is basically reserved for soliciting funds from members. Telephone solicitation is used to complement the direct mail program, raising 15% of the PAC's revenue. Although premiums have not been used to promote responses, thank-you notes have been found to be an effective way to encourage additional contributions. Nonetheless, the average contribution is substantially lower than that of the other PACs studied, a fact Mr. Brown cannot explain. The small size of its contributions may conceivably be compensated for by the fact that LAPAC strives to make its members "total activists." Grassroots participation in local campaigns is strongly encouraged, especially focusing on the mobilization of church groups. Thus, resource mobilization for LAPAC involves using the mass media to identify constituency for both its financial and political support.

Unlike LAPAC, NOW/PAC is not concerned solely with the abortion issue. NOW/PAC is also different from LAPAC in that it is a separate segregated fund which has its overhead covered by the affiliated organization—the National Organization for Women. Because of this affiliation, the PAC must solicit only from NOW's active membership list, and must make its political decisions in conjunction with local NOW chapters. The annual PAC appeal is basically a discussion of needs and an expression of support for specific candidates and issues. The PAC relies on the other periodic mailings of the parent organization to inform and educate members on the need for their support. Thus, NOW/PAC does very little to mobilize members beyond its annual solicitation. Although individual chapters may also prompt members to volunteer in campaigns supported by the PAC, this mobilization is not directed from the national level.

Differences in the success of *resource mobilization* among groups depend to a large extent on whether the PAC is multi-issue or focused-issue and which issues are involved. In addition, mobilization may differ according to the degree of expertise involved in (1) utilizing direct mail; (2) building loyalty among members; (3) providing additional incentives for participation; and (4) developing local organizations to augment mobilization programs.

RESOURCE EXPENDITURES: CAMPAIGNS AND CANDIDATE SUPPORT

Table 4.4 offers a summary comparison of expenditure characteristics of the selected PACs. Not only does this chart provide a synopsis of the expenditure repertoire of each group, it also indicates which groups favor specific tactics. Thus, while all PACs allocate some of their funds for direct contributions to candidates, fewer groups make these contributions as "in kind" services. More interesting is the fact that conservatives tend to favor independent expenditures and stress a nonincumbent support strategy—rational approaches for groups attempting to counter their minority status in Congress through the strategic expenditure of superior financial resources.

Over the years, NCEC has developed a strong commitment to provide "wholesale" campaign services to progressive candidates in marginal races. Thus, most of its direct contributions to candidates are "in kind" services: campaign planning, research, fund raising, media consulting,

TABLE 4.4. Repertoire of Resource Expenditures for Selected Liberal and Conservative PACs

Do the following PACs:	NCEC	CSFC	ADA/PAC	NCPAC	Handgun control	Gun Owners of America	NOW/PAC	LAPAC	Christian Voice
1. Cover fund-raising and administrative costs in their expenditures?	Yes	Yes	No	Yes	No	Yes	No	Yes	Yes
2. Conduct polling and other campaign support activities?	Yes	Yes	No	Yes	Yes	No	No	No	No
3. Conduct candidate schools?	No	Yes	No	Yes	No	Yes	No	No	No
4. Support fieldmen to gather information or assist campaigns?	No	Yes	No	Yes	Yes	Yes	No	Yes	No
5. Give direct contributions to candidates?	Yes	Yes	Yes	Yes	Yes	Yes	Yes	Yes	Yes
6. Give in kind contributions to candidates?	Yes	Yes	No	Yes	No	No	No	No	No
7. Use independent expenditures either positively or negatively?	No	No	No	Yes	Yes	Yes	No	Yes	Yes
8. Rely on local chapters or grassroots organizing?	No	No	No	Yes	Yes	No	Yes	Yes	Yes
9. Use predominantly a nonincumbent (or anti-incumbent) strategy?	No	Yes	No	Yes	Yes	Yes	No	Yes	Yes

precinct targeting, and polling. In addition, the PAC puts a substantial effort into gathering information on races and disseminating this to interested liberal groups through a "Targeting Seminar." Because of the experience and expertise of NCEC, as well as its extensive information network, progressive candidates and PACs alike rely on NCEC's judgments about running campaigns.

Despite the multitude of political services in which NCEC is engaged, it must still devote 53% of its financial resources to covering fund-raising and administrative costs. According to the PAC's financial statement for 1980, 47% of the expenditures were for political programs, whereas 39% was spent on fund raising and 14% on operating expenses. Nonetheless, these figures are reasonable considering the PAC's independent status and its reliance on direct mail fund raising.

To maximize the effectiveness of its contributions, NCEC retains political consultants and pollsters to assist individual campaigns as needed. The decisions of whether to contribute and what to contribute are made after a substantial body of information has been gathered from polls, candidate interviews, and discussions with local individuals, officials, and journalists. The information network of NCEC has grown extensively; thus, it does not even need fieldmen to assist in gathering information about the local idiosyncracies of the districts.

If this wealth of information leads NCEC to decide that the race is marginal but could be won and that a deserving progressive candidate is involved, the PAC consults with the candidate to determine what kind of assistance is needed. The primary criteria for deciding what services are provided for a selected candidate is what Mr. Hemenway calls the "saliva test." When a candidate realizes how desperately he needs a service, such as a targeting poll, NCEC will consider providing it. The PAC will not force assistance on a campaign that will presumably ignore it.

Although NCEC is extremely experienced in resource expenditures for in kind contributions and political services, it purposely avoids other strategies such as candidate schools, independent expenditures, and grassroots organizing. The PAC prefers to have candidates receive training either from the Democratic National Committee candidate schools or through head-to-head consultations with NCEC staff. NCEC also avoids independent expenditures, primarily because the PAC would be in constant violation of the FEC restriction that there be no contact with candidates. Even if this contact could be avoided, NCEC is concerned that independent expenditures would be counterproductive more often than not. The PAC can be more effective by directly providing the expertise necessary in campaigns, and may even use its campaign planning services to inform candidates of needs they were not aware they had.

As for grassroots organizing, NCEC assists candidates in developing their own local volunteer programs, although the PAC itself does not have chapters or local organizations. The NCEC often accomplishes the task of grassroots organizing as part of its fund-raising services to candidates. A mainstay of NCEC programs is arranging fund-raising parties and events where candidates can solicit financial and political support, as well as gain media exposure. The proposed celebrity program will augment this fund-raising and organizing service to NCEC candidates.

Like the NCEC, the CSFC must raise funds to cover all of its expenditures, thus accounting for the small proportion of expenditures that are contributed to candidates. According to the PAC's audit for 1980, only about 20% of total expenditures went for contributions and other campaign related programs, including consulting, polls, publications, and conventions. Among these special projects were several candidate schools, costing a total of almost $30,000, with only about $7,500 covered by "tuition" payments. Another 25% of the PAC's total expenditures was spent on administrative costs, and fully 55% was absorbed by fund raising. Given the fact that the PAC's mail solicitation program is extremely efficient (a 40% response rate and large average contribution), the proportion of expenditures that must be devoted to fund raising and administrative costs is presumably kept to a minimum.

In making political contributions, the CSFC will not support incumbents, nor does it (often) merely give checks to candidates to use as they like. Instead, the PAC provides a wide range of in kind contributions—whatever is needed to make the campaign a winner. Most, if not all, CSFC money comes with strings attached, including the requirement that someone from the candidate's campaign staff must attend a CSFC Candidate School. Paul Weyrich insists that candidates who have a chance to win do not resent the directions given by CSFC, but recognize that they are intended to strengthen the campaign. If candidates resist the CSFC's terms, Mr. Weyrich pulls out of the race; all but one of the campaigns he has pulled out of since 1976 have eventually lost. The moral for conservative candidates is: It is better to win with CSFC's expertise than to lose without it.

Paul Weyrich is extremely careful about which campaigns the CSFC enters, gathering information on the strengths and weaknesses of candidates from a host of sources. Refusing to rely on polls alone, the CSFC maintains seven to ten fieldmen who are based in local areas and can get a "feel" for the campaign. The fieldmen may then encourage the candidate to conduct a poll and send CSFC the results. The key is to locate the most conservative candidate who is electable in a district where the incumbent or opponent has a "re-elect margin" of under 54%. If, in addition to these factors, the fieldman indicates there is a conservative base of support in the district, then Mr. Weyrich is likely to recommend to the board of directors that CSFC enter the race.

In addition to direct involvement in campaigns, the CSFC engages in various other campaign-related activities. As previously noted, it is considered by many to be the source of reliable information on conservative candidates and worthwhile campaigns. The CSFC also has a political staff of twelve and hired consultants to teach candidate schools and assist campaigns. Yet the CSFC has not moved in two strategy directions which tend to appeal to the other conservative PACs—independent expenditures and grassroots organizing. Independent expenditures are shunned because CSFC money can better be spent by providing expertise in cooperation with the campaigns. Furthermore, focused issue groups are more likely to use independent expenditures in order to assure the visibility of their issues, while the CSFC supports a general conservative ideology. As for organizing local chapters or volunteers to assist campaigns, the CSFC simply does not consider this to be its role. Rather, according to Mr. Weyrich, "The general purpose of the CSFC is to find out which campaigns are viable and which aren't, and to communicate that information to other interested groups."

Whereas the NCEC and CSFC are large-scale PAC operations which provide a range of campaign expertise, ADA/PAC is a modest operation with one tactic—direct contributions to progressive candidates. Because of its status as a separate segregated fund, ADA/PAC is able to have all of its operating expenses covered by the parent organization. The PAC itself works in conjunction with local ADA chapters in awarding direct contributions to candidates. Although the trustees toyed with making independent expenditures as well, this tactic was rejected because increased competition for mailing lists was deemed counterproductive.

Following a request for support by a local ADA chapter, the decision to back a candidate is based on information about the status of the campaign and the records of the candidates. Nonincumbents are assessed on the basis of a personal interview and campaign literature. Incumbents are evaluated in terms of their legislative record and the viability of their campaigns. Although ADA/PAC made an effort at affirmative action in 1980, its primary concern was to assist marginal races that had not received much money from other sources. The decision to back a candidate must then be approved by the local chapter members. Although there is no presumption of additional voluntary campaign assistance on the part of local chapters, this varies from chapter to chapter. Occasionally, the mobilization of local members becomes an additional political resource. At the national level, the professional expertise of the PAC is limited to the services of a single staff member (part-time), resulting in reliance on the tried and true strategy of direct contributions and little else.

In contrast with ADA/PAC, NCPAC resembles a conservative Goliath facing a liberal David. Although NCPAC was formed to provide campaign expertise and support to conservatives, it is best noted for its pioneering efforts in independent expenditures. Over $2 million was spent on Target '80, the negative campaigns which sought to oust the most objectionable liberal senators. Independent expenditures provide versatility in two important respects: the PAC may spend unlimited sums in a campaign if it operates without any contact with the candidate's committee. Furthermore, independent expenditure campaigns can be double-edged. Rather than trying to improve the challenger's "favorable" rating, they may seek to push up the incumbent's "unfavorable" rating. The latter strategy has been used even before the incumbent has an opponent; in fact, it may be necessary to undermine the support of a candidate perceived to be strong in order to persuade a challenger to oppose him. NCPAC claims that the key of its success in both direct and indirect expenditures has been to point out the anomaly of liberal legislators representing basically conservative constituencies.

Because NCPAC has tremendous financial resources, it is engaged in the entire range of resource expenditures. After financing its administrative and fund-raising costs, the PAC still has plenty of money to conduct polls and candidate schools. In addition, NCPAC establishes and funds the efforts of local committees in states and congressional districts. These committees are not the equivalent of local chapters, however, as the individuals involved need not even be NCPAC contributors. Rather, as noted previously, their purpose is to coordinate NCPAC expenditures in concert with the efforts of local groups.

Focused-issue PACs share most of the characteristics of resource expenditures that the multi-issue PACs have, but they tend to be more selective in their approaches. In particular, focused-issue PACs see real advantages to using independent expenditures and local organizations to maximize their electoral impact. Since most focused-issue groups have a smaller base of financial support than the large multi-issue PACs, they may not engage in the full range of campaign-related expenditures, including fieldmen, polling, or candidate schools. They also tend to lack the resources for providing in kind contributions, preferring either to give a simple grant or to reserve their political expertise for use in independent expenditure campaigns.

Although both the Handgun Control, Inc. PAC and the Gun Owners of America Campaign Committee are concerned with the same focused issue, they have very different bases of support and use diverse strategies for resource expenditures. Handgun Control rests its campaign-related activities on the use of negative independent expenditures to defeat targeted incumbents who oppose gun control. Television ads, emotionally charged speeches by handgun victims, and distribution of literature at candidate appearances are all used to heighten the public's awareness of the handgun issue and to undermine the support of incumbents. Whereas a candidate is not likely to run for office solely on the basis of his gun control views (nor are voters likely to support him on the basis of this alone), marginal candidates can find their support eroded by the loss of the five to ten percent of the voters who vote against them because of their pro-gun stance. Thus, Handgun Control devotes very little money or effort to direct contributions or positive campaigns to promote a candidate. Instead, the PAC attempts to blanket selected districts with appeals designed to raise the priority of the handgun issue and increase its negative impact on the electoral strength of gun control opponents.

Gun Owners of America has a larger financial base than Handgun Control, but the overhead of the latter is largely covered by its parent organization. According to the PACs financial report for 1980, the basic noncampaign related expenses for the gun control PAC totalled $20,476 and the parent organization absorbed the additional costs of membership services, public relations, membership development, fund raising, and administration, totalling $705,484. This figure is comparable to the CSFC's fund-raising and administrative costs—costs that this nonaffiliated PAC had to cover through its own expenditures and fund-raising efforts. According to the Handgun Control, Inc. PAC financial report for 1979 and 1980, total expenditures were $162,513—about $38,000 in administrative costs (23%) and about $122,000 (75%) in campaign-related expenses such as consulting, advertising, direct mail, and contributions to candidates. This figure also includes $23,000 for the production of a film on handgun control. Note that only $6,300 (less than 4%) of the PAC's expenditures were direct contributions to candidates.

In addition to independent expenditures, Handgun Control is moving toward a reliance on grassroots organizing as the second major component of its expenditure tactics. While efforts at local organizing were stymied in 1980 because no single congressional district had enough supporters to form a core organization, the PAC intends to broaden its member base significantly. Although there were only 50,000 to 60,000 supporters in 1980, 250,000 individuals responded to ads after the attempt to assassinate President Reagan. These new members will be contacted to participate in local independent expenditure campaigns to gather information on candidates, to schedule appearances by local handgun victims and screenings of the gun control film, and to stir up controversy over this issue in key districts. By dovetailing grassroots mobilization with saturation television ads and other media campaigns, Handgun Control aspires to insure that the gun control issue remains a priority political concern in national elections.

In contrast to Handgun Control, Gun Owners of America has a slightly more diversified set of electoral tactics, although independent expenditures are key and grassroots organizing is being explored for future races. Although GOA relies on information from other PACs rather than conducting its own polls, it utilizes many of the other resource expenditure strategies. Candidate schools are run in California to assist those who cannot attend other schools usually held on the East Coast. Free-lance fieldmen are hired during elections to visit campaigns, gather information, and to lend a hand if necessary. Direct contributions are given in races, but in kind contributions are seldom made.

By far the two largest expenditures of GOA are administrative or fund-raising costs and independent expenditures. Independent expenditures are made for the same tactical reasons that Handgun Control uses them— they are the best way to magnify the political clout of the approximate five percent of the voters who strongly support the right to bear arms. In 1980, the bulk of independent expenditure money supported President Reagan's campaign. Executive Director Bill Saracino expects GOA to become more heavily involved in independent expenditures in future elections. Unlike Handgun Control, however, these campaigns will not necessarily be negative. Instead, GOA will evaluate whether attacks on gun foes or support for anti-gun controllers will be more effective in different races. Furthermore, although GOA has preferred not to back incumbents, it will probably feel committed to support incumbents they helped elect in 1980, especially if these are facing stiff challenges. Thus, the general strategy has been predominantly nonincumbent; however, strategies may change as the PAC achieves its objectives and sees its candidates elected.

The primary tactic in the abortion issue, as in the gun control issue, is to raise its saliency in campaigns to mobilize that margin of voters who will decide on the basis of this focused issue. Of the two groups studied on this issue, NOW/PAC is the more conventional in its resource expenditure approach. Although it is an affiliated PAC, only some of its operating expenses are absorbed by the parent organization. As for the funds spent on campaign-related activities, direct contributions are the predominant mode of expenditure. Direct contributions are awarded after the decision of a nine-member PAC committee (three NOW officers, three board members, and three politically astute members) and the approval of the state organization.

In making decisions, the committee relies on COPE reports and other information shared among liberal groups to determine a candidate's issue stance and viability. In making contributions, NOW/PAC has never taken a negative approach, nor does it tie any strings to its donations. As an electoral bonus, candidates often benefit from volunteer assistance by local NOW members.

While NOW/PAC stresses a positive approach in giving direct contributions to candidates, LAPAC counters with what are frequently negative independent expenditures. Like NOW/PAC, LAPAC stresses the local mobilization of supporters to maximize its political clout. Coordinators (15 in 1980) are appointed in each campaign to inform other groups of LAPAC's efforts, although not necessarily to work with these other organizations and especially not with the official campaign staff. The primary reason for this separation is not simply because groups making independent expenditures must have no contact with the candidate's own committee, but for an important strategic concern: Because abortion is such a volatile issue, Director Paul Brown prefers LAPAC to be the focus for any hostile reactions to their campaigns. This way, he hopes to avoid having a backlash effect hurt the candidates he seeks to help.

In addition to conducting negative independent expenditure campaigns at the local level, LAPAC and its coordinators promote grassroots mobilization among supporters. A particularly interesting tactic for this is a workshop on political action presented to church groups. About 50 workshops were conducted in 1980. Yet another unusual approach was to place leaflets on cars during church services. Thus, LAPAC demonstrates the innovative spirit that often characterizes the resource expenditure strategies of focused-issue groups. In addition, the nature of the abortion issue leads LAPAC to rely on religious affiliations as the best way to identify and mobilize members.

As with resource mobilization tactics, examination of the resource expenditures of individual PACs shows great diversity depending on the type of PAC and professional expertise of its leaders regarding campaign services and political organizing. Furthermore, as table 4.4 indicated, there is not even a single expenditure strategy that is identified only with conservative or liberal PACs. Instead, multi-issue PACs tend to have an extensive repertoire of resource expenditures, including polling, candidate schools, and "in kind" expenditures. On the other hand, focused-issue groups rely more heavily on independent expenditures and grassroots organizing.

RELIGIOUS POLITICAL ACTION COMMITTEES

Part of the justification for the previous, detailed analyses of resource mobilization and resource expenditure patterns among liberal and conservative PACs was the claim that many of these findings would also apply to religious PACs. Although ideology does not strongly affect the behavior or success of PACs when other technical factors are taken into consideration, does the religious foundation of a PAC alter any of these strategic considerations?

In resource mobilization, the Christian Voice PAC relies largely on direct mail solicitation, as do each of the other PACs studied. With a house file of 40,000 and an average response rate between 7 and 10%, its program is comparable to the others studied, although the average contribution of between $12 and $14 is low. Individual mailings focus on specific issues or candidates, thus requiring careful targeting. Late in 1981, the PAC initiated a telephone solicitation program to supplement its direct mail program.

In building the loyalty of contributors, Christian Voice continues to educate supporters about key issues and races. Mr. Jarmin, National Director, believes that individuals respond without additional incentives partly because they enjoy receiving this information, but largely because they are motivated by their religious convictions and believe their contribution will make a difference. In addition, the Christian Voice lobby has local chapters that overlap in membership with the PAC, and the PAC itself is significantly involved in grassroots political activism, reinforcing the contributors' sense of political efficacy.

For Christian Voice, local organizing is far more important as a resource expenditure tactic for political influence in campaigns than as an enhancement to resource mobilization. Christian Voice Moral Government Fund is similar to the focused issue groups studied here in its reliance on grassroots organizing tied to independent expenditures. The key strategy is to target races where the incumbent is vulnerable, then to disseminate through churches a Christian voting "report card" of selected roll call votes by that legislator. Information on races is obtained from national polls or shared findings from other PACs. If an approximate five percent change in the vote might oust an objectionable incumbent, the Moral Government Fund goes to work.

In disseminating these report cards, the PAC relies on contacts with local members or ministers, people often affiliated with the local lobby chapter and who, as individuals, provide a valuable pool of dedicated volunteer labor. These "Christian Activists" then make arrangements to distribute the report cards at local churches and to persuade ministers to encourage their flocks to vote and become involved.

Unlike the Moral Majority, the Christian Voice PAC prefers that its contacts be lay persons. Mr. Jarmin believes that there will be less strife among denominations and greater ease in mobilizing lay people of different denominations to cooperate if their leader is not strongly identified with a given sect. The objective of these Christian voter education programs is to encourage and enable Christians to make a more informed and intelligent judgment on election day. Other grassroots activities related to this objective include voter registration and "get out the vote" drives.

Like the gun control and antiabortion PACs, Christian Voice adopted a predominantly anti-incumbent approach in 1980. Before voters can be persuaded to change their allegiance, Mr. Jarmin notes that, "We have to give people a reason to change horses by exposing the bad voting record of the incumbent." In the future, the PAC may modify this strategy to use pro-challenger information as well as campaigns to protect the incumbency of vulnerable legislators they helped elect in 1980. As the political situation changes, the tactics used must also adapt.

The Christian Voice Moral Government fund case indicates that religious groups are similar to the liberal and conservative PACs in considerations of resource mobilization and expenditures. In fact, religious groups face the same tactical decisions as these other PACs, although there are certain factors peculiar to religious PACs which pose additional problems and others which are definite advantages.

The first problem peculiar to religious groups arises from the notion of the separation of church and state and the limitations placed on the political activities of corporations with tax-exempt status. Three other problems are related to the religious convictions of members. First, any cooperative efforts among religious groups must counteract traditional doctrinal and denominational rifts which could undermine political unity. Second (and related to this), mobilization efforts must overcome the antipolitical bias certain denominations have had in the past. Mr. Jarmin notes that there is a significant shift in the civic responsibility of evangelical Christians who have come to believe that much of the evil in society is the result of their overlong neglect of politics. Finally, although congregations are ready-made grassroots organizations, one must be cautious about adopting their ministers as ready-made leadership figures. Ministers are identified not only with specific denominations but also they have prior obligations to their ministry in these congregations; thus, they may not be as capable of dedicated political work as a lay person might be.

There are three advantages to the reliance upon religion as the identifying and motivating factor of a group's constituency. As noted above, the task of grassroots organizing is usually already partly done, since there is a foundation of existing church congregations on which to build. Furthermore, the religious motivation for behavior can be pervasive and powerful. Mr. Jarmin claims that he has received numerous compliments from candidates on the dedication of Christian Voice volunteers: "Their religious motivation provides a value framework for everything they do in life, and this is true of politics no less than of anything else." Related to this religious zeal is the fact that other incentives for participation (such as premiums) are less necessary for individuals driven by the convictions of their faith. Leaders have merely to ask and it shall be given unto them.

Despite these special considerations related to religious PACs, the force of the argument remains. Examination of the resource mobilization and expenditure tactics of religious and liberal and conservative PACs has demonstrated that the spiritual or ideological predispositions of the groups do not adequately characterize or explain their behavior. Instead, some tactical decisions are affected by whether PACs are multi-issue or focused-issue. Others differ depending on the issue concerned. Research suggests that remaining variations are due to the expertise of PACs in using different approaches. The technical constraints and tactical decisions facing PACs are similar regardless of whether the groups are liberal, conservative, or religious.

ACKNOWLEDGMENTS

The assistance of the following individuals is gratefully acknowledged:

ADA/PAC: Amy Isaacs, Americans for Democratic Action, August 7, 1981—personal interview.

Christian Voice Moral Government Fund: Gary Jarmin, National Director, October 26, 1981—telephone interview.

CSFC: Paul Weyrich, National Director, August 19, 1980—telephone interview; June 2, 1981—personal interview. Elaine Hartman, Finance Director, July 15, 1980—personal interview; June 2, 1981—personal interview; October 13, 1981—telephone interview.

Gun Owners of America: Bill Saracino, Executive Director, October 14, 1981—telephone interview.

Handgun Control, Inc. PAC: Charles Orasin, Executive Vice President, August 6, 1981—personal interview.

LAPAC: Paul Brown, National Director, August 5, 1981—personal interview.

NCEC: Russell Hemenway, National Director, September 11, 1980—telephone interview; October 30, 1981—personal interview. Eileen Fischer, NCEC fund raiser, August 6, 1980—personal interview.

NCPAC: Steven DeAngelo, Press Secretary, August 6, 1981—personal interview; October 1, 1981—telephone interview.

NOW/PAC: Alice Chapman, Treasurer, August 5, 1981—personal interview.

Morton Blackwell, Special Assistant to President Reagan, December 9, 1981—telephone interview.

III | The
Constituency

5 | THE MORAL MAJORITY CONSTITUENCY*

Anson Shupe and William Stacey

Much of the research on the New Christian Right has been inconclusive and largely inferential. Moreover, there is little or no research on the character and extent of popular support for the movement in the Southern Bible Belt where support should logically be strongest and where the electronic church is most heavily syndicated (Hadden and Swann, 1981, pp. 156–157).

The Dallas–Fort Worth Metropolitan Area (Metroplex) offers an ideal opportunity to survey opinion on Moral Majority, Inc., the flagship organization of the New Christian Right, and to probe the demographics of its supporters. The Metroplex, with a population of almost 4 million, is located in north-central Texas in what has been often called the buckle of the Southern Bible Belt. The Texas headquarters of the Southern Baptist Convention and the nation's largest Southern Baptist congregation are located in Dallas; the headquarters of the James Robison Evangelistic Association and the conservative Religious Roundtable, of which Robison is an active charter member, can be found in nearby Fort Worth. The

* This study was not funded by any governmental, university or denominational agency.

103

Metroplex has been the scene of various heavily publicized New Christian Right events and controversies: the 1980 National Affairs Briefing, where presidential candidate Ronald Reagan and other conservative politicians and clergy appeared, a 1981 antiabortion rally attended by Jerry Falwell, James Robison, Phyllis Shlafley and conservative political lobbyists Howard Phillips and Paul Weyrich, an intense "Freedom of Speech, Freedom to Preach" protest campaign in which evangelist James Robison was refused the purchase of airtime on a local television station after he criticized homosexuals, and a series of sensationalized murder divorce trials involving a controversial Fort Worth millionaire who was converted to born-again Christianity by Robison.

THE DALLAS–FORT WORTH STUDY

A sample of 905 respondents was drawn from the Dallas–Fort Worth Metroplex during the early summer of 1981 (see Shupe and Stacey, 1982). A total of 771, or 85 percent, returned useable questionnaires. Sixty respondents in the sample were either black or Hispanic; in order to preserve racial and ethnic homogeneity within the sample, they were removed from the study, leaving 711 respondents for whom data were analyzed.

While the Metroplex sample, drawn from an urban and economically prosperous region, does not reflect the same demographic characteristics as a representative national sample, it has significant national implications. The extent of Moral Majority support in this location should approximate support for the New Christian Right in other urban areas of the Southern Bible Belt. While support in the Dallas–Fort Worth Metroplex speaks only indirectly to the appeal of the New Christian Right in other sections of the nation, the failure to find strong support here casts doubt on finding it elsewhere.

Supporters of Moral Majority were identified by the following questions: Have you ever heard of the Moral Majority?; If so, how do you feel about the Moral Majority? The first question permitted a yes/no response, while the second provided space for an open-ended reply. The nondirective question offered respondents the opportunity to give a wide range of answers. Examples of comments coded as *favorable* included: "They are Angels of Mercy"; "I am for them"; and "Glad this viewpoint is being brought out for discussion—it is a majority view." Examples of comments coded as *unfavorable* included: "I disagree very strongly with their views and tactics"; and "They are a bunch of holier-than-thou ———s." Comments such as "I guess it's okay if it's okay for you" or "I haven't decided yet" were coded as *neutral*.

Of the 711 Bible Belt nonminority respondents, 26 percent claimed to have never heard of the Moral Majority; 28 respondents gave no response to the question of whether they heard of the movement. Of the 70% who had heard of Moral Majority, only 111 (16% of the nonminority sample) made favorable comments. Those holding unfavorable sentiments (31%) outnumbered the latter by two-to-one.

MORAL MAJORITY SUPPORTERS: ATTRIBUTES AND ATTITUDES

As Table 5.1 suggests, supporters of the Moral Majority do not appear to differ significantly from nonsupporters in their basic social, economic, or demographic characteristics. Both groups are roughly similar with re-

TABLE 5.1. Dallas-Fort Worth Metroplex Sample Characteristics

Characteristics	Supporters of moral majority (%)	Indifferent to moral majority (%)	Nonsupporters of moral majority (%)	Total %	N
Age					
Under 35	41	39	44	41	288
Over 35	59	61	56	59	422
Sex					
Male	51	33	53	42	297
Female	49	67	47	58	411
Education					
H.S. or less	21	44	15	31	221
Some college	44	31	36	35	246
College graduate	35	25	49	34	327
Income					
Less than 20,000	21	29	21	25	161
20–29,999	18	26	26	25	158
30–39,999	23	19	20	20	126
40,000 or over	38	26	33	30	191
Occupation					
White collar	60	50	70	58	389
Blue collar	16	17	11	15	101
Other	24	33	19	27	185
Voting behavior					
Yes	85	72	88	79	558
No	15	28	12	21	149
Church attendance					
Seldom	9	19	26	20	114
Now and then	19	32	17	25	151
Every week	72	49	57	55	334

gard to age, sex, education, income, and voting behavior. One noticeable difference is in occupational classification; more of the nonsupporters (70%) hold white collar occupations than do the supporters (60%).

The most significant difference appears in the church attendance measure. Seventy-two percent of Moral Majority supporters attend every week compared to 57% of the nonsupporters. Moreover, as Table 5.2 reveals, supporters come disproportionately from the ranks of fundamentalists. Support steadily decreases from fundamentalist to moderate or liberal denominations.

The political conservatism of Moral Majority is grounded in issues which have been debated in and out of the courts and among preachers and the laity for decades. The most critical assumption behind Moral Majority positions seems to be a strong concern with the negative impact of a trend toward a secular culture on traditional institutions in American society, especially the church, education, and the family. Three interrelated dimensions of the "world-view" expressed by the New Christian Right were identified in the research: opposition to teaching values clarification in public schools (i.e., sorting out personal rather than biblical priorities for making responsible decisions about alcohol, tobacco, drug use, and premarital sexual relations), opposition to secular humanism (i.e., human-centered rather than God-centered morality), and opposition to humanistic perspectives (i.e., atheism) in public education. Table 5.3 indicates strong support among Moral Majority sympathizers for the basic premises of Majority's platform.

Another focus of the research concerns attitudes toward the basic issues

TABLE 5.2. Relationship between Denomination and Support for the Moral Majority

Moral majority	Fundamentalist[a] (%)	Conservative[b] (%)	Moderate[c] (%)
Supporters	29	19	14
Indifferent	62	56	52
Nonsupporters	9	25	34
	100	100	100
Total	$N = 75$	$N = 238$	$N = 163$

$\chi^2 = 22.6$ Gamma $= .29$ $P < .001$

[a] *Fundamentalist:* Baptist (not Southern Baptist): Church of the Nazarene; Pentacostal; Seventh Day Adventist.

[b] *Conservative:* Southern Baptist; Church of Christ; Christian Church; Disciples of Christ; Lutheran.

[c] *Moderate:* Episcopalian; Methodist; Presbyterian.

TABLE 5.3. Views of Moral Majority Supporters[a]

Views	Supporters of moral majority (%)	Indifferent to moral majority (%)	Nonsupporters of moral majority (%)
1. Values clarification should be a part of every school curriculum			
Agree	81	86	78
Disagree	19	14	22
2. Secular Humanism undermines Christianity			
Agree	80	56	34
Disagree	20	44	66
3. One of the major problems in education today is that secular humanists have been allowed to determine the textbooks used in the public school system			
Agree	80	58	37
Disagree	20	42	63
Total	$N = 111$	$N = 156$	$N = 190$

[a] Employing Chi-square and Gamma statistical tests of association all relationships were significant $P < .001$.

of the Moral Majority platform. These issues include abortion, women's rights, sex education, evolution versus biblical creation theory, and prayer in public schools. Table 5.4 presents the response to questions on these issues.

Perhaps the most salient issue is the 1973 Supreme Court's decision legalizing abortion. The decision has been heatedly debated among all segments of the population, and represents *the* major legislative priority of Moral Majority. Table 5.4 reports that a larger proportion of supporters than nonsupporters agree with the "pro-life" position. While the finding was anticipated, a surprising 34% of the supporters dissent from the Moral Majority position. Another surprise is that 41% of its sympathizers disagree with the Moral Majority position on the Equal Rights Amendment.

The traditional family orientation of Moral Majority shapes its views on education and the role of the public school system. Many in the New Christian Right feel that much of the worst in American society is the result of an emerging secular culture arising from public education. The New Christian Right expresses four major concerns with public education:

TABLE 5.4. Responses Toward Political Issues of the Moral Majority[a]

Issues	Supporters of moral majority (%)	Indifferent to moral majority (%)	Nonsupporters of moral majority (%)
1. Abortion is a sin against God's law			
Agree	66	55	40
2. I believe in the ERA to guarantee women equal rights			
Agree	41	75	65
3. Evolution should be taught in school			
Agree	46	56	81
4. The Biblical account of creation should be taught in school			
Agree	88	74	64
5. I think prayer should be allowed in the schools			
Agree	95	90	78
6. Sex education should be taught in the schools			
Agree	62	82	88
Totals	$N = 111$	$N = 345$	$N = 202$

[a] Employing Chi-square and Gamma statistical test for association all relationships were significant $P < 0.001$.

the teaching of evolutionary theory as scientific fact; the neglect of biblical creation theory as a viable alternative; the absence of prayer in the schools; and the opposition to sex education as part of school curricula. As expected, Table 5.4 indicates that a larger proportion of supporters than nonsupporters disagree with the scientific explanation of evolution, agree with teaching the biblical concept of creation, and feel that prayer should be allowed in school. Yet a very high percentage (62%) also agree that sex education should be taught in school. While one might infer that their favorable response to the values clarification question resulted from a misunderstanding of the term, such a misunderstanding on the issue of sex education is unlikely. Similar evidence of a lack of consensus can be seen in that a significant proportion (46%) of supporters want evolutionary theory taught in schools. Thus it can be concluded that while many supporters may prefer creation theory to evolutionary theory, they do not wish to see the former taught to the exclusion of the latter.

Beyond dissension within the ranks of Moral Majority supporters, Table 5.4 also shows a considerable amount of disagreement between the non-supporters and the indifferent. For example, 64% of the nonsupporters express a clear mandate for teaching the biblical account of creation in schools and 78% support reintroducing prayer in public schools, while 40% feel abortion is a sin against God's will and 35% do not believe that the Equal Rights Amendment is necessary to protect women's legal rights. In sum, the disagreement over these issues among Moral Majority supporters and nonsupporters mirrors the disagreement in the overall culture of this generally conservative region.

According to the Reverend Jerry Falwell, the political goal of Moral Majority is to "line people up—at the polls" (*Newsweek*, Sept. 21, 1981). In order to consider the relationship between general political ideology and religion, a six-item civil religion scale (adapted from Wimberly et al. 1976) was included in the questionnaire. An additional item to directly measure sympathy for religious involvement in politics was also included. The results are presented in Table 5.5.

The pattern of responses to individual items in the civil religion scale shows significant differences among respondents. The most conservative respondents tended to be supporters of the Moral Majority. But even among supporters a great deal of dispersion was found, especially on the last question. This divisiveness is ironic since the Moral Majority represents, if anything, a revitalization movement in American civil religion. Fort Worth evangelist James Robison, for example, has been outspoken about infusing politics with conservative Christian morality and stated: "We are taking 1,000 preachers to Washington and show them how to integrate politics with religion" (*Fort Worth Star-Telegram*, September 26, 1981). The dispersion on the final item is of signal importance for a movement claiming to be able to mobilize its supporters at the ballot box: almost 38% of the Moral Majority supporters did not feel that religion should be involved in politics!

ACCOUNTING FOR SUPPORT

The most important socio-demographic variables for the analysis of Moral Majority support are education, occupation, employment status, length of residence in Texas, and social participation (Table 5.6). The relative importance of each of these factors was assessed using multiple

TABLE 5.5. Civil Religion and Sentiments Toward the Moral Majority

Statement	Supporters of moral majority (%)	Indifferent to moral majority (%)	Nonsupporters of moral majority (%)
1. I consider holidays such as the 4th of July religious as well as patriotic			
Agree	27	20	8
2. We need more laws on morality			
Agree	65	63	19
3. National leaders should affirm their belief in God			
Agree	81	73	45
4. If the American government does not support religion, the government cannot uphold morality			
Agree	55	61	25
5. We should respect presidential authority			
Agree	97	96	92
6. To me, the flag is sacred			
Agree	71	80	55
7. I think religion should be involved in politics[a]			
Agree	62	34	17
Total	$N = 108$	$N = 344$	$N = 213$

[a] Not included in the Civil Religion Scale

regression techniques. Because religious denomination was found to be an important predictor of Moral Majority support (see Table 5.2), it was employed as a control variable in the analysis.

As anticipated, education is strongly and negatively associated with support for Moral Majority. However, this relationship is only significant in the total sample. All the other associations are in the directions one might predict but are not significantly associated with support for the Moral Majority. This can be explained by the relative homogeneity of the sample (i.e., white middle-class homeowners in the Southern Bible Belt).

Another set of questions in this study derives from previous research

TABLE 5.6. The Effects of Socio-Demographic Characteristics on Support for Moral Majority Employing Multiple Regression Analysis

Variable	Total sample		Fundamentalist		Conservative		Moderate	
	r	$r_c^{2\,a}$	r	r_c^2	r	r_c^2	r	r_c^2
Education	−0.16*	0.026	0.05	0.002	−0.13	0.02	−0.03	0.001
Occupation	0.09	0.001	−0.09	0.007	−0.08	0.003	0.14	0.018
Employment status	−0.01	0.001	—	—	0.06	0.005	0.02	0.002
Length of residence in Texas	0.09	0.005	0.05	0.013	0.06	0.002	0.08	0.006
Social participation	0.01	0.001	0.17	0.022	0.11	0.008	0.14*	0.029

* Significant $P < .05$.

^{a} r_c^2 = Proportion of variation explained by each additional variable.

on the relationship between religious and political behaviors. Social science literature suggests that media religiosity, religious orthodoxy, church religiosity, and civil religious sentiments should be important predictors of Moral Majority support. Table 5.7 reports the results of a regression analysis using these independent variables. In the overall sample, media religiosity has the strongest relationship with support for the Moral Majority. Religious orthodoxy accounts for about half as much of the variation, while civil religion accounts for little of the variation in support. Church religiosity explains virtually nothing and is not significant.

Table 5.7 indicates the importance of religious affiliation in identifying Moral Majority support. Among the clusters of denominations, the strongest support came from fundamentalists. Moral Majority support is much less pronounced among persons of conservative or moderate religious persuasion.

Among fundamentalists, the independent variables explain 49% of the variance in support for the Moral Majority. Media religiosity and religious orthodoxy are the strongest predictors of support for the Moral Majority. Church religiosity is more important and civil religion less important among fundamentalists than for the overall sample. Among conservatives, media religiosity is the only significant predictor of support. Among moderates, none of the independent variables are significant at the 0.05 level.

For all groups, attitudes of civil religion are not as important as might be expected; in other words, when Moral Majority supporters "attend"

TABLE 5.7. Effects of Religious Attitudes and Behavior on Support for the Moral Majority Employing Multiple Regression Analysis[a]

Variable	Total sample		Fundamentalist		Conservative		Moderate	
	r	$**r_c^2$	r	$**r_c^2$	r	$**r_c^2$	r	$**r_c^2$
Media religiosity	0.33*	0.110	0.53*	0.283	0.27*	0.072	0.14	0.021
Religious orthodoxy	0.32*	0.057	0.48*	0.154	0.24	0.023	0.11	0.006
Civil religion	0.30*	0.018	0.27	0.001	0.20	0.008	0.20	0.029
Church religiosity	0.19	0.003	0.44*	0.052	0.11	0.000	0.01	0.001
	$R = .44$	$R^2 = .20$	$R = .70$	$R^2 = .493$	$R = .32$	$R^2 = .105$	$R = .29$	$R^2 = .08$

$**r_c^2$ = proportion of variation explained by each additional variable.

* Significant P < .05.

[a] *Religious Orthodoxy* refers to items concerning Biblical literalism and inerrancy, belief in heaven and hell, salvation as the gift only of those accepting Jesus Christ as Savior, and Satan as an actual active personality. A *Church Religiosity Scale* contained items on frequency of church attendance, enrollment as a church member, denominational membership, and frequency of financial contributions to a church congregation. Finally, a *Media Religiosity Scale* contained items on frequency of listening to religious radio broadcasts, frequency of watching religious television broadcasts, and making financial contributions to television evangelists' programs. Further details on these last three scales are provided in the Appendix.

TABLE 5.8. Distribution of Religious TV Viewers

	Fundamentalists		Nonfundamentalists	
Program	N	%	N	%
Pat Robertson ("700 Club")	19	30.6	45	12.7
Billy Graham	16	25.8	64	18.1
Oral Roberts	16	25.8	53	15.0
Local church services	13	21.0	84	23.8
Other programs	10	16.1	29	8.2
James Robison	8	12.9	21	5.9
Jimmy Swaggart	7	11.3	5	1.4
Jim Bakker (PTL)	6	9.7	5	1.4
Rex Humbard	5	8.1	9	2.5
Robert Schuller	4	6.5	20	5.6
Kenneth Copeland	3	4.8	0	0.0
Ernest Angley	2	3.2	1	.3
Jerry Falwell	1	1.6	8	2.3
Miscellaneous others	3	4.8	10	2.8
Total programs watched		113		354
Total respondents		62		244
Mean number of programs watched		1.82		1.45

to media religious messages, they appear to be more interested in the "religious" than the "civil" or political dimension. In support of this conclusion, Table 5.8 reveals that the most frequently viewed televangelists were *not* political. At the top of the list is Pat Robertson's "700 Club," which contains some civil religious messages but none that are overtly partisan. Billy Graham, who explicitly repudiated the New Christian Right, and Oral Roberts, who declined to become involved, tie for second. Local church services and other programs take third and fourth places. Political televangelists Robison and Falwell place sixth and thirteenth.

CONCLUSIONS

Our analysis of Moral Majority support in a Bible Belt metropolitan area that had been saturated with New Christian Right exposure offers three important conclusions.

First, contrary to the claims of fundamentalist preachers like Jerry Falwell, there is no evidence of a sizable constituency in support of religious involvement in politics. Among those who could identify the Moral Majority, the most visible of New Christian Right groups, Metroplex respondents rejected the notion of organized religion's involvement in the political arena by a margin of two-to-one. Only 16% made favorable comments about Moral Majority, while 31% opposed it. The majority of respondents were indifferent and could hardly be said to constitute a mass citizenry poised for political mobilization. National opinion polls (e.g., Gallup, 1980; Peterson and Sussman, 1981) report similar findings. Indeed, given the Bible Belt location of our sample, this study may likely have overestimated national Moral Majority support.

Our second conclusion is that Falwell and other leaders of the New Christian Right seriously overestimate the amount of agreement among sympathizers on the issues they hold dear. Divisions and inconsistencies seem to be the rule rather than the exception. An unambiguous Moral Majority position on any issue or cluster of issues does not emerge from the analysis.

Finally, while Falwell claims that Moral Majority is a political, not a religious, movement (Falwell 1981a, 1981b), the analysis of its grassroots support indicates otherwise. Among Protestants, support for the Moral Majority increases markedly with the level of religious orthodoxy. Fundamentalists are twice as likely to support Moral Majority than moderate Protestants. Conservative Protestants are slightly more supportive than moderates. Among Roman Catholics, a group which Moral Majority claims as an important ally, fewer than 1:10 express support. In the Metroplex sample the strongest support for the Moral Majority comes from sectarian, fundamentalist Christians and is weakest among Catholics and members of main-line denominations who jointly comprise the vast majority of Christians in the United States.

The defense of a cherished lifestyle from the perceived ill effects of secularization and a wish to correct the failures of modernity present a plausible framework for understanding the goals of the New Christian Right, particularly in light of the strong fundamentalist element among its supporters (see also Lorentzen, 1980; Page and Clelland, 1978). However, there is an additional factor contributing to its political impact. Falwell and Robison in particular have managed to co-opt some of the publicity that surrounds the antiabortion, anti-pornography and antievolution movements. By appearing at events like the 1981 Dallas Pro-Life Rally, by holding press conferences, and by reiterating claims of popular support that have only recently begun to be seriously questioned, New Christian Right leaders create the impression of a massive following (Martin, 1981). At the same time, they lay claim to a broad consensus among their supporters. Our analysis suggests that the constituency of the New Christian Right is much more limited and much less unified than Reverend Falwell and others would lead us to believe.

ACKNOWLEDGMENT

We wish to express thanks for assistance in this study to Kristy Smith, JoAnne Nawn, Susan Stacy, and Ed Vaughn for their valuable assistance in this project.

APPENDIX

Religious (Christian) Orthodoxy Scale

(Response Scores: Strongly Disagree = 1, Disagree = 2, Agree = 3, Strongly Agree = 4; range = 4–16; 1 = ≤ 8; 2 = < 12 > 8; 3 = ≥ 12)

I believe the Bible is the inspired Word of God and literally true in all its details.

I believe there are such places as heaven and hell.

Eternal life is the gift of God only to those who believe in Jesus Christ as Savior and Lord.

Satan is an actual personality working in the world today.

Church Religiosity Scale

How often do you, yourself, attend a church?
Every week or almost every week (3) Only now and then (2) Very Seldom (1) Not at all (0)
Are you enrolled as a member of that church? Yes (1) No (0)
What is the denomination of the church you usually attend?
Can Name It (1) Cannot Name It/No Denomination (0)
How often do you make a financial contribution to this church?
At least once a week (3) 1 or 2 times a month (2) Several times a year (1) Almost never (0)

Media Religiosity Scale

I listen to religious broadcasts on the radio:
Daily (6) Several times a week (5) Weekly (4) Several times a month (3) Monthly (2) Several times a year (1) Never (0)
I watch religious broadcasts on television:
Daily (6) Several times a week (5) Weekly (4) Several times a month (3) Monthly (2) Several times a year (1) Never (0)

If you do watch religious programs on television, which ones do you recall watching most frequently?

(One point per program mentioned)

Have you ever sent in a donation or contribution to a television evangelist, preacher or program?

Often (4) Occasionally (3) Rarely (2) Never (1)

$(1 = \leq 3, 2 = \, < 8 > 3, 3 \geq 8)$

6 SOUTHERN BAPTIST CLERGY: VANGUARD OF THE CHRISTIAN RIGHT?

James L. Guth

Part of the nation's largest Protestant denomination and long famous for both theological orthodoxy and traditionalist values, Southern Baptist ministers would seem to be tempting targets for Christian Right recruitment. Press accounts of the Right's activities teem with prominent Southern Baptist names, leading many secular observers to see the Southern Baptist Convention (SBC) as a hotbed of Christian Right activism (*Conservative Digest*, 1981; Covert, 1981). Yet the picture is more complex than this interpretation suggests. Over the past few years, a coalition of social action "liberals," SBC bureaucrats, and "denominational loyalists" has staunchly resisted and, for a time at least, forestalled any SBC alliance with the Right. But the battle has just begun; close observers wonder whether the Convention's enormous financial, organizational, and popular assets will be enlisted in the armies of the Right.

Southern Baptist ministers are split down the middle in their feelings about the Christian Right despite their common denominational affiliation and evangelical theology, often considered prime indicators of ministerial political orientation (Hadden, 1969; Quinley, 1974; Jeffries and Tygart,

1974). This suggests the need to dig deeper for the roots of the Christian Right, roots which might be uncovered more easily among a group of clergymen representing a wide range of social backgrounds, educational experiences, regional origins, and current church and denominational responsibilities.

This chapter will attempt to answer several questions: How large is the Right's beachhead among Southern Baptist ministers? What are the characteristic theological and political orientations of ministers on both sides? What are the social backgrounds of Christian Right supporters and opponents? What relationship do these bear to the theological and political views of the contending groups? What organizational variables influence attitudes toward the Right? Finally, what is the future for the Christian Right among Southern Baptists?

THE SURVEY

To gather data to answer these questions, we sent a nine-page, 110–item questionnaire to a random sample of 756 Southern Baptist ministers, drawn from approximately 40,000 "pastors" listed in the SBC's *1980 Convention Annual*. Although the sample thus excludes assistant pastors, ministers of music, and "evangelists," it does include the Right's most obvious targets. Questions sought to elicit opinions on issues agitated by the Right, on ministers' social, educational, and political background, on their attitudes toward political activism, and on their relationship with their own congregations and with SBC institutions.

The questionnaires were mailed on November 14, 1980. After one follow-up letter and two additional mailings, the survey elicited 453 usable responses. Returns indicated that at least 16 other members of the original sample had died or left the ministry. Thus, the response rate for the reduced sample was slightly over 61%. Evidence from the survey itself and postal returns indicates that Southern Baptist ministers are a very mobile lot and that many of the nonrespondents never received the questionnaire. Still, the response rate is comparable to that in other recent studies of ministers, despite the considerable number of Southern Baptist ministers with modest educational backgrounds (cf. Quinley, 1974, pp. 316–317; Connecticut Mutual Life, 1981, p. 275). A comparison of the characteristics of respondents with those known of Southern Baptist ministers as a whole (gleaned from various issues of the Southern Baptist *Quarterly Review*) indicates that they are quite representative, with the possible exception of being slightly better educated. Thus, response bias is not an insuperable problem for interpretation and generalization.

Our central concern was the ministers' response to the politics of the Christian Right. They were asked to react to several groups, including Moral Majority, Religious Roundtable, Christian Voice, the SBC's own Christian Citizenship Corps, and the liberal Evangelicals for Social Action. Ministers were given four response categories for each group: "I am a member"; "I have heard about and generally approve"; "I have heard about and generally disapprove"; and "I have not heard about or can't evaluate." They were also urged to add their own open-ended comments (and did).

Moral Majority was by far the best-known and most controversial, making support for this organization the best indicator of Christian Right penetration of the SBC. A surprisingly small number of these Southern Baptist ministers were actually members (3.3%, $N = 15$), but another 42.6% ($N = 193$) were "sympathizers," while 46.6% ($N = 211$) were "opponents." Only 4.4% had not heard about or could not evaluate Moral Majority, and 3.1% did not answer the question. The relatively high level of support is qualified somewhat by reservations that many "sympathizers" expressed about the tactics, political associations, or priorities of Moral Majority. With these overall distributions in mind, we can move on to the main issue: which Baptist ministers are likely to endorse or oppose the Christian Right?

MINISTERIAL IDEOLOGY

Earlier studies of ministerial politics have found a close link between theological and political views. Clergy scoring high on theological orthodoxy generally are political conservatives, while theological liberals tend to be political liberals as well. Presumably, then, Moral Majorityism should be associated with theological orthodoxy. But traditional measures of theological orientation cannot be used to test this proposition here, as these ministers proved to be monotonously orthodox, with overwhelming majorities believing in life after death (99%), that Jesus was born of a virgin (96%), that the Devil actually exists (94%), and that the Bible is without errors in its original form (86%).

Nevertheless, as recent SBC meetings attest, there are vital theological differences among Baptists that these traditional items do not tap. As an alternative measure of theological orientation, we asked ministers to classify themselves as fundamentalist, conservative, moderate or liberal— all terms commonly used in SBC doctrinal battles. (Note that "moderate" replaces the usual "neo-orthodox" category, meaningless to most Southern Baptist clergymen.) The ministers were not reluctant to label them-

TABLE 6.1. Theological Self-Identification and Moral Majority Support

	Fundamentalist	Conservative	Moderate	Liberal
Members (%)	11.7	0.8	0	0
Sympathizers (%)	52.3	45.1	16.4	0
Opponents (%)	27.9	45.8	80.6	100.0
Not heard (%)	6.3	4.2	1.5	0
N	(109)	(253)	(66)	(3)

selves (often with emphasis supplied); there were fewer write-in comments or qualifications on this item than on almost any other.

Theological self-identification does help in locating Moral Majority supporters, as Table 6.1 demonstrates. Quite clearly, Moral Majority members are fundamentalists, sympathizers are fundamentalists and conservatives, while opponents are drawn mostly from conservative and moderate ranks. Looked at from the opposite direction, fundamentalists are overwhelmingly supportive, conservatives are badly split, while moderates and liberals oppose Moral Majority by large margins. What specific theological elements predisposed ministers toward one or another position is not clear, but Moral Majorityism is concentrated among the theologically conservative.

Is it also found among political conservatives? This is also rather difficult to test, as almost 70% of the respondents call themselves conservatives in politics, with most of the rest claiming the moderate label. But, as Table 6.2 indicates, support for Moral Majority does come disproportionately from conservative ranks. Although the political moderates oppose Moral Majority by large margins (72.6%–23%), a substantial minority of political conservatives join in disapproving the organization; in fact, they constitute a majority (54.5%) of all opponents.

Do theological and political viewpoints make distinct contributions to Moral Majority support? Some observers claim that Moral Majority is

TABLE 6.2. Political Self-Identification and Moral Majority Support

	Conservative	Moderate	Liberal	Don't know
Members (%)	4.4	0	0	0
Sympathizers (%)	51.4	23.0	20.0	40.0
Opponents (%)	36.5	72.6	80.0	50.0
Not heard (%)	4.4	2.7	0	10.0
N	(305)	(111)	(5)	(10)

essentially religious fundamentalism masquerading in political garb, while others contend that it is simply the Republican New Right at prayer. While we cannot settle the argument as to whether the moral traditionalism or the economic conservatism of Moral Majority is more central to its appeal, the survey data provide some hints. Controlling for the political philosophy of ministers, we find that theological perspective (and presumably the associated moralism) has an independent impact; among both political conservatives and moderates, theological fundamentalists and conservatives are more likely than theological moderates to approve Moral Majority. The impact of political conservatism is also partially independent of religious orthodoxy: among all three theological orientations, political conservatives favor Moral Majority more frequently than do political moderates.

Thus, both the cultural fundamentalism and the economic and political conservatism seem to serve as complementary attractions. Nevertheless, it is probably the combination which attracts *members;* those in the sample are almost all political conservatives and fundamentalists. For the Right's "core supporters," this identification of religion and politics seems especially important. When asked their reactions to the statement that "it would be hard to be a true Christian and a political liberal," all the Moral Majority members agreed (and "strongly"), while 67% of the sympathizers and only a fraction (37%) of the opponents did.

As a further attempt to locate the ministers politically, we asked their party identification: 44% claimed to be Democrats, 27% Republicans, and 22% independents. As might be anticipated, Moral Majority support was strongest among Republicans and independents, while opposition was more concentrated among Democrats (see Table 6.3). Within each partisan group, we find again that theological orientation influences attitudes toward Moral Majority. Among Republicans, Democrats, and independents, the fundamentalists are most supportive, conservatives next, and theological moderates the least. As might be expected, it is among independents that theology is most helpful in predicting attitudes toward the Right.

TABLE 6.3. Party Identification

	Republican	Independent	Democratic
Members (%)	5.0	4.2	1.5
Sympathizers (%)	51.3	41.9	37.9
Opponents (%)	33.9	49.6	54.0
N	(109)	(112)	(185)

Many clergy also seemed to be in the throes of a partisan transition. To test whether "Moral Majorityism" is a part of a larger realignment of traditionally Democratic Southern ministers toward new loyalties, we asked them whether they had become more Republican, more Democratic, more independent, or had not moved much "over the past few years." Almost all (87%) of the Moral Majority members had become more Republican or independent, the sympathizers had moved toward the GOP (40%) or independence (14%), while the opponents had not moved much (57%) or had become more Democratic (8.5%). Over all, 40% of the Republicans, 26% of the Democrats, and 23% of the independents reported having moved toward the Republican Party. Even among Democrats, only a negligible number moved toward the Democratic Party.

To summarize, then: Moral Majority members and sympathizers differ from their opponents in several ways. They are more likely to be theologically very conservative, adhere to conservative political beliefs, view theological and political conservatism as inseparable, and be in transition from a Democratic identification toward Republican or independent status.

SOCIOECONOMIC INFLUENCES

What impact does schooling have on these pastors' view of the Christian Right? Table 6.4 portrays the impact of a college degree, controlling for background. The figures suggest that a college education does little to modify the views of ministers from farm and blue-collar homes; Moral Majorityism remains potent in college-educated ministers in these groups. What is striking is the massive "shift" among white-collar and professional ministers; among those without a college degree, pro-Right sentiment is very strong, but for those with a degree, the Right is apparently repugnant.

TABLE 6.4. Effect of a College Degree

	Farmers		Blue-collar		White-collar		Business and professional	
	ND[a]	CD[a]	ND	CD	ND	CD	ND	CD
Members and sympathizers (%)	49.0	50.0	44.7	46.4	62.4	41.7	59.0	34.2
Opponents (%)	37.3	41.9	43.4	49.5	25.0	55.0	36.3	63.4
N	(44)	(57)	(67)	(95)	(21)	(58)	(21)	(40)

[a] ND, no degree; CD, college degree.

TABLE 6.5. Effect of a Seminary Degree

	Farmers		Blue-collar		White-collar		Business and professional	
	ND[a]	SD[a]	ND	SD	ND	SD	ND	SD
Members and sym-pathizers (%)	52.1	48.8	44.5	45.8	68.4	40.7	73.4	28.6
Opponents (%)	35.4	42.6	44.5	49.4	26.3	54.2	20.0	68.6
N	(48)	47)	(63)	(83)	(19)	(59)	(15)	(35)

[a]ND, no degree; SD, seminary degree.

Why the impact of a college education should differ so significantly from group to group is not clear. Perhaps upper-status students prefer "liberalizing" institutions or majors, while lower-status ministers attended less prestigious institutions or chose more vocationally oriented studies (cf. Selvin, 1960; Hendricks, 1977).

Or perhaps this gap reflects the added effects of theological training. While only 9.9 and 12.5% of all professional and white-collar ministers have not spent time at seminary, 41.4 and 31.6% of all blue-collar and farm-reared pastors have never been to seminary. Table 6.5 delineates the effects of a seminary degree. (The comparison is with those who have never attended seminary. Those who have attended but who did not receive a degree are omitted.) A seminary education reduces the gaps between supporters and opponents among farmers' sons, gives opponents a slight edge among blue-collar offspring, and results in truly massive "shifts" among the sons of middle-class families.

If both a college and a seminary education tend to reduce Moral Majority support among ministers, what is their combined effect? Table 6.6 summarizes data on the four possible combinations of educational background. Of the four combinations, ministers with both a college and a seminary degree are most antithetic to Moral Majority. This is hardly

TABLE 6.6. Combined Effects of College and Seminary

	Both degrees	Col./no sem.	Sem./no col.	Neither degree
Members (%)	2.3	3.2	0	6.1
Sympathizers (%)	36.0	51.6	53.8	40.9
Opponents (%)	57.1	40.9	36.5	40.2
Not heard (%)	1.7	2.2	5.8	9.1
N	(175)	(93)	(52)	(132)

a surprise. What is less expected is the majority backing for the Right among those with one, but not both, degrees. These mixed categories are actually more supportive of Moral Majority than the "neither" group. Whatever may be the case among lay supporters of the Christian Right, among ministers, at least, the movement appears to benefit from the initial stages of upward educational mobility among traditional religionists (cf. Hendricks, 1977; Guth, 1981).

Of course, the labels "college graduate" and "seminary graduate" represent many different kinds of educational experience. The combined impact of college and seminary degrees, for example, may reflect several factors. At Southern Baptist seminaries a college degree has long been a prerequisite for theology degree programs. Most of those entering probably possessed a college major in a traditional liberal arts subject, even before experiencing the "liberalizing" influences of theological study. Ministers without a college diploma could enter a degree program oriented toward pastoral care and church administration, one unlikely to have the same effect. The ministers in the sample with only a college degree often have a technical or business major and were called to the ministry relatively late in their career. Thus, we should not expect ministers in these "mixed" categories to exhibit the same tendencies as those with both degrees, even if only to a lesser extent. But their education has given them personal and organizational skills which may be very useful politically.

Although we can do little more than speculate on most such issues, we do have data to study one kind of difference in educational experience: seminary attended. On an *a priori* basis we could assume that the various Southern Baptist institutions might have differing influences on those who attend them, as they vary in prestige, theological bent, and political orientation. Southern Baptist Seminary in Louisville is the oldest, most prestigious, and reputedly the most "liberal" of these institutions, while Southwestern Baptist Theological Seminary in Fort Worth is the biggest and most "conservative." The other denomination-sponsored institutions— Southeastern Baptist Seminary, Golden Gate Seminary, New Orleans Seminary, and Midwestern Seminary—fall somewhere in between on the theological and political spectrum. On the far "right" are various independent (and typically fundamentalist) institutions outside the Convention, which nevertheless train a significant number of Southern Baptist pastors: Dallas Theological Seminary, Criswell Center for Biblical Studies, Luther Rice Seminary, and several others. Table 6.7 provides data on these institutions' students.

Southern Seminary-trained ministers are the core of the opposition to Moral Majority, while Southwestern supplies a slightly larger group of supporters than opponents. The other Baptist schools turn out consider-

TABLE 6.7. Baptist Seminaries and Moral Majority

	Southern	Other Baptist	Southwestern	Fundamentalist
Member (%)	0	1.1	3.0	8.3
Sympathizer (%)	25.0	38.9	46.6	47.9
Opponent (%)	69.6	53.7	47.5	35.4
Not heard (%)	1.8	3.2	1.0	8.3
N	(56)	(95)	(101)	(48)

ably more opponents than supporters. There are, of course, several possible explanations for this pattern. Southern may attract the most "liberal" students because of its reputation; it may draw on ministerial aspirants primarily from the most "liberal" geographic areas within the Convention; it may work with a somewhat different social clientele; or, perhaps, it may change students in a different direction when they are in residence. At least three of these explanations seem partially correct. Discussions with Baptist ministers and college chaplains indicate that prospective ministers do sort themselves out in accordance with their own views and the theological reputation of the seminary. Also in line with the conventional wisdom among Baptists, the data show that the Southeast is clearly the most anti-Christian Right of SBC territories, while the Southwest is much more pro-Right. On the other hand, Southern does not draw from a "favorable" social clientele; in fact, Southern students are much more likely than Southwestern students to come from farm and blue-collar homes. But Southern students from every social background are more anti-Right than their Southwestern counterparts.

The interrelationships of social class background and education with Moral Majority support are intricate and not easy to disentangle. This preliminary look suggests the following tentative conclusions: first, that Moral Majorityism is strongest among ministers from farm backgrounds and weakest among ministers from professional homes; second, that support for the Right is increased among those who have either a college or a seminary degree, but not both, while those with both degrees are the core of opposition; and finally, that Moral Majority orientation among ministers varies with the nature and tradition of their seminary as well.

THE ORGANIZATIONAL CONTEXT

Ministers do not work in a vacuum, of course, motivated only by their own background and beliefs. They live within a rich organizational context defined by their own congregation and the increasingly elaborate associational life of local, state, and national SBC institutions. All these might influence the minister's orientation toward the Christian Right. In this section, we can do no more than explore briefly a few of the survey's many leads.

Presumably the minister's attitude should be influenced most by his own church. In the Baptists' "congregational" polity, the minister stands with fewer formal defenses vis-à-vis his congregation than his counterparts in more hierarchically organized denominations enjoy. But it is also true that the intensity of this relationship allows the possibility for ministerial manipulation by a skillful or charismatic pastor (Ingram, 1981). In any case, whether because of greater congregational influence or because of ministerial opportunity, Moral Majorityism should vary with the nature of the minister-church nexus.

First, the minister's political orientation should reflect to some extent the church's social class composition. Again, if the literature on traditionalist religion is any guide, working-class and perhaps lower-middle-class churches should provide the friendliest environment for the Moral Majority. In this survey, ministers were asked to classify their congregations as primarily working class, lower-middle, upper-middle, or mixed. Although asking ministers to act as amateur sociologists has obvious risks, the results (and many clarifying comments offered by respondents) suggest that their judgments were reasonably accurate (cf. Hadden, 1969; Sapp, 1975). Members and sympathizers are clearly located in working class and mixed congregations, while opponents are more widely distributed in several church environments.

If Right-favoring ministers are reflecting the traditionalist values of their lower-status congregations, we should expect that they will perceive their political attitudes closely comporting with those of their members. For the most part they do, but the picture is a little more complex. As Table 6.8 suggests, a majority of pastors in all three political categories see themselves holding about the same political views as their people, but

TABLE 6.8. Minister's Views Compared With Congregation's

	More conservative (%)	About the same (%)	More liberal (%)
Members	33.0	53.3	6.7
Sympathizers	22.0	75.1	2.1
Opponents	9.5	63.0	23.2
Not heard	10.0	75.0	5.0

a substantial number of Moral Majority members and sympathizers characterize themselves as more conservative, while a quarter of the opponents find themselves more liberal.

This suggests the possibility that for most ministers, the sources of their attitudes toward Moral Majority are internal, but that activists feel more comfortable in holding such views in working-class congregations—and perhaps experience less restraint in laboring for the political kingdom. This would comport with some evidence from the sociology of religion that working class congregations are less likely than others to challenge the pastor's authority (Newman and Wright, 1980; Avery and Gobbel, 1980). In fact, in this sample, Moral Majority members and sympathizers do perceive fewer limits imposed by their congregations. Members see their congregations supporting clerical involvement in politics, while sympathizers see overwhelming, though less enthusiastic, support. Opponents, however, expect greater congregational opposition to any political activism. Each of these expectations is probably linked in some degree to the social class composition of their churches.

The local congregation is only one influence on ministers, albeit a vital one. The Southern Baptist Convention is another. Over the past three decades the SBC has gone from a loose federation of autonomous churches to an increasingly centralized, rationalized, and coordinated bureaucratic entity (Baker, 1974; Harrison, 1959). Every Baptist minister is deluged by information from and contacts by the SBC and its agencies. Perhaps the extent of a minister's involvement with and attitude toward the SBC would affect his response to the Christian Right. As Martin Marty (1980) has observed, the Right is essentially a "parachurch" movement, spearheaded by independent Baptists such as Jerry Falwell, historically at enmity with the SBC. Also, deep involvement in Southern Baptist affairs would seem to preclude development of the intricate web of personal and ideological ties with the nondenominational and independent churches which dominate the movement (cf. Lorentzen, 1980). Thus, we hypothesize that pastors marginal to the SBC's organizational life or alienated from its institutions would be most attracted by the Right.

As one test of this proposition, we looked at the frequency of a pastor's attendance at SBC annual meetings as a "messenger" from his church, almost a routine event for many Baptist ministers. As Table 6.9 shows, the few Moral Majority members tend to be frequent attenders, but among sympathizers and opponents the expected relationship holds. Looking at the distribution of political groups by years attended, it is evident that frequent attendance at SBC conventions reduces the appeal of the Christian Right.

TABLE 6.9. Attendance at SBC Annual Meeting

	Years			
	Never	1–2	3–5	6 or more
Members (%)	2.5	2.6	4.8	4.2
Sympathizers (%)	48.8	44.4	35.5	39.9
Opponents (%)	37.2	47.9	54.8	51.0
Not heard	8.3	4.3	1.6	2.8
N	(118)	(116)	(60)	(139)

Of course, the minister's attendance depends both on his own financial resources and on his church's willingness to pay his expenses—both factors closely related to church size. Perhaps ministers from large churches are disproportionately opponents of Moral Majority and are also able to attend meetings more often. A look at the relationship of church size to Moral Majority strength indicates that this is a possibility. The relationship is curvilinear: the smaller churches (1–300 members) parallel convention averages, the medium-size churches (300–500) are the core of Moral Majority support, while churches over 500 members have the fewest pro-Right pastors. Do these patterns eliminate the tie between attendance and opposition to Moral Majority? No. In fact, in most size categories frequent convention attenders are less likely than their nonattending counterparts to be friendly toward the Right. The one major anomaly is among ministers in churches over 1000 members, who as a group are quite strongly opposed to Moral Majority, but whose Right-leaners are diligent attenders.

As the theological and political Rightists have made a sustained effort over the past few years to get supporters to the annual meetings, some of the impact of involvement in Baptist organizational life may not be measured well by these attendance figures. A more appropriate test might be a minister's evaluation of Southern Baptist institutions. Ministers were asked to rate the job being done by several SBC "commissions," "boards," and institutions. For present purposes the most important of these ratings were those of the seminaries (at the center of much theological controversy raging within the SBC) and the Christian Life Commission, the liberal social "conscience" of the Convention and long a target for the Right (Shurden, 1981).

As Table 6.10 shows, ministers who regard the Moral Majority with favor are generally disenchanted by or alienated from the work of these denominational agencies. Opponents of Moral Majority, on the other

TABLE 6.10. Institutional Assessments

	Seminaries				Christian Life Commission			
	Excellent	Good	Fair	Poor	Excellent	Good	Fair	Poor
Members (%)	1.5	2.4	5.1	11.8	2.2	2.3	3.7	7.0
Sympathizers (%)	23.1	41.1	62.2	67.6	22.6	38.2	46.3	66.7
Opponents (%)	65.7	49.4	27.6	17.6	67.7	50.9	41.5	24.6
Not heard (%)	4.5	4.8	5.1	2.9	4.3	4.6	7.3	1.8
N	(127)	(164)	(98)	(34)	(90)	(166)	(86)	(57)

hand, are overwhelmingly "organizational loyalists." This pattern, incidentally, holds for all the institutions rated, not just the "sensitive" seminaries and CLC, although the extent of disenchantment varied somewhat from one to another.

SUMMARY AND CONCLUSIONS

This profile of the Southern Baptist clergy has established some of the ideological, social, and organizational sources of the Christian Right. Clerical supporters of Moral Majority are likely to be very conservative in both theology and politics, Republican (or at least moving away from Democratic loyalties), and from modest socioeconomic backgrounds. Few have both a college and a seminary education and many are marginal to Baptist organizational life.

For the most part, these findings indicate that Moral Majority's future within the SBC is not very bright. The Right draws its strength from the very social types which are becoming rarer in Southern society: the farm-reared minister with modest (though not negligible) educational accomplishments. The increasing educational level and "professionalization" of the Southern Baptist clergy seem likely to diminish the number of conservative militants. At the same time, the continuing and rapid urbanization and upward mobility of Southern Baptists, and the organizational rationalization of their churches, will reduce the number of churches with favorable climates for Christian Right activists.

There are some countervailing influences which need more exploration, however. The data hint that the large Southern Baptist seminaries may be experiencing the same influx of strongly conservative prospective ministers as other theological institutions. This trend, despite the seminaries' best efforts, may result in larger numbers of conservative clerics.

Should the Rightists acquire control of SBC seminaries—as they have pledged to do—the resulting transformation might also augment their reproduction. Should that happen, however, the SBC as presently constituted would probably cease to exist, as many urban and other moderate churches would pull out. A more likely eventuality, given the moderates' clear organizational advantages, is that many conservative ministers and churches might withdraw, perhaps providing the core of a new Baptist denomination. In either case, the Christian Right would maintain an organized presence in Southern religious and political life, but would hardly dominate either.

IV | Ideology

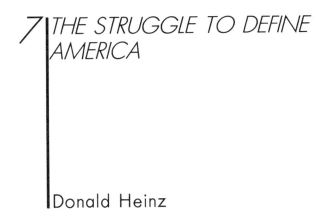

7 | THE STRUGGLE TO DEFINE AMERICA

Donald Heinz

The New Christian Right is engaged in the creation of a countermythology which contends against at least two mythologies—secular humanism and liberal Christianity. Their attack on secular humanism and liberal Christianity brings to light two shadow mythologies within the New Christian Right's own house.

MYTHOLOGY AND COUNTERMYTHOLOGY

Secular humanism is a malleable mythology. Because it is so often a screen upon which the New Christian Right projects all that is hostile to its own mythology, it deserves to be defined in its own right by those who espouse it. A group discovers or creates its own myth; often, that myth takes on a life of its own and continues to evolve. Part of that evolution is the view of the myth by its fiercest opponents.

Secular humanists are widely agreed on two major tenets: the rejection of any supernatural conception of the universe and an affirmation that

133

ethical values are human and have no meaning independent of human experience. Thus, the human is placed at the center of ethics and world-view construction. For many secular humanists an additional tenet is the preeminence of reason and the scientific method.

The Humanist Manifestoes of 1933 and 1973 assert that traditional theism is an unproved and outmoded faith, that the universe is self-existing and not created, that any faith which places God, ritual, or creed above the human is to be rejected, and that ethics is autonomous and situational. It may be noted in passing that not every humanism which wishes to favor the human wishes to disfavor God, and also that there is a long tradition of Christian humanism in western civilization.

In the perception of the New Christian Right, secular humanism is characterized by godlessness, moral relativism, and permissiveness regarding decency issues. Specific issues associated with secular humanism are a toleration of pornography, a fostering of an abortion culture, the legitimation of homosexuality as an appropriate lifestyle, an attempt to delegitimize the traditional family as normative or even ideal, creeping socialism and welfarism, a disinterest in strong national defense, and an attack on public religion as a key dimension of American culture and society. That is an unwieldy bill of particulars.

Crucial to the New Christian Right's mythology is the conviction that secular humanism has twisted the First Amendment to mean the separation of God from government and society. Even more important, secular humanism is seen as having accomplished the "establishment" of its own mythology by the government and in the public school system. Issue after issue of the monthly *Moral Majority Report* dwells on this theme.

Robert Bellah (1978) has described a phenomenon that he chooses to call liberalism or radical secularism, which may be related to what the New Christian Right calls secular humanism. According to Bellah, liberalism emerged in the United States in a life and death struggle with Puritanism. Giving ontological primacy to isolated, even atomistic, individualism and using contract as its fundamental model of social relations, it has gradually increased its dominance over other elements of the American cultural tradition. In alliance with scientific technology, it has become the most powerful solvent of traditional culture. This radical secularism, the faith of America's cognitive elite, "seeks to eradicate from our public life every trace of common belief having any religious dimension whatsoever" (p. 369).

A variety of mythological contenders, including secular humanists or radical secularists, have used Jefferson's language of a wall of separation as a red herring whenever the religious dimensions of American society or religious claims to access to public symbol production are at issue.

If analyses of Bellah or the New Christian Right are close to being correct, this secular faith has become sedimented into the cultural assumptions of contemporary intellectuals who significantly control symbol production. Thus, a kind of deprogramming would be necessary for them to consider alternative options or to rethink what they believe to be their inclusive pluralism. A successful countermythology could function as just such a deprogramming.

There is another "story" against which the New Christian Right has mounted its countermythology. Evangelicals and fundamentalists in this century have regularly criticized and denounced the ecumenical movement and liberalism in Protestant denominations. In recent decades, the National Council of Churches—the umbrella organization for mainstream Protestantism in this country—has become the symbolic target. The NCC has been attacked for representing a value system and worldview that appears to the New Christian Right to be much closer to secular humanism than to historic Christianity. Such a view is, of course, not a total fabrication. The welcoming of the Enlightenment and the alliance with modern science (and perhaps even with modernity) have been clearly stated goals of Protestant liberalism since the 19th century and, more recently, of Roman Catholic liberalism as well. Some commentators would argue that liberalism married the faith to an atheistic and scientific culture and that conservatism married it to a nationalistic culture. If so, this is another example of contending mythologies.

In May 1981, the National Council of Churches released a message to its member churches entitled "The Remaking of America," which confirms the thesis that we are seeing a contest over opposing American stories and that the use of rhetorical and political symbols is connected to the contest. In this document, which was reprinted in *Christianity and Crisis* (July 20, 1981, pp. 207–210), the Reagan Administration proposals are said to "threaten the vision of America as the model and embodiment of a just and humane society." The Reagan reversal of a national commitment to promote the general welfare "is contrary to the best insights of both Christian faith and the national creed." Reagan is seen as turning America's public lands into booty, seeking peace through military predominance rather than negotiation, and muting America's advocacy for human rights because of a selective preoccupation with terrorism. More dangerous than these specific tendencies is "the pattern that they pose, the vision of America and its values that lie behind them." The drafters of the document see in the new administration's philosophy a confronting of the nation with "a crossroads choice between alternative visions of the meaning and purpose of America." The writers claim their vision "has deep roots in religious faith and biblical images of divine intent and human possibility," but they acknowledge that both visions "have vied for supremacy throughout the nation's history." The New Christian Right would seem to be correct in charging Protestant liberalism with hypocrisy for the latter's charge that an evangelically legitimated religious-political program is inappropriate in the American system.

There are also clashing symbols within the New Christian Right's own house. Strong political involvement was typical of nineteenth century evangelicalism, but in a "great reversal" twentieth century fundamentalism and evangelicalism have generally been politically quietistic (Moberg, 1972). Premillennial dispensationalism had become the dominant eschatological belief of most fundamentalists and many evangelicals (Sandeen, 1970). Such a view typically produces a mood of cultural and political pessimism in response to the strong expectation that life on earth will turn steadily worse until Christ returns to rapture the elect from the earth and then, shortly after, returns with the elect to reign on earth.

In a pamphlet, *Christians in Government: What the Bible Says* (1980), Jerry Falwell finds it necessary to provide answers to typical fundamentalist responses to his campaigns. Some are wondering why they should work for national change if they will be rescued by the rapture soon to come. Others wonder why they should try at all to redeem the country if biblical prophecy assures that things are going to get worse and worse. Gary North (1981), a biblical reconstructionist, has offered a more pointed analysis of this mythological dilemma within the fundamentalist camp. Reflecting on the National Affairs Briefing in Dallas which he attended, he writes:

> Here were the nation's fundamentalist religious leaders . . . telling the crowd that the election of 1980 is only the beginning, that the principles of the Bible can become the law of the land. . . . Here was a startling sight to see: thousands of Christians, including pastors, who had believed all their lives in the imminent return of Christ, the rise of Satan's forces, and the inevitable failure of the church to convert the world, now standing up to cheer other pastors, who also have believed this doctrine of earthly defeat all their lives, but who were proclaiming victory, in time and on earth. . . . Thousands of people were cheering for all they were worth—cheering away the eschatological doctrines of a lifetime, cheering away the theological pessimism of a lifetime.

The rapture was out; the sovereignty of God was in. North, who longs to reconstruct a society based on Old Testament law, thinks the savory odor of the opposition's blood has overwhelmed official theology. North wonders about the resolution of such schizophrenia.

> If they preach victory, the old-line pessimists will stop sending in checks. And if they start preaching the old-line dispensational, premillennial earthly

defeatism, their recently motivated audiences may abandon them in order to follow more consistent, more optimistic, more success-oriented pastors.

It is often claimed that apocalyptic thought and literature only arise in desperate times, in times when only a direct and dramatic intervention of God could right earthly wrong. If this is so, then a marked shift away from apocalyptic pessimism may signal a significant upward mobility for American fundamentalism. Their social location is no longer that of the despised, the disinherited, the poor. The New Christian Right, preparing to take possession of a newly reformed America, would seem to be a long way from *The Late Great Planet Earth* (Lindsey, 1970), which sold ten million copies in the early 1970's.

But there is another shadow in the house. The mythology that the New Christian Right protests may be a mythology in which it has strong roots. The utilitarian individualism which is so much a part of the prevailing mythology seems to be a crucial element in the mind set of many of those allied with the New Christian Right. The frank utilitarianism of so many altar calls and fundamentalist invitations has often been remarked on. The linking of moral renewal and national stature and wealth in the current rhetoric is additional evidence. How deeply imbedded in the secularism against which it protests is the New Christian Right? Sometimes religious crusades direct attention away from the enemy within. Moral reform movements can be reaction formations (Freud) in which the world is chosen as an easier target than the self.

SEIZING ACCESS TO SYMBOL PRODUCTION

If the New Christian Right is engaged in a contest over the meaning of America's story, and if public symbols are the key instruments through which overarching systems of meaning are discovered and constructed, then gaining access to symbol production (generation, selection, definition, dissemination, and control) is indispensable. Since 1980, the New Christian Right sees itself as having stormed its Bastille and freed its story from forces which had the power to imprison it and hide it from public consciousness. Television, schools, and family are the major areas of conflict over symbols. Important symbols themselves, they are also the means of access to symbol production for which the New Christian Right is contending.

All observers are agreed that the role of television evangelists, or the electronic church, has been fundamental in the coming to public consciousness of evangelicalism in general and of the New Christian Right in particular. Newly aware of their numbers and their potential financial and political power, evangelicals began an aggressive cultivation of television which simply left mainstream Protestantism and Roman Catholicism far behind (Hadden, 1981; Armstrong, 1979). Not content with local station handouts prompted by benign FCC regulations, they began to buy time and pay well for it. Their new access to this crucial medium is startling confirmation of the old American truth that money talks. The electronic evangelists knew well what was on the minds and in the hearts of millions of evangelicals, who had regularly been ignored by others, and they offered something to supply the demand. The mythology they were marketing turned out to have an enthusiastic audience willing to consume it and, to pay to have it continued. Their success became a not unambiguous symbol of their new respectability and their arrival in the American mainstream.

Ben Armstrong (1979), the executive director of the National Religious Broadcasters, has suggested a national audience of 130 million for the electronic church. William Martin (1981) has argued that figure is wildly inflated. Martin proposes a weekly viewing audience of 7 to 10 million, with occasional peaks up to 23 million. It is estimated that 1 billion dollars in contributions are received yearly. In addition to their wide use of the national networks, fundamentalists and evangelicals are said to own and operate 1300 radio stations and 40 television stations.

Television was more than a symbol of having arrived; with television, the New Christian Right gained crucial access to symbol production. The medium of television had been the chief means, in the view of the New Christian Right, through which secular humanism was being implanted in the public consciousness. Now they were going to use this medium to tell their own story, to propagate a countermythology. The success they experienced was a heady transfusion for those who had been labeled (often on television) a backwater, a laughing stock, a defeated power that history had left behind and that deserved to be ignored.

The emergence of Reverend Donald Wildmon's Coalition for Better Television can be understood in this context. It is a protest against the perceived arrogance and indifference of the networks. It is a protest against those who, like Norman Lear, are perceived to function as secular popes of television entertainment. It is a protest against television's denial of a mythology that the New Christian Right was certain is in continuity with the American past and with current calls for decency and for honoring family values.

To protest the exclusion of one's own mythology may lead to protests against the marketing of other mythologies. Eventually such protests may take the form of calls for control. According to the New Christian Right, the mythology of secular humanism needs to be regulated and limited, and perhaps delegitimized and eliminated. Outraged cries of censorship are red herrings. Analysts on the left have always seen that all advertising and other forms of corporate support are forms of censorship. Economic and ideological interests have regularly determined what could be shown on television; it is no accident that the anti-Vietnam film *Hearts and Minds* could not be shown on CBS. There are also other than economic kinds of censorship. *TV Guide* (June 6, 1981) reported how a Los Angeles psychologist, Newton Deiter, "persuaded the networks to submit scripts involving homosexual characters to his Gay Media Task Force for review." Deiter said he is also assisted by "agents in place." Even with the apparent success of the New Christian Right, it remains unthinkable that anyone in the media would submit scripts which concerned Christian Right mythology to any of its representatives for review and correction. None of this is to argue that television could not become a medium open to all contending mythologies, but this has not yet been the case.

For the New Christian Right, the public school stands as a primary symbol of their control, or lack of control, over decisions that directly affect their lives. The school is a symbol of the neighborhood, of grassroots, of the family extended. Federal intervention in the school is experienced as an intrusion of the government at a deeply resonant symbolic level. Whatever else the rapid growth of alternative schools in recent years means—and it may mean virulent racism and resurgent know-nothingism—it means a war over competing mythologies and a battle for access to symbol production.

The symbols of school prayer and Bible reading have proved remarkably opaque to most commentators. The New York prayer declared unconstitutional by the Supreme Court in 1962 was worded: "Almighty God, we acknowledge our dependence upon Thee and we beg Thy blessings upon us, our parents, our teachers and our country." The Supreme Court interdict was interpreted as a direct attempt to seize control of an institution which mediated the story and value system of the family and local community. To deny school prayer and, later, Bible reading, was to attack an American story that had been consecrated by the historical presence of God. It is not that evangelicals thought a brief prayer would accomplish significant Christian indoctrination, as many mainstream Protestant critics seemed to believe. Rather, school prayer serves to acknowledge the hallowing presence of God throughout the school day.

In the Supreme Court decisions, the New Christian Right saw direct federal interference with its First Amendment liberties. The bitter pill was the secular arrogance of a ruling that a religiously legitimated education is not to be permitted in American public schools. For religious legitimation of the school, of education, of the school day is what such a prayer accomplishes, just as the Bible and religious oaths function to accomplish something similar in other areas of American life.

The argument of the New Christian Right cannot simply be dismissed as the product of a backwater group's inability to recognize that pluralism has become the American way. Robert Bellah (1978) has discussed the dilemmas involved in a contest between the needs of pluralism and the need of a normative center. In an address titled "Cultural Pluralism and Religious Particularism," Bellah (1981) insisted that to argue, as a secular culture seems to, that there is or can be no *public* meaning for religion or religious truth (or that none should be allowed) is, in effect, to argue that there is no religious truth. Thus, religion is effectively reduced to the irrelevant, the private, the psychological. The irony is that evangelicals have often seemed to hold precisely such a position. Only the increasing encroachments of a secular culture upon their ever narrower space have forced them to reevaluate their position. The New Christian Right has come to see that to exclude any religious legitimation from the public American story is to exclude religion completely. Moreover, it is to set up a rival story in its place—a secular story. Against that secular story the New Christian Right is mounting its countermythology and attempting to regain access to the school as a primary agency of symbol production.

The fight to have creationism taught in public schools may be viewed in the same light. While that fight is being legitimated by an appeal to "scientific creationism," there is a more cogent argument to be made. Evolution, as the New Christian Right seems to intuit, is not simply a neutral methodology of modern science. It has become a key symbol of an alternative story—a story that includes human autonomy, the noncreation of the world, the rejection of transcendence, and the triumph of secularism. Since such a mythology has been erected upon a scientific methodology, the New Christian Right wants to use the Genesis account as a key symbol of an opposing mythology. Much of the current discussion fails to consider the power and significance of the major opposing symbols and the level at which this argument is being enjoined.

A similar struggle underlies textbook controversies, which Page and Clelland have argued are best understood as examples of the politics of lifestyle concern. Remarking that what they call cultural fundamentalism was once the dominant lifestyle in the United States and that school board elections, educational policy decisions, and textbook selection are often considered nonissues in the realm of politics, they note: (p. 276):

> The fact that this is so is a measure of the cultural hegemony of the educational strata and the economic elites which largely have set public school policy. . . . Such cultural modernists can be elected in issueless school board contests on the basis of their skilled use of such resources as time, community prestige,

and verbal and organizational abilities. They can then, without conflict and even without self-consciousness, "subvert" or change educational policy (expropriate the means of symbolic production) in order to socialize youth to their own construction of social reality, that is, to their own lifestyle.

At some deep level, articulated or not, the cultural fundamentalists understand what is happening to them. Even as the educational establishment goes about its business with no self-consciousness about lifestyle questions or the power they hold in the socialization process, these fundamentalists are seeing a major contest between competing mythologies.

The great power of the public schools as socializers is precisely the reason why the school has become such a salient symbol. To surrender a religious undergirding of education, to surrender cultural control or influence is to surrender a primary area for the implanting, development, and maintenance of symbolic universes. Anabaptist groups have always seen this and so withdrew their children from public high schools. Roman Catholics have seen it and so founded their own schools. Mainstream Protestantism, at least at the official level, seems remarkably out of touch with this issue. Perhaps its commitment to modernity makes it a nonissue.

The family is being called the issue of the 1980's. It may be the issue on which the New Christian Right can ride to power. Why has the family become a salient issue for American society and what is its significance and potential as a symbol for the New Christian Right?

A common theory of the modern family is that following industrialization and modernization the nuclear family lost its economic function and came to specialize in emotional services. Christopher Lasch (1975) comments:

> Whereas kinship served as the unifying principle of earlier forms of society, the modern social order rests on impersonal, rational, and "universalistic" forms of solidarity. In a competitive and highly mobile society the extended family has no place. The nuclear family, on the other hand, serves industrial society as a necessary refuge. It provides adults with an escape from the competitive pressures of the market, while at the same time it equips the young with the inner resources necessary to master those pressures.

But for many reasons the family can now no longer be relied on for such services. Emotional and leisure services are sublet. The individual becomes the purchaser of such services throughout the interpersonal marketplace. But those who cannot afford to pay for alternative intimacy or networks of meaning will be alone and lost in an alien world, if the family too is gone.

The experience of family dislocation and breakdown invites attention to the family as an important symbol. It is possible that certain interests will want to focus frustration away from economic and structural issues and onto the family. But the concern about a crisis in family life is nevertheless real. There are many ways to account for it. In a helpful brief introduction to the theory of German sociologist Arnold Gehlen, James Hunter (1981) summarizes his analysis of the effects of modernity upon institutions. De-institutionalization progresses in the private sphere, while in the public sphere institutions are strong but faceless, rationalized, and technocratic. While choices multiply, the background of stable institutional patterns recedes. A crisis of individual and communal identity occurs.

Whether because it finds the traditional family stifling or because it aligns itself with the modernity Gehlen describes, the so-called radical individualism of secular humanism ignores the problem of the family or even celebrates its demise. In contrast, Rosemary Reuther (1980) notes that nineteenth century feminists were careful to keep the issue of the family in their own camp: "The message of 19th century feminism was that women had to reform the entire public political order in order to protect the home!" (p. 235).

The New Christian Right finds in the family a means to recover a lost meaning as well as a lost past. It has become a primary symbol of the worldview, and the story they offer as a countermythology. The family is both a symbol for that mythology, and its primary and necessary socializer. Forces in government, the media, and education are seen to be delegitimizing the traditional family, challenging the family as the fundamental unit of society, and arguing for alternatives. Mediated by intellectuals, federal regulators and managers, and media entrepreneurs, these alternative symbols would come together in a different story than the one the New Christian Right wishes to make normative. The role of federal brokers of alternative "worlds" has already been seen in the arguments over Head Start programs. Blacks claimed government was getting a head start in delegitimizing the black family and inserting itself as the primary socializer—into a bureaucratically defined American way. The seemingly bizarre objections of the New Christian Right to programs for battered wives and abused children may be seen in this light. There is the fear that homes for battered women will become anti-family indoctrination centers. Restructuring or redefining the family is a powerful means of creating alternative myths. To gain control of definitions is to gain the power to stabilize or de-stablize the myth for which the New Christian Right is contending.

If a resurgent movement becomes powerful enough it may move beyond the demands for access to symbol production or for equal cultural space for its own myth; it may seek control of symbol production in an effort to dislodge all opposing myths. The Family Protection Act, conceived and strongly pressed by the political and religious right, is an attempt to enforce a particular myth by writing its definition and maintenance into law.

The family is a powerful symbol of great resonance on many levels. It is therefore possible for it to function effectively as a code for other agendas as well, such as capitalism, militarism, and patriarchy. However, the examination of such possible agendas is not being undertaken in this chapter. Even as they function to resonate with individual needs or lend themselves to worldview construction, symbols can unload great emotional power on political or economic agendas.

SYMBOLS: THE POWER TO CREATE AN ALTERNATIVE WORLD

What is it about symbols which gives them such political power? Symbols are signs which humans generate and discover as they create meaning and interpret the world. The symbol is a sign which includes in itself that which it signifies and points beyond itself to a larger meaning. The symbol invites, discloses, puts together. The word once meant a token carried by the parties to an agreement. (How many such common tokens are there today?) When symbols touch or imply the ultimate, they may be experienced as an eruption of the sacred. If they seem to touch the nature of things, they may be seen as occasioned by a "surplus of ontological substance." Symbols relate to the sacred dimension of society itself. They are generated by collective effervescence as society constructs or discovers its own larger meaning [Durkheim, 1965 (1917)]. When mythologies contend against each other, there is the implication that some sacred dimension of society has been repressed or is now being revitalized. As movements struggle to tap some sacred core, one may observe which symbols are ascendent and which are in decline.

Symbols bear the power to bring a symbolic world, a universe of meaning, into existence. They become ordering forces in everyday life. Life is created and lived out as an extension of the symbol, in which one discovers life-giving and enlightening power. Symbols may help to recover a lost past or summon a new future (Streng, 1976).

But there are forces that cripple the power of symbols. Secularization may be defined as the process by which more and more sectors of society and culture are withdrawn from the domination or interpretive power of religious symbols. Thus, symbol-generated meaning is likely to recede where secularization is advanced. Secularization, then, by weakening the power of symbols to help modern people "locate" and interpret their existence, contributes to the feeling of homelessness in the cosmos. Literalizing a symbol may also strip it of its power. Secularization inevitably literalizes symbols; but other forces, such as the opponents of a myth, may also succeed in disconnecting a symbol from the sacred or from ontological meaning.

Relating to symbols by drawing meaning from them and attempting to disseminate such meaning is a significant form of expressive social action. Wallis and Bland (1979), in their study of a moral crusade rally, show how expressive rather than instrumental goals may dominate. The participants sought an opportunity for evangelistic witness (perhaps to result in long-term assimilative reform) and for expressing their solidarity with important moral issues. The care and tending of symbols may develop social networks of meaning and put one in touch with deep religious and psychological reservoirs of identity and commitment. Such symbols as family and school can function as consciousness-raisers that mobilize a sense of participation in larger meaning and may effectively invite entry into the political process. Abortion and national defense, for example, seem to resonate for many at levels deep enough to return them to the polls.

A charismatic leader evokes a deep response from the public by touching the symbolic dimensions of consciousness in such a way that responding to such a leader makes meaning, recovers identity, and revitalizes roots. Consciously or unconsciously, such a leader takes hold of the symbols that will resonate with the public and bring the leader to power and influence. Social change occurs when a charismatic leader attends to the symbolic needs of the populace that have been neglected. A movement emerges around these symbolic dimensions which promises revitalization, new direction, or legitimation for a particular way of life in a time of bewilderment and loss. It remains for others (usually intellectuals, in Max Weber's view) to rationalize these symbols so that an all-encompassing social action is charted. Thus expressive social action, meaningful in itself, may move to instrumental goals and entry into the political process, if there is structural conduciveness, significant leadership, and a readiness to conceive one's goals politically. Orrin Klapp has written: "Heroes take people on vicarious journeys, but crusades take them on real ones" (McPherson, 1973, p. 170).

What possibilities present themselves to those who engage in political action armed with a host of religious symbols? Peter Berger (1969) defined religion as the positing of a sacred cosmos. The rendering of a particular lifestyle or political order as transcendently legitimate or as corresponding to the ultimate nature of things, Berger calls the construction and placement of a "sacred canopy." It is to clothe an order or movement or story, built of many symbols, with divine sanction. The contest over the meaning and course of the American story is a contest over whose sacred canopy shall prevail. There are recurring attempts to topple one system of meaning and erect another in its place. For worldview construction and maintenance, religion is always available with its power to legitimize. It specializes in questions of meaning or the lack of meaning (theodicy).

When symbols are interpreted or experienced as religious, they gain a larger resonance.

When a religious worldview has successfully been constructed, there is need to maintain it and perhaps enforce it. Gusfield (1963) argues that a coercive reform movement is likely to arise as a response of a newly powerful but previously disenfranchised, social class that perceives its world view to have been abandoned by status elites. A movement that clothes its countermythology in religious symbols and legitimates its story with God or religion, may attempt to enforce its reality definitions by arguing they are part of the nature of the universe—God's will.

The New Christian Right has tapped into symbols which turn out to be powerfully resonant in the lives of many people. In the experience of participants and approving followers a dimension of the sacred, of society's ideal or larger image of itself, has been touched. Perhaps in the current strife between contending mythologies, followers of the New Christian Right are discovering or intuiting a dimension of society that has been repressed or ignored but which they now experience as necessary, promising, and fulfilling.

Single issues, symbolic of a larger lost world now to be regained, have come together into a strong political thrust because these were first expressive issues that resonated with large numbers of people. Employing such symbols garners emotions and deep levels of meaning and transfers them to political action. Identity, meaningfulness, and emotional power connected to a symbolic homecoming, the recovering of a lost world, are unloaded onto particular movements or courses of political action. Such political action runs, as it were, on symbol power. The student, civil rights, and women's movements were similarly generated, mobilized, and empowered.

The New Christian Right found a particular kind of Christianity available as an antidote to alienation and decay in the social system and as a legitimizer of a recovered traditional story. Choosing evangelical Christianity for this purpose is continuous with a long revival tradition in which repentance and new national life under Christian auspices have been offered in the midst of despair, crisis, or loss. Just as fifth century B.C. post-exilic Judaism struggled to recover roots and find structures continuous with the past, the New Christian Right calls for a "rebuilding of the walls of Jerusalem." Nehemiah's prayer for Jerusalem (Nehemiah 1:5–11) has become a favorite of the New Christian Right in its own calls for national repentance and reconstruction. If the leaders of the New Christian Right are sufficiently convinced of the religious legitimacy of their countermythology, if they perceive God as calling for and the country as requiring their story, and if they perceive there is sufficient power to accomplish it, worldview enforcement will be part of their agenda. Federal regulations, laws, and social sanctions can function as enforcers of a symbolic universe. Agencies in the social system can be mobilized to police reality definitions.

That, however, is not new. The Organizational Safety and Health Administration (OSHA), the Environmental Protection Agency (EPA), nonsexist textbook requirements, affirmative action, legally entitling abortion clinics not to notify the parents of minors are examples of writing particular stories of reality into law. The New Christian Right understands itself as a countermythology to that story currently established and enforced in the United States.[1]

None of this is meant to argue that there can be no symbolic universe with sufficient cultural space for several competing mythologies—several stories contending to offer the most satisfactory interpretation of the American experience. But there is the likelihood that loyalty to a larger social system and commitment to democratic rules of conflict will vary with one's expectations of and perceived past treatment by that system. Persistent calls for civility in the present mythological contest by representatives of the center will not resonate with those who feel that the center is itself a liberal construct which is being used normatively. If that is so, civility is a centrist virtue espoused by those who regularly find that the system, or currently dominant cultural definitions, works for them. In the perception of the New Christian Right, the present normative pluralism, carefully defined, has seriously limited its cultural space and access to symbol production. It is not a symbolic universe in which the Right's story has been granted free access; hence, it wills to seize access to symbol production and mount a countermythology. Meanwhile, opponents want to literalize the symbols of the New Christian Right and disconnect them from sacred power—whether this power resides in God or in society's larger imagination.

CONCLUSIONS

Seizing access to or control of symbol production gives a social movement the opportunity to create an alternative world through the power

---

[1] When mythologies compete, an important dimension of worldview maintenance and enforcement is the control of labeling. Radical psychiatrists R. D. Laing and Thomas Szasz have already seen this in their own profession. Homosexuals made a concerted and successful effort to change the way in which homosexuality is labeled by the American Psychiatric Association. Labeling wars are fought to determine which lifestyles, behaviors, symbols will be publicly recognized as deviant and worthy of sanction as harmful departures from prevailing definitions of reality. Labeling may be compared to witchhunting at previous times in history, but it also should be seen as a sophisticated, modern process through which deviance is identified and official reality is enforced.

of symbols. Drawing meaning from symbols is an important form of expressive social action, but in the case of the New Christian Right, it has led to instrumental political goals as well. The move to political power was apparently possible because the movement had tapped symbols powerfully resonant in the lives of many people, symbols which may promise a recovery of the sacred or of a lost dimension of society. A variety of single issues symbolize a larger lost world now waiting to be regained. The movement comes to run on symbol power. Fundamentalist Christianity is the transcendent symbol that legitimizes this attempt to recover a particular story by clothing it with a larger validity. If the recovery of public space for a lost story is successful, the enforcement of that story through coercive reform may follow.

This interpretation allows critical analysis to move beyond hypotheses that have insufficient complexity and power of explanation, and which probably have built-in bias. Any analysis of a social-religious movement that proceeds from a perspective labeling the movement as inappropriate to the American system or *prima facie* illegitimate and worthy of scorn does not promise new insight into the complexity of social action nor real understanding of the intentionality of its participants.

Given the interpretation argued in this chapter, however, one can move on with further research that prejudges none of the current contenders for the meaning of the American story, but which poses critical questions for all of them. Further, this interpretation invites additional critical analysis of the New Christian Right on terms appropriate to the movement and promising fruitfulness—once pejorative labeling is cleared away. Some suggestions follow.

Symbols are never one-dimensional; they are also always subject to manipulation by leaders and movements with diverse ends. The ambiguity in the symbols of the New Christian Right (and of its opponents) needs to be explored. The multiple worlds to which these symbols may be pointing need to be uncovered. The choices of specific symbols and the ignoring of others need critical examination. Are the chosen symbols open-ended, inclusive, enlarging, or are they repressive and narrowing? Do they promise an enlargement of human experience, a greater ability to make sense of one's world? Do they resonate with the need for a normative center?

Evaluating symbols for their power to aid in the public tasks that lie ahead may require some consensus about what those tasks are. Just such a consensus has yet failed to emerge, as was evident in the bicentennial year. The call for a reinstitutionalization of the private sphere and a recovery of the power of mediating institutions may be examined in this connection.

Finally, it is time to begin a critical examination (sociological, theological, biblical, historical) of the public stories that are currently being recommended to give meaning and purpose to the American experience. When its symbols have been put together, what is the nature of the symbolic universe toward which the New Christian Right points? How crucial are the needs going unmet by the worldviews dominant among current status elites?

8 THE LIBERAL REACTION

James Davison Hunter

What has long been a source of amusement or of superficial contempt has recently become the cause of serious concern on the part of the liberal community in North America. Those on the far right of American political theory and praxis have rarely been taken very seriously by those who fashion themselves the vanguard of social and political thought. But with the emergence or increased visibility of such groups as Moral Majority, the National Conservative Political Action Committee, Christian Voice, and the Conservative Caucus *and* the election of a conservative Republican president, such nonchalance has been rapidly laid aside.

The last major campaign waged by the harsher elements of political conservatism in the 1950's resulted in an embarassment for the nation and in an experience that was altogether unsavory, if not personally damaging, to liberals. To be sure, much of the present concern is articulated by a generation haunted by the memory of the "Red Scare" and McCarthyite "witch-hunting." Motivated either by a desire for self-preservation or out of a concern for avoiding the very real social dislocation of what is perceived as a potential neo-McCarthyism, or both, the liberal

149

community is determined not to let history repeat itself. In response, a loosely structured coalition of liberal groups has begun to orchestrate a large-scale effort to mobilize resources against the New Right.

Interestingly, in the 1950's it was the secular Right that inflicted the greatest harm to liberal interests and ideology. This was principally due to the far-reaching influence of Senator Joseph McCarthy and his Senate Committee on Un-American Activities. The religious Right, headed by such figures as Carl McIntyre, Billy James Hargis, and Major Edgar Bundy, was clearly an ideological bedfellow of McCarthyism lending religious legitimation to the inquisitions of the period. It even conducted its own exposes and public discreditings of liberal church leaders and theologians (Gaspar, 1963). The credibility of the religious Right, however, was linked directly to the credibility of the secular Right—Senator McCarthy in particular, but also such groups as the John Birch Society. Thus, when the secular Right began to lose ground in the face of increasing resistance from intellectuals (Einstein was the most famous), the news media (the *Washington Post* and the *New York Times* were the most vocal), the Congress and the Eisenhower Administration and the general public, the religious Right also began to falter.

Since the secular Right was the key mover in the last campaign, one might then suppose that, in the present generation, it would be against the secular Right that liberals would direct the greatest part of their energies. But this is not entirely the case. While most of the criticism of the New Right is of a general nature, directed to both the religious and secular elements, there appears to be a general division of labor in terms of the emphasis of countermobilization. In the most broad terms, it has been the labor unions which have organized against the secular Right (conservative politicians, lobbies, PACs); it has been the "New Class" of knowledge workers (educators, the media, liberal churchmen, intellectuals) that has organized against the New Christian Right.

THE LIBERAL REACTION

The response to the New Christian Right has been notable yet varied in strength. Liberal strongholds such as the American Civil Liberties Union (ACLU), the National Organization for Women (NOW), the National Abortion Rights Action League (NARAL), the National Education Association (NEA), and the National Council of Churches (NCC) have offered significant opposition on behalf of their own organizations mostly in terms of national media campaigning and direct mailings to its membership. One should not fail to mention the anti–New Right challenge of local groups such as the San Diego Ecumenical Convention, Thinking Majority (NOW affiliates in Texas and in Arkansas), and Free Voices (an Alaskan affiliate of the Voices of Reason) which sponsor rallies, produce educational material and make public debate and repudiation of the political agenda of the religious Right. Most salient and significant are the national organizations established solely for the purposes of opposing the Right. Among these are People for the American Way (a nonprofit educational foundation established in 1980 by Norman Lear which directs most of its energy into a direct mail and mass media countering of the "pervasive negative messages of the moral majoritarians"), Americans for Common Sense (a citizen's coalition established by former Senator George McGovern designed to "present a substantive, issue-oriented alternative agenda to the slogans of the New Right . . ."), Moral Alternatives in Politics (an ecumenical consortium which encourages Jewish and Christian clergy to speak publicly on the issues posed by the Christian Right), and Interchange Resource Center (a clearinghouse for information on the New Right whose "material shows right-wing connections and manipulation of issues").

It is clear from a cursory review of the programatic dimensions of these organizations that the Christian Right has generated a significant backlash among liberals. Of primary concern, is not a descriptive review of the activities, programs and policies of the liberal reaction, but rather an examination of the substance of the liberal disagreement with the New Christian Right. What is the ideological rub which so irritates liberal sensitivities?

In this chapter, a variety of literature will be examined—articles from liberally oriented periodicals; direct mail and membership mailings from such liberal organizations as PAW, the ACLU, NARAL, Interchange, NOW, and others; advertisements; and editorial comment from periodicals and newspapers—in the attempt to determine what, in fact, the liberal complaint is. This information can be read two different ways. How one group criticizes another may also be understood as an implicit statement about that group—its values, assumptions, and ideological precepts. The liberal critique of the New Christian Right will be examined to determine what it may say about those liberal groups making the criticism.

THE LIBERAL COMPLAINT

In reviewing the large and stylistically diverse corpus of literature that addresses the New Christian Right, several common themes become apparent. While each theme is related to the others, for analytical purposes each can be regarded as distinct.

The first theme focuses on the issue of *values and ideals*. The Christian Right is said to be characterized by moral absolutism; that is, under the conviction of an unpliable, supramundane (indeed universal) system of moral strictures. "[Jerry] Falwell's ideology denies the pluralistic society in favor of one directed by 'absolute' Christian values . . ." (Jenkins, 1981, p. 22). This absolutism is itself based in what is variously termed a "parochialism" or "narrow-minded," "dogmatic, authoritarian reli- gion"—"a closed intellectual system, without possibility of change or ad- mission of error" (Asimov, 1981). Proceeding from this is what a PAW brochure calls a "rigid and absolutist set of positions on what is and is not 'Christian,' implying that there is only one Christian position on any given political issue."

At the core of the liberal objection is the accusation of intolerance implied by this absolutism. The religious Right, according to a spokesman of the ACLU, is "militantly intolerant." "Their leaders," as another PAW brochure claims, "want to silence dissent and exclude from fullest citizen- ship anyone who disagrees with them." They "label as amoral, ungodly and un-American anyone who disagrees with them." Or, as Norman Lear, writing in the 1981 PAW quarterly report has said, to "disagree with *their* conclusions on numerous matters of morality and politics is to be labeled a poor Christian, or unpatriotic, or anti-family." Moreover, such a view holds, according to MAP, that "others are lax or corrupt in their faith, disparages the authority and authenticity of other religions, and would constrain the rights of groups with which it disagrees." Or, as the inaugural statement of PAW proclaims, "the danger of the Religious New Right is that they attack the integrity and character of anyone who does not stand with them." Consonant with this disposition is the unwilling- ness to engage in conversation with those of a different persuasion. "Gen- uine dialogue, leaving open the possibility of mutual change, is by defini- tion unknown to Fundamentalists. 'We will talk *to* you, but never actually *with* you' " (Scanzoni, 1980, pp. 847–849).

The pragmatic consequences of the religious Right's moral absolutism is, it is held, "the imposition of values and beliefs upon others." "The radical right . . . seems less interested in attacking these *public* evils (social injustices) than in legislating *private* morality and, by so doing, imposing its standards on *all* citizens" (Connors, 1980, p. 1002). Imposing their ideals upon the will of the people largely means legislating against the Equal Rights Amendment, the Gay Rights Bill, abortion, gun control, and sex education in public schools; or for prayer in public schools, the teaching of evolution as part of the public education curriculum and the Family Protection Act. A PAW brochure summarizes: "their declared goal is the enactment of laws that will prohibit everything which goes against their narrow interpretation of the will of God." Their agenda is intellectual and moral uniformity.

What intensifies the anger of liberals against the religious Right is the perception of an unjustifiable "self-righteousness" which underlies their absolutism. Organization trademarks such as Christian Voice or Moral Majority clearly imply self-righteousness since, it is contended, no groups can legitimately claim to represent the Christian perspective or the moral point of view on social and political issues to the exclusion of others. What is Christian or what is moral, it would be argued, depends on one's perspective. Backlash to this kind of boldness surfaces in the form of accusations that the religious Right's leaders are arrogant, bigoted, fanatic, profoundly immature, demagogic, and self-righteous. While not directly representative of all liberal opinion, the following commentary does summarize ideas which, in spirit, would receive wide huzzahs in liberal quarters: "fundamentalism is not a religion but a misanthropic cult replete with self-appointed gurus professing indelible blue prints of the moral life, where unquestioned obedience is part of the pact, and where to think and to be skeptical is to be evil" (Michalsky, 1981, pp. 15–51).

A second theme of criticism focuses upon the *methods* by which the religious Right carries out its agenda. On this, the Christian Right is characterized as being *irresponsible if not unprincipled*. In the public record this accusation varies in degrees of severity.

At one level, those of the New Christian Right are accused of reducing into the classic Manichean duality of good versus evil/right versus wrong the very complex issues that constitute social and political reality in modern times. Their program, it is held is one based upon slogans and simplifications that are offered as solutions to the anxiety brought about by rapid social change (Park, 1980). Even more than simplification, these groups tend to sensationalize the issues they oppose through exaggeration or emotive infusion. As former Senator Thomas McIntyre (D–N.H.) contends in *The Fear Brokers*, "many of the beliefs held by the New Right are also shared by millions of other Americans but . . . it is the subtle blending, the exaggeration of what may well be valuable attributes and the intolerance of other viewpoints that make the New Right political philosophy an unacceptable distortion."

Liberal opinion is not usually so benign, however. Typically, the claims of distortion are voiced in more vitriolic and sinister terms. Claims of deliberate manipulation on the part of the religious Right may also be heard. Manipulation takes two forms. On the one hand, there is the "exploitation of traditional values to further their ends." In one media campaign, the ACLU claims that the Moral Majority is "dangerously deceptive. They appear to represent American patriotism, because they wrap themselves in the American flag and use words like 'family' and 'life' and 'tradition.' " (ACLU advertisement). Former Senator George Mc-Govern argues:

> The New Right's close identification—some would say preemption—of the classic political support elements of religious groups, the family, and patriotism (God, mother and the flag) has made it difficult to create a public dialogue and political discussion on the serious issues of our time. Instead the New Right has, in effect, set the agenda for political discussion heavily weighted against any who would dare oppose them [McGovern, 1981; cf. Bryant, 1979].

The second form of manipulation occurs through the blurring of the role distinctions between religion and government. Most of the critics of the New Christian Right agree to the right of these groups to apply religious values in the arena of public action. Yet at the theological level, proponents are accused by some of manipulating biblical concepts for their own ideological purposes. More than this, there is the accusation that the agenda of the Christian Right is to establish itself as a "power over government" (Cousins, 1981, p. 8). The issue, then, for most is not the influence of government but the control of government. It is the fear, among many liberals, that the religious Right has, through skillful machinations, gone beyond what is deemed the legitimacy of the former to the illegitimacy of the latter. From an ACLU advertisement: "Their agenda is clear and frightening: they mean to capture the power of government and use it to establish a nightmare of religious and political orthodoxy."

At the extreme, one may even note claims of sinisterness of the harshest kind. The political ideology of the Moral Majority has been labeled "false doctrine and malicious propaganda"; Jerry Falwell has been likened to Adolf Hitler and the Ayatollah Khomeini and accused of self-deception and hypocrisy (Lamont, 1981, p. 19; Fore, 1980, p. 1004). Likewise, there is the accusation that New Right groups will knowingly bend to irrationality and deceit in order to accomplish their intentions.

The third theme of criticism directed at the Christian Right centers on the *cultural climate of negativism* which it creates. Negativism in this context may be understood as a pervasive pessimism—a general attitude of resistance based upon suspicion. This spirit of negativism derives from several factors. One major factor is identified as the "fear and hysteria" which the New Right groups are "whipping up." Labeled "fanatics," "extremists," "fear brokers," "zealots," "militants," and "patriots of paranoia who feed upon today's cynicisms," they are accused of practicing the " 'politics of polarization', setting up group against group, with blatant overtones of sexism, racism, classism, and prejudice against the poor" and the " 'politics of intimidation' to silence those who oppose (their) positions." In an Americans for Democratic Action (ADA) publication the statement is made that New Right groups "deliberately trigger popular waves of irrational fear."

Perhaps the principal source of this negativism derives from the use by these groups of conspiratorial ideas with attendant scapegoats. Frequent associations are made between the present situation and the "red scare" of the McCarthy era—"only the faces of the demagogues and the object of their suspicions has changed" (Harnack, 1981, p. 2). "What has replaced the communism of the 1950's in the present era is secular humanism." This may be defined as a naturalistic moral philosophy in which man is viewed as the measure of all things—there are no standards other than humanly created ones; the human factor is the determining factor in deciding the moral and the social good (Berger, 1979). Humanism "is becoming the object of so much distortion and fear" (Harnack, 1981, pp. 5–6). As PAW announces, "the catch-all term 'secular humanism' is used to describe an array of perceived evils and political enemies that can be blamed for all of society's ills." Overall, proponents of the religious Right "exaggerate the influence of humanism," and at times create "an image of humanists as self-centered, narrow and aimless people who would think nothing of snuffing their grandmothers should they become inconvenient" (Jenkins, 1981, p. 22). The combined effect of all of these things, it is maintained, is the creation of a social and cultural climate of distrust and resentment which the religious Right uses to enhance its own political stature.

The final theme of criticism speaks to the net effect of the previous themes and focuses on issues of *substance*. Here the foreboding judgment is made that the New Right, and especially the New Christian Right, is *antidemocratic, indeed totalitarian* in its impulse.

Many would contend with Richard Neuhaus that "they really don't understand the ethical and philosophical traditions of democracy or how to bring about change in a pluralistic society" (quoted in *Newsweek*, September 15, 1980). In many respects, this opinion is related to the belief that the religious Right is opposed to civil liberties; that, as the ACLU argues, "the new evangelicals are a radically anti-Bill of Rights movement." It is widely held that this coalition "would do violence to the American tradition of religious pluralism"; that they "don't share the First Amendment commitment to diversity and tolerance"; and as such, that their agenda "seeks to undo freedoms guaranteed in our . . . Bill of Rights." From an ACLU advertisement we read:

> [T]heir kind of 'patriotism' violates every principle of liberty that underlies the American system of government. It is intolerant. It stands against the First Amendment guarantees of freedom of expression and separation of church and state. It threatens academic freedom. And it denies to whole groups of people the equal protection of the laws.

This intolerance for diversity of belief and opinion is "not the American way." More than this, these trends, it is often maintained, portend a "religious facism" characterized by political repressions; the hidden agenda of the religious Right, according to a Friend of the American Way Proposal for funding, is " 'to overturn the present structure in this country' by 'Christianizing America' " so that "pluralism will be seen as immoral and evil, and the state will not permit anybody the right to practice evil" (cf. Ribuffo, 1980).

The threat of the New Christian Right is articulated even more precisely. Writes Ira Glasser of the ACLU: "The Moral Majority's agenda, if adopted, would result not in freedom, but in massive governmental intrusion into family life." To be sure, the threat of totalitarianism sometimes goes beyond implication. Notes Edward Morgan:

> The new right, consciously or not, is stealing not only the tactics but the philosophy of Communism. They are poisonous toadstools, which if not plucked and discarded in the bud, could well grow into an American-style totalitarianism [Morgan, 1980:7].

The sum of the liberal complaint then is that by maintaining values and ideals which are absolutist and intolerant, employing methods of simplification, exaggeration, distortion and cunning manipulation, and creating a social atmosphere of negativism through the fostering of fear and distrust, the Christian Right has spawned a political agenda which is unwittingly antidemocratic and even totalitarian in its thrust. The seriousness with which the liberal community takes the new religious Right is plain. To be sure, there are few if any issues in the past century which have evoked such unilateral and resolute reaction on the part of such a broad coalition of liberal groups.

THE LIBERAL COMPLAINT CONSIDERED

The New Christian Right may or may not stand justly accused of all of these things. Assessing the merits of the criticisms voiced is not, for the moment, germane to the reading. What *is* interesting, however, is the fact that the opposition has consistently made very similar claims on all counts about its accusers. As it was previously mentioned, the criticisms of a group may say as much about the group doing the criticizing as about the group being criticized. In an analytical "double-take," is it possible to find within the liberal complaint conventions similar to those of the Right they decry?

Though the liberal community as a whole prides itself on its cosmopolitanism, its unabashed defense of the freedom to think and behave according to individual wishes with the provision that the exercise of those rights does not inflict harm on others, it too has its own parochialisms. The literature clearly reveals its own absolutism. As survey data has shown, there are very few individuals, even the most liberal, who would privately maintain a policy of unrestricted lifestyle choice and tolerance for either themselves, their spouses or especially for their children (Yankelovich, 1981a, pp. 5–10). Notwithstanding, the ideal of tolerance is held up as an orthodoxy in its own right. For most liberals, intolerance is utterly intolerable and can be adequately met only with an equal measure of vehemence. The limits of sectors of the liberal community to tolerate politically legitimate positions deemed choice-restrictive, and thus intolerant, is well illustrated by the editorializing of the renowned biochemist, Isaac Asimov. Commenting on the New Christian Right in *Macleans,* Asimov writes:

> And it is these ignorant people, the most uneducated, the most unimaginative, the most unthinking among us, who would make of themselves the guides and leaders of us all; who would force their feeble and childish beliefs on us; who would invade our schools and libraries and homes. I personally resent it bitterly . . . [Asimov, 1981].

The issue, it would appear, is not tolerance versus intolerance, but rather where to draw the limits of moral acceptability. Consider the irony of the National Council of Churches' statement defining its views on "the *proper* role of Christians in politics" holding, among other things, that "no group can legitimately claim to represent the 'Christian vote' to the exclusion of others." (emphasis added) What is implied is something of a paradox: the Christian position is that there are no normative Christian political positions.

The issue of liberal absolutism becomes more clear when examining the symbol of liberal civility—dialogue. As much of a penchant liberals and liberal groups have for it and have expressed the need for it, there is little indication that liberal groups have actually sought dialogue with New Right groups. As it has been shown, most liberals perceive the Christian Right as intransigent in its positions. It has been reasoned: "Why dialogue with those who will only talk *to* you" (an indication that they have made up their mind) "and not *with* you." Yet it is clear that most liberal groups are equally intransigent in their positions. One would hardly expect, for example, the National Abortion Rights Action lobby to be willing to change its opinion on abortion or the gay rights lobby to change its mind on the rights of homosexuals. When liberal groups call for dialogue, it is not unreasonable to suppose that their objective may not be "mutual understanding of unreconcilable opinions" but the extraction of compromise from their opponents. Clearly the very same could be said for conservative groups.

On the issue of self-righteousness, it would be unnecessary to elaborate on the self-righteous flavor of organizational names as Americans for Democratic Action (a name which implies that if you do not support their objectives, you must not favor democratic action), People for the American Way, "a national voice for liberty": (which of course implies that if one disagrees with the views of PAW, one must be opposed to the American Way and liberty), and the American Civil Liberties Union, "the organization that protects the Bill of Rights" (with at least a *past* history of approaching civil liberties selectively) (cf. Ribuffo, 1980). The list could be extended. New Right groups, then, are not alone. Names of organizations are often appropriations of valued ideas. The reality is that most groups that bear a standard are and must be self-righteous to one degree or another. There is little evidence that liberal organizations and their leaders are less so on this point. The only significant difference is that the religious Right tends to ground its self-righteousness in religious symbols. This would seem to give the latter an ideological advantage among certain sectors of the American population.

Similarly, liberal groups are also given to dubious methods for furthering their objectives. One of the more common distortions results from portraying all Evangelical Christians as a political and religious monolith (right-wing religious fanatics) which, as several have documented, they are patently not (e.g., Hunter, 1983). Distortion is also a product of sensationalizing their opponent's positions or the conflict they experience with their opponent. It is difficult, in fact, to find a moderate voice in the liberal reaction. Indeed it could be argued fairly that the nature, present effects, and potential power of the Christian Right as a whole have been either grossly misperceived or deliberately misrepresented; but in either case, with the result being the casting of their opponents in an unfavorable image (to their advantage). With regard to the issue of ideological manipulation, organizations promulgating a liberal point of view are typically as eager to preempt American symbols for their own purposes as are those on the New Right (cf. Ward, 1981, p. 64).

The liberal coalition evidences similar tendencies in spirit, as well. Sensation and exaggeration, regardless of the party and the object of disfavor, foster fear, mistrust and resentment. On the liberal side this is accomplished when it is claimed, for example, as NARAL literature claims, that "with shocking speed they [the New Right] are now within their reach of their goal—control of our nation's political processes"; or as the Americans for Democratic Action claim in "A Citizen's Guide to the New Right," that their's is "a cynical and calculated effort to create a colossal new movement, to destroy the Republican and Democratic Parties, and to rule the United States"; or at the extreme, that "the result of a political takeover by the religious right" might "bring into existence a kind of Christian Nazism (with the Bible as *Mien Kampf*) whose manipulated multitudes goosestep mercilessly over the godless" (Michalsky, 1981, p. 52). "Constitutional scholars, bishops and rabbis are worried. So am I, and so are thousands upon thousands of your fellow citizens. I hope you too are worried . . . ."

Making what may fairly be called extreme comments such as these also sharpens existing polarities and intimidates those who know little or nothing about the New Right. Adding to this are the conspiratorial themes suggested by some. In this case, the New Christian Right is presented as the *bete noir*—"the greatest immediate threat to our pluralistic society [is] the growing power of the Religious New Right." "[Y]our welfare and the causes which you most passionately defend are in danger, jeopardized by the relentless growth of the New Right."

Finally, there is more than a vague antidemocratic sentiment implied in this literature. Liberals are incensed that the religious Right has an agenda which implies to them that those who disagree with the Right are immoral, non-Christian and un-American. Yet in the statements of policy made by liberal groups, the implication is that if one disagrees with their agenda (the Equal Rights Amendment, legalized abortion, gun control, busing, gay rights, etc.), one is against the Bill of Rights and individual freedom, against civil liberties, against the First Amendment and therefore undemocratic and "against the American Way." In a clear example of this, the ACLU writes of the New Christian Right in an advertisement:

> These groups have clearly had alarming success. They have been pivotal in blocking passage of the E.R.A. in fifteen states. Public school boards all over the country have banned books and imposed prayer and other religious ceremonies. State legislatures have begun placing increasingly severe restrictions on a woman's right to have an abortion. And there is mounting pressure to pass laws requiring the teaching of the Biblical account of creation as an alternative to evolution.
>
> We will meet the anti-Bill-of-Rights forces in the Congress, in the courts, before local and state legislatures, at school board hearings. Wherever they threaten, we will be there—with lawyers, lobbyists, staff and volunteers—to resist their attempts to deprive you of your liberty and violate your rights.

Through a reading of the statements and literature of the various New Right groups—especially those of the Christian Right, one may quickly see that when qualifying for overstatement and occasional misrepresentation, the liberal complaint is largely justified (Barnhart, 1981). The themes, by and large, hold true. Nonetheless, when People for the American Way claim that "[w]e will meet the moral majoritarians on their own ground," they speak for others in a sense they probably did not intend.

To be sure, each coalition has its own form of moral absolutism with regard to public policy. This includes their own form of parochialism, their own definitions of what is tolerable, their own kind of moral impositions, and their own expressions of self-righteousness (Stein, 1981, pp. 23–27). Organizations and spokespeople from each side also employ questionable techniques for carrying out their agenda. Neither side is given to much subtlety. Each simplifies, sensationalizes, and exaggerates claims. Both groups attempt to discredit each other with pejorative labels. Each coalition also contributes variously to a cultural atmosphere of negativism by polarizing the political realities and intimidating potential supporters. Indeed, each group tends to scapegoat the other—the opposition is either to blame for present conditions or will be to blame for future conditions. Finally, within each coalition one may note the claims or the implication that they are the true patriots or conversely, that the other has un-American, antidemocratic, and even totalitarian tendencies.

After all of this, it is clear that each coalition as a whole sounds remarkably similar to the other. The pronouncements of each have a certain interchangeable quality to them. This is not to say that there are no differences between both groups. For one, their goals are different. For the liberal coalition, the goal is civil liberties, variously understood. For the New Christian Right, the objective is the "preservation of the traditional American style of life." Moreover, within and between both groups one may find varying degrees of integrity and varying levels of sophistication. Nonetheless, in terms of style, technique, and effect, the phrase "the Right is the Left and the Left is the Right" comes close to the mark in describing the New Christian Right and the liberal community.

ON DEMOCRACY

Upon careful reflection, it becomes obvious that both coalitions are divided by more than differing opinions on different issues. Each is characterized by its own "cultural system" or "symbolic universe." As such, each brings to the political arena a different set of assumptions about the nature of social and political (*ipso facto,* moral) reality.

The New Christian Right maintains assumptions for which there was much broader popular consensus prior to the 1960's. Most importantly, these assumptions are grounded in a long-standing tradition of moral and social propriety—American in flavor but Judeo-Christian at the core. Variations are apparent, yet general themes hold: life (from conception) is sacred; not only genitalia, but also role and psyche differentiate the human species into male and female; the natural sexual relationship between humans is between male and female and that this relationship is legitimate only under one social arrangement—marriage between one male and one female; the nuclear family is the natural form of family structure and should remain inviolable from outside (state) interference; the American experience is one that respects religious symbols and authority (especially those that are Protestant) and it is essential that this respect be transmitted successively to future generations (principally through the educational apparatus); and American tradition and life is fundamentally superior to those found in other societies, and are worthy of both protection (military if necessary) and transmission.

The liberal community generally holds assumptions which *positively reflect* a social world that has undergone drastic social and cultural change (Yankelovich, 1981b). At base, it assumes that the universe is material in its nature and origin; that all social reality, including ethical proscriptions and normative codes, is exclusively a human construction and therefore relatively defined; and that reason and the empirical method in conjunction with an opaque conception of the human good is the crucible that determines what is right and wrong, legitimate and illegitimate—and ultimately what is good and evil. (The human good is subject to multiple definitions, varying with interest and circumstance.) It is a world view that is open-ended and malleable.

Each coalition carries into the political arena a different assortment of vested interests. Those of the New Christian Right are basically in line with the interests of the larger business class in America and find their justification in conservative political and free market economic ideologies (Hunter, 1980). Liberal interests, on the other hand, are essentially identical with New Class vested interests (Gouldner, 1979; Bruce-Briggs, 1980) and are, by and large, legitimated by an ideology of political reformism and a quasi-economic collectivism (all defined as "public interest").

These cultural systems are clearly more complex than the abbreviations presented here. Nonetheless, what is important is that they bear on political praxis in direct ways. The most obvious way is with regard to specific political issues for which there has been wide publicity—abortion, ERA, gay rights, SALT II, etc. Apart from the logic for or against (for most, logic has little to do with their position on an issue), the assumptions and the interests of each cultural system will preclude or endorse the proposals from the outset. (For example, abortion is murder and must be stopped if human life is defined as beginning at conception. Legalized abortion is morally acceptable and therefore a viable public policy if life is defined as not starting until birth or perhaps the third or even second trimester of pregnancy.)

These also bear on broader issues. One of these is the constitutional relationship between religion and government, the nature of the separation between church and state. Modernization means, among other things, an increasing institutional differentiation and specialization of structure and function. For those whose assumptions and interests reflect a world in which there is greater institutional overlap between, for example, religion and politics or religion and education, the political initiatives of the Moral Majority will present little difficulty. For those whose assumptions and interests reflect a world accustomed to a relative institutional autonomy (especially from religion) the political activism of the Christian Right cannot help but appear highly irregular and even reactionary.

Another issue is that of government intrusion into private life. Each group accuses the other of this infraction. Both, in their own way, are correct. The enactment of law that endorses a shifting cultural climate will be perceived as an intrusion by those who resist the present cultural changes; the reversal of these laws or the attempt to prohibit their enactment will be perceived as an intrusion by those who approve of these changes and whose interests are served by them. The liberal reaction is ultimately grounded in a different constellation of values, assumptions, and interests than those of the Christian Right. They are "worlds apart."

On the issue of democracy, both groups are simultaneously right and wrong. Both are incorrect to imagine that the other does not understand the traditions of democracy, because—*in practice* both do. They both have effectively organized grassroots support for their political platforms, have generated publicity to make known their causes and to garner greater popular support, and have effectively lobbied to influence elected political officials. All of this is well within the boundaries of legal-political propriety. They both are partially correct, however, when they claim that the other has an unwitting anti-democratic motive. The anti-democratic impulse which resonates in the pronouncements of each group is not simply the unofficial political and social intolerance which we have seen each group has for the other. Officially such intolerance does not exist. Each side has publicly claimed that it would defend the right of the other to exist and to exercise free speech.

What hints of the anti-democratic is the deliberate attempt on the part of both to *monopolize the symbols of legitimacy* (patriotism, Americanism, family, First Amendment, etc.). In a democratic forum, there occurs a strange form of double talk: at once we are told that a group is guaranteed a right to exist and to exercise free speech; at the same time, it is judged illegitimate by virtue of the substance of its message (unpatriotic, un-American, etc.) and by implication, should not exist and should not voice its opinion. Put in more strident terms, since this group is a danger to our society, we would be better off as a society if it did not exist and did not publicize its opinion. The distinction between the descriptive and the prescriptive is very small and one that is not always easily maintained. The process of moving from the latter to the former (such that what should be by implication redefines what is in actual policy) is, cognitively, a precariously easy move to make and its consequences are profoundly undemocratic. Yet both sides in this contest are cavalier in their use of these powerful symbols of legitimacy and illegitimacy. In as much as this is true, the spirit of democratic tolerance is strained.

In a society as large and diverse as American society, sharply different views of the world are predictable. Democracy is predicated upon this sort of plurality. Yet as the patriarchs of sociological thought maintained, in advanced industrial societies democracy is most vibrant not when innumerable individuals voice their opinion, but when individuals come together into associations or coalitions to exert a much greater influence upon the political process. In this light, what can be said for the contest between liberals and the New Christian Right? It could be reasonably argued that, *not by their respective pronouncements but by their net effect, American democracy is enlivened.* Through counterbalancing each other, democracy is invigorated.

If this speculation turns out to be true, it is made possible only because each group has imposed limits upon its absolutism and in turn, limits upon its intolerance for the other. Democracy clearly is built upon a plurality of value and opinion. However, it can thrive only when the plurality upon which it is based is a *civil* plurality—a tacit agreement among all parties, despite their differences, to work within certain legally prescribed, nonviolent, channels of political action and dissent. Thus, in spite of the attempt of both groups to monopolize the symbols of legitimacy against the other, both the liberal community and the Christian Right have made that agreement. Both have, in fact, publicly reaffirmed their commitment to it. The experiment which is America would not then seem to be on the brink of disaster, as both sides would have us believe. Clearly, American democracy has withstood more vigorous tests than the present one and will undoubtedly withstand more serious tests in the future.

V | *The Cultural Environment*

9 | THE POLITICAL REBIRTH OF AMERICAN EVANGELICALS

Robert Wuthnow

For many years it was believed that evangelical religion and politics did not mix. Evangelicals were thought to be so preoccupied with personal piety, Bible verses, and visions of unearthly rewards that the practicalities of political life could not be countenanced.

This view was, of course, completely at odds with historical studies showing that evangelicals had played a significant role in the Prohibition movement in the early part of the century, that they had been a major force in the antislavery movement during the nineteenth century, and that they had actively participated in the drive for independence in the century before that. It was, however, firmly supported by the results of quantitative empirical research.

Between 1953 and 1974 the relations between conservative theological convictions and political activity were examined in more than a dozen empirical investigations. These studies were conducted in different parts of the country, included church members and clergy from a number of different denominations and from the general public, and employed carefully designed questions aimed at measuring theological views, to which were related an assortment of political activity and attitude measures.

Without exception, these studies indicated that evangelicals were less inclined toward political participation than were their less evangelical counterparts.

Impressed by the regularity of these findings, social researchers went on to suggest theoretical interpretations. For the most part, these interpretations focused on the social psychology of the individual. They assumed a need for cognitive consistency and argued that conservative religious beliefs were inherently incompatible with an active interest in politics. As one prominent group of researchers concluded:

> . . . the thrust of evangelical Protestantism is toward a miraculous view of social reform: that if all men are brought to Christ, social evils will disappear through the miraculous regeneration of the individual by the Holy Spirit. Thus evangelicals concentrate on conversion, and except for occasional efforts to outlaw what they deem to be personal vices, evangelical Protestant groups largely ignore social and political efforts for reform [Stark, et al. 1971 p. 102].

By the end of the decade, these confident generalizations would prove to be patently false.

THE EVIDENCE OF REBIRTH

Journalism has more than amply documented that evangelicals became increasingly active in politics toward the end of the 1970's. They conducted mass mailings, leafletted church parking lots, raised money for political causes, and lobbied for legislation. Evangelicals were hardly waiting passively for miracles; they had become a highly mobilized political force.

Media reports sometimes gave the impression that this fervor was limited mostly to a few particularly active organizations. But research studies show otherwise. Between 1976 and 1981 ten studies, seven national and three local, compared the political activities and attitudes of evangelicals with those of persons with other religious views. With no exceptions, evangelicals were the most politically involved. A 1976 Gallup poll showed that born-again churchgoers were just as likely as other churchgoers to be registered to vote and that they planned to vote, and concluded that they would have been more likely to vote than other groups had differences in demographic composition been taken into account.[1] A 1978 study of Protestant clergy in North Carolina demonstrated that clergy with evangelical orientations preached sermons on a

---

[1] These data were analyzed by Crippen (1981), showing that 78 percent of both born-again churchgoers and non-born-again churchgoers were registered to vote in 1976 and that 67% of both groups said they were planning to vote.

wide variety of contemporary social issues, including sex and violence on television, crime, drug abuse, ERA, pornography, abortion, school prayer, and the conduct of public officials more often than did clergy with more liberal theological views (Koller and Retzer 1980). In a November 1978 Gallup study conducted for *Christianity Today,* 31% of the evangelical Protestants said it was very important "for religious organizations to make public statements about what they feel to be the will of God in political-economic matters," compared with only 17% of the non-evangelical Protestants. By a margin of 62 to 40%, the evangelicals were also more likely to say that "religious organizations should try to persuade Senators and Representatives to enact legislation they would like to see become law."[2] These differences, moreover, remained when factors such as region, age, income, and education were taken into account. A related study of nearly 2000 clergy found that evangelical pastors were more supportive of these kinds of actions than were evangelical laity and just as supportive of them as were nonevangelical pastors (Henderson, 1980). Both studies showed, however, that evangelism and spiritual growth continued to be regarded as the church's top priorities among evangelicals.

Research in 1980 and 1981 further substantiated these findings. An ABC-Harris survey conducted in September 1980 found white evangelicals by a margin of 74 to 53% for white nonevangelicals agreeing that "it is fitting and proper for religious groups to support candidates and to be active politically to restore morality to public life." The same study showed evangelicals less supportive of strict separation of church and state. A national survey conducted in 1980 for the Connecticut Mutual Life Insurance Company found that persons scoring high on a scale of conservative religious commitment were more likely to have voted in local elections than were persons scoring low on the scale (Connecticut Mutual Life, 1981). Another national study, conducted by Gallup for the American Research Corporation in March 1980, reported that evangelicals were more likely to be registered to vote than were nonevangelicals and just as likely to say they planned to vote, despite being overrepresented in politically inactive demographic segments of the population.[3]

---

[2] These figures were compiled by Hunter (1981) who divided the sample into five religious groups: Evangelical Protestants (persons who believed the Bible to be the word of God and believed that it was not mistaken in its teachings, believed that Christ is divine, and believed that Christ is the only hope for salvation and/or had had a powerful religious experience involving Christ and a sense of conversion), Liberal Protestants (not meeting the requirements listed for evangelicals), Roman Catholics, Non-Christians (mainly Jews and Greek Orthodox), and Secularists (self-defined as nonreligious).

[3] These and subsequent Gallup figures were made available to the author by George Gallup, Jr.

A local study of Protestant clergy in South Carolina revealed perceptions of greater support from parishoners for political activities among evangelical ministers than among clergy with liberal theological views (Guth, 1981). Another local study, conducted in one Congressional district in Alabama, provided indirect evidence: in this predominantly evangelical district, 78% of the respondents said they were against strict separation of church and state, 67% felt God had answers for social and political issues, and 43% approved of the Moral Majority's being involved in politics (Penfield and Davis 1981). Finally, a Roper poll for NBC in April 1981 gave evidence that "extreme fundamentalists" were particularly likely to take an activist stance toward politics: 53% thought religious groups should get involved in election campaigns in the way the Moral Majority had, compared with a national average of 28%; 28% had worked in a political campaign as a volunteer, compared with a national average of 25%; and 60% had written to their Senator or Congressman, compared with a national average of 44% (Milavsky, 1981).

The contrast between these results and those from studies conducted prior to the middle seventies could not be more distinct. Researchers during that period uniformly concluded that evangelicals were indifferent to politics and opposed to churches and clergy becoming involved in political issues. One survey of the literature in 1973 concluded that "active involvement in political issues appears so alien to the laity they may well regard those who engage in it as not of their own church, that is, as deviant from their conceptions of proper religious behavior" (Winter, 1973). Another study asked a panel of twenty-five leading social scientists, historians, and theologians to rank religious groups, first in terms of theological conservatism, and then in terms of concern about social and political issues. Those at the top of the first list were almost always placed at the bottom of the second (Hoge, 1979).

While the empirical studies conducted prior to the mid-1970's varied in quality and representativeness, there was strong consistency in the results. One of the first, conducted among Episcopalians in 1953, examined the extent to which laity supported clergy speaking out on political issues, endorsing candidates, and getting people out to vote. The authors concluded "obviously, primary support for such functions will not be found among those with a traditionalistic orientation toward religion and the church" (Ringer and Glock, 1954–1955). One of the most compelling studies, done in 1971 among 600 church members in Indianapolis, found that orthodox religious belief correlated negatively with support for clergy being involved in political activities; this relation was especially strong among the more religiously committed (Gibbs, *et al.*, 1973). An earlier study of Protestants in Indiana had suggested much the same thing, showing that writing letters to political officials and joining community aid groups were less common among evangelicals than among nonevangelicals (Davidson, 1972). Another study, done about the same time in New York state, reported that persons scoring high on an index of traditional religious orthodoxy were more likely to agree with the statement "churches should stick to religion and not concern themselves with social, economic, and political questions" than were low scorers (Broughton, 1978). Still another survey, done in North Carolina in 1972, found that those who denied belief in an afterlife, in God, and in the truth of the Bible were more likely to have voted and to have been involved in political discussions than were believers (Wimberly, 1978). And finally, a study using national data collected in 1972 found that members of fundamentalist denominations were less likely than members of mainline denominations to be involved in political clubs or in civic groups, to have voted, to have been interested in the 1972 election, and to value the importance of political participation (Hendricks, 1977).

The patterns found among the public were also found among the clergy. A study of more than 1500 Protestant clergy in California in 1968 found that traditional orthodox beliefs were negatively associated with having delivered a sermon on a controversial political or social topic, having organized a social action group for the church, having taken a stand from the pulpit on a political issue, and favoring one's denomination taking official positions on important issues of the day. Its author concluded, "clergymen who adhere to traditional Protestant orthodoxies and an otherworldly conception of Christianity are generally politically conservative and socially inactive; those who possess what we have termed 'modernist' religious views are the most liberal in their political positions and the most outspoken in their activist behavior (Quinley, 1974, p. 292). The same patterns were found in a national survey of mainline Protestant clergy in 1972 (Tygart, 1977), in a survey of Presbyterian clergy in 1973 (Hoge, 1976), and in a national study of denominational officials and seminary professors in 1974 (Schuller et al., 1980).

It may have been that these studies were biased against evangelicals. Many of the studies conducted in the late 1960's and early 1970's were concerned with civil rights activism and it is possible that even the ones which asked neutrally worded questions may have carried connotations about civil rights because of their overall purpose. Evangelicals were deeply divided over the tactics being used to achieve civil rights legislation and may for this reason have scored artificially low on political involvement. An additional difficulty with these studies stems from the fact that many of them were conducted among church members in mainline denominations. In these contexts conservative evangelicals were likely to be in disagreement with the official views of their denominations and, consequently, may have wished them to keep silent politically. Nevertheless, the evidence seems sufficiently consistent and comes from a sufficient variety of sources to suggest that evangelicals were definitely less supportive of political activism in the early 1970's than they had become by the late 1970's.

Evidence from other sources also points to this conclusion. A content analysis of the leading evangelical periodical *Christianity Today* showed a dramatic rise in attention to political issues during the 1970's: only twelve articles in 1969–70 were devoted to political themes (5.5% of the total), compared with thirty-two articles in 1979–80 (15.4%).[4] Qualitatively, the articles in the latter period also tended to encourage greater political involvement, whereas the earlier ones had been largely critical of involvement. In one of the few articles dealing with political themes in the earlier period, for example, Malcolm Nygren concluded, "when the church tries to become a political leader, it harms both its own mission and the world it seeks to help" (1969, p. 9). A decade later, in contrast, the magazine editorialized, "as good disciples we must take seriously the lordship of Jesus Christ over every aspect of human thought and life, including man's political life, and we must function as Christian citizens of the state" (Christianity Today 1980, p. 11). The same editorial, incidentally, endorsed the lobbying efforts of the New Christian Right, lauding "their deep commitment to social and political change."

The shifting mood of evangelicals toward politics from the late 1960's to the late 1970's was also evident in other publications. In a widely read article published in the May 1966 *Readers Digest* J. Howard Pew, a prominent evangelical and board chairman of Sun Oil, advised readers against political activity, citing the example of Christ who "refused to enmesh himself or his followers in the economic, social and political problems of his day—problems certainly as serious as those we face today. . . . He made it crystal clear that we are to seek 'first the kingdom of God and his righteousness'—carefully pointing out that 'the kingdom is within you' " (p. 53). By comparison, the late 1970's witnessed an outpouring of evangelical literature which argued directly against this position. New evangelical periodicals appeared that were heavily oriented toward political themes. These included *Sojourners, The Other Side, The Wittenburg Door,* and the National Association of Evangelicals' *Washington Insight.* Established journals such as *United Evangelical Action* and *Christian Life* began publishing interviews with political leaders, announced

---

[4] A total of 219 articles for 1969 and 1970 and 208 articles for 1979 and 1980 were content analyzed by the author.

political rallies, and carried ads for political groups. A number of books were written as well, arguing that evangelicals should become more politically responsible. Theologian Carl F. Henry reflected the broader mood among many evangelicals when he challenged conservative Christians to quit regarding "evangelism as the only morally significant force in national life" and to develop a "philosophy of social and political involvement" (1980, p. 19).

During the same period, the so-called electronic church also began to take on increasingly political overtones. Although popular broadcasts such as Charles E. Fuller's "Old Time Revival Hour" and Billy Graham's "Hour of Decision" had attracted large audiences since the early 1950's, a new generation of religious broadcasters emerged in the 1970's attracting audiences far larger than ever before. Whereas a study in 1963 found that only 12% of all Protestants regularly watched or listened to religious broadcasts, according to Gallup polls this figure had more than doubled by the late 1970's: in April 1978, 28% of the public claimed to have watched a religious broadcast in the past thirty days; in November 1978, 29% claimed to have been viewers in the past week; in 1980, 50% said they had watched in the past year; and in 1981, 27% said they had watched more than one religious program in the past month. Among evangelicals the figures were considerably higher, indicating that more than half were occasional viewers and at least a quarter were heavy viewers. Some of the leading broadcasters, of course, refrained completely from issuing political pronouncements (for example, Oral Roberts, Rex Humbard, and Jimmy Swaggart). But others, such as Jerry Falwell, James Robison, Pat Robertson, and Jim Bakker, turned increasingly to political and social issues. Viewers, for their part, seemed to be responsive to these appeals. One study, for example, showed that more than a third of "700 Club" viewers checked "to learn about politics and what's right and wrong in America today" as a very important reason for their viewing; nearly a quarter checked learning "who to vote for and what kind of laws to accept" (Gantz and Kowalewski, 1979).

Most visibly, of course, the political rebirth among evangelicals was evident in its organized political efforts. State chapters of Christian Voice and Moral Majority participated in a number of campaigns to oust liberal Congressmen in the 1980 elections. They contributed funds and worked through local pastors to mobilize evangelical voters. Besides special interest groups, evangelicals also participated politically through their official organizations. In Florida the National Association of Evangelicals (NAE), representing more than 3 million evangelicals nationwide from 60 denominations, actively supported Anita Bryant's campaign against homosexuality and protested school district edicts forbidding Christ to be mentioned in conjunction with Christmas celebrations. While the NAE refused to take an official stand on the Equal Rights Amendment, its Women's Fellowship supported organizations seeking to block ERA. The NAE also hired a full-time lobbyist who testified on behalf of political appointees, publicly sympathized with the views of Moral Majority and Christian Voice, encouraged NAE members to write letters of support for Reagan administration policies, and was frequently cited as a kindred spirit by New Right leaders, such as Richard Viguerie and Paul Weyrich.

All of this was in stark contrast to the virtual political uninvolvement of evangelicals during the preceding two decades. At mid century, only one evangelical lobbying effort was in existence (Ebersole, 1951). Later, personalities like Carl McIntire and Billy James Hargis became widely known for their political pronouncements against Communism. But these figures never managed to attract more than a small fringe of evangelicals and failed completely in establishing active political organizations. On a broader scale, evangelicals had not been mobilized politically and had not shown much interest in politics as individuals, and their theological views seemed to provide ample reason for not becoming involved.

THE SHORTFALL OF THEORY

How is it, then, that the same religious convictions can so thoroughly discourage political activity at one moment and only a short while later promote it so enthusiastically? How is it that the biblical piety of evangelicals could have blinded them to political concerns at the beginning of the 1970's but only a few years later have allowed them to become politically mobilized?

The question yields no obvious answer if we insist on viewing religious convictions as neat intellectual dictums governed by canons of rational consistency and elective affinity. As long as religious systems are regarded as static clusters of beliefs organized around simple tenets, such as the quest for individual salvation, events like the political rebirth of evangelicals can scarcely be explained, except as anomalies. It is little wonder, given this view of religion, that social scientists have largely abandoned the study of religion for the greener pastures of Marxian theory, status politics, and resource mobilization.

And yet, the enduring religions of the world have never been so easy to dismiss nor so simple to reduce. They have been, and remain, vastly complex. Religious systems are dynamic configurations of symbolism and ritual whose character has scarcely begun to be comprehended. This symbolism contains a structure within itself which defines the very categories in which religious thought takes place. Neither the political involvement of evangelicals, nor the nature of religion more generally, can be understood unless careful attention is given to the symbolism of which religion is comprised.

The political awakening of evangelicals may have received impetus from a number of events—the Supreme Court decision on abortion in 1973, the IRS proposal in 1978 to invoke racial quotas in Christian schools, the efflorescence of the electronic church, to name a few. But religious symbolism itself remained the most vital aspect of evangelical thought, and it was this symbolism that defined the ideological context in which the connections between religion and morality and between morality and politics were understood. Those in the vanguard of the evangelical movement knew this well. As conservative organizer Paul Weyrich explained, "It is a war of ideology, it's a war of ideas, it's a war about our way of life" (quoted in Range, 1981b, p. 99).

THE STRUCTURE OF EVANGELICAL IDEOLOGY

Religions are comprised not only of symbolism about relations with the divine, but by symbolism about the relations among mortals as well. These relations, the domain of "morality," bear close connections with the realm of the sacred. The symbols that inspire awe as objects of worship are also likely to be invoked as sources of authority for conceptions of morality. And the activities accorded moral significance in the world of men may well have implications for one's relation to the divine. Conceptions of morality, therefore, generally fall within the definition of what it means to be religious. This is clearly the case among evangelicals, for whom morality is codified in divinely inspired biblical injunctions.

The nature of morality, however, is also subject to cultural definition. In modernized societies both morality and religion have evolved in the direction of being matters of conscience—of individual preference and personal life style. In this conception, individuals are expected to exercise responsibility over their own behavior and to govern themselves sufficiently to forestall the collapse of collective institutions through lapses in moral behavior. Associated with this understanding is the assumption that individuals must be free to make their own moral choices. As a result of this freedom a certain range of moral expression must also be tolerated. Except in cases of extreme negligence, public institutions must not enter the domain of morality. These institutions also contain their own safeguards that enable them to function smoothly despite variations in individual moral performance. Implicit in the modern understanding of morality, therefore, is a distinct demarcation between private morality and public institutions.

Although the line separating private morality from public institutions has never been absolute, it was blurred at least temporarily as a result of several highly symbolic events during the 1970's. Undoubtedly the most significant of these was the Watergate episode. This event not only dramatized an actual connection between private morality and the collective good, but indicated that purely private conceptions of morality may have serious negative repercussions for the society as a whole. Watergate became a collective ritual in which personal immorality came to symbolize evil in the corporate society. This drama was chiefly resolved by the election of President Jimmy Carter in 1976. In Carter, the connection between private decency and the collective whole gained personification.

Watergate was only one of the episodes that blurred the distinction between morality and collective life. Criticism of the Vietnam war as an act of public immorality, the various legislative actions taken in the aftermath of Watergate to institutionalize morality as a matter of official concern, and major Supreme Court decisions symbolically linking government with morality in the very act of attempting to protect private conceptions of morality also had this effect. Morality came to be viewed as a public issue rather than in strictly private terms. This shift was reflected clearly in the periodical literature of the decade. The total number of discussions about morality and ethics in this literature increased, as did the number of separate headings under which these discussions took place, as well as the number of separate institutional sectors in which morality was treated as a significant issue.[5] In short, the wall that had separated private morality from public institutions broke down.

By the end of the 1970's, the distinction between private morality and collective institutions had become so sufficiently ambiguous that critics openly challenged the former privatistic conceptions of morality and called for greater official concern for the relation between moral issues and the public good. Meg Greenfield editorialized in the *Washington Post*, writing just prior to the 1980 election, "We have refused to view practically any indecency, outrage or pathological assault on our sense of rightness in any way except as a civil-liberties problem—protecting the abstract right of the sickos to come to dinner." In a similar vein the *Wall Street Journal*, putting the issue in partisan terms, charged that the

---

[5] Content analysis of the *Readers' Guide to Periodical Literature* conducted by the author showed that the number of entries concerning morality and ethics increased from 55 to 87 between 1969 and 1979, the number of category headings increased from 13 to 18, and the number of institutional spheres (e.g., military ethics, journalistic ethics, business ethics, etc.) increased from 6 to 12.

earlier view of politics and morality had "come to stand for the proposition that it makes no difference to the well-being of the polity whether, for example, the populace is heterosexual or homosexual, the traditional family is preserved or not, some 'lifestyles' are considered exemplary or not" (Bennett and Eastland, 1980).

In evangelical thought, the connection between private morality and the collective good had always been present. Evangelicals steadfastly maintained that personal morality necessarily had public consequences. This view had been incorporated into the American civil religion from earliest times by the Puritan colonists and had surfaced repeatedly during the eighteenth and nineteenth centuries. It held that a nation cannot be great unless it is good. Surely God would bring collective judgment on those who permitted immorality to exist in their midst. The book of Proverbs, in a much quoted passage, made this abundantly clear to evangelicals: "Righteousness exalteth a nation; but sin is a reproach to any people" (Prov. 14:34 AV). For evangelicals, morality had never been a matter of privatistic withdrawal, as critics in the academy had so often mistakenly accused. Now, at the end of the 1970's, they found a version of their view being expressed in far quarters, including the nation's major news media and the White House itself.

Along with the expanded definition of morality, the 1970's also modified the public definition of evangelicalism itself. The election of Jimmy Carter to the White House—the first President since Woodrow Wilson to have claimed an adult conversion experience and the first since James Garfield to hold membership in an evangelical denomination—was a major symbolic victory for evangelicals. Carter's campaign brought evangelicals into the forefront of media attention. *Time, Newsweek, U.S. News & World Report,* and the *Saturday Evening Post* all carried feature stories about evangelicals in 1977. CBS produced a prime-time documentary titled "Born Again," featuring such prominent evangelicals as Charles Colson, Eldridge Cleaver, and Senator Harold Hughes. Colson's book *Born Again* made the best-seller list and celebrities like Roger Staubach, B. J. Thomas, and Natalie Cole openly professed their evangelical faith. Startled by the sudden attention, but obviously pleased, the National Association of Evangelicals' official publication declared, "We did not expect to have our proverbial lights so abruptly exposed from underneath their bushels" (Maust, 1978, p. 8).

The national attention that evangelicals received in the 1970's forged a symbolic link between their own identity and that of the larger society, giving them a sense of political entitlement which made it more conceivable to speak out on moral issues. Evangelicals perceived themselves as having a special message to bring to the American people. Theirs was a message based on the biblical values they had so long sought to preserve. It was in the best interest of the whole society that evangelicals responsibly draw attention to these values. Evangelical writer Harold O. J. Brown put the issue forthrightly: "In America, Christians are custodians of the values of our civilization. If we exclude ourselves or allow ourselves to be excluded from participation in public policy making whenever political and spiritual concerns overlap, then we are depriving our whole society of the richest source of ethical insight" (Brown, 1977, p. 112).

Others drew a direct connection between the enhanced opportunities that the sudden prominence of evangelicals in the media and in government had provided, suggesting that increased public responsibilities accompanied these opportunities. The biblical injunction "to whom much has been given much will also be required" was implicitly invoked. Evangelist Billy Graham wrote, "The new prominence of evangelicals has given us significant access to the mass media, and as a result many people listen to what we have to say. Will we use this visibility for God's glory in the coming decade?" (Graham, 1980, p. 25). Another writer commented, "What the media's coverage of Christians and their beliefs most demand is responsibility" (Maust, 1978).

Evangelicals had become an identifiable collective unit having both the public recognition and the internal sense of responsibility necessary to take part in the political sphere. The shifting definition of morality that had occurred during the same period helped to channel the evangelicals' newly felt political obligations into an activist direction. Morality was one issue on which evangelicals agreed. They remained deeply divided in many other ways—theologically, denominationally, geographically. But on questions of morality they were unified. In the 1978 Gallup study mentioned earlier 97% said they were opposed to premarital sex, 95% expressed opposition to abortion, and 89% were opposed to homosexuality (Hunter, 1981). Virtually every empirical study showed close connections between evangelical beliefs and conservative moral views.

Now that morality and politics had come to be discussed in the same breath in the media and among government agencies themselves, taking action on moral issues necessarily meant taking part in political affairs. The two could no longer be easily separated. It was, indeed, evangelicals' convictions about morality that most clearly motivated them to take a more active role in politics. A survey conducted in 1980 by the Opinion Research Corporation found that 72% of those who thought morals had been getting worse felt religious groups should be having more political influence, compared with only 13% of those who thought morals had not gotten worse (Silverman, 1981). This study did not examine evangelicals separately, but in the 1978 Gallup study it was possible to do so.

There, evangelicals showed distinctly different patterns from liberal Protestants. Using views on abortion as an indicator of attitudes about morality, 68% of the evangelicals who thought abortion was never acceptable felt the churches should try to influence legislation, compared with 63% of those who thought it was sometimes acceptable, and only 50% of those who thought it was always acceptable. In other words, the more strongly opposed one was to abortion, the more likely he or she was to favor political action from religious organizations. Among liberal Protestants, just the opposite was true. Only 33% of those who felt abortion was never acceptable favored churches influencing legislation, compared with 40% of those who felt abortion was sometimes acceptable, and 46% of those who felt it was always acceptable.[6]

The most likely explanation for these divergent patterns is that antiabortion evangelicals wanted churches to speak out because they assumed the churches they knew best would speak out against abortion. Antiabortionists in liberal denominations, in contrast, probably assumed their churches would speak in favor of abortion, and therefore were less inclined to want them to speak at all.

Evangelicals' commitment to the preservation of traditional morality, together with the growing politicization of morality more generally, provided the symbolic linkage necessary to legitimate evangelicals' awakening interest in politics. For evangelical leaders, morality was broadly conceived and therefore had ramifications for a wide range of political issues. In a radio broadcast against homosexuality Jerry Falwell asked rhetorically, "Is it any wonder that we are the laughing stock of the world? Is it any wonder that nations and terrorists thumb their noses at this once proud land?" To others, declining moral standards were responsible for social ills, ranging from crime to declining SAT scores.

If morality was indeed the mainstay of national health, evangelicals could hardly stand by, knowing that God had given them both the answers and the opportunity to voice their answers, while the social fabric deteriorated. In the biblical prophets evangelicals had dramatic examples of persons who had been called to speak out against moral decay, and evangelical leaders consciously adopted these as models. In prophetic tones evangelist James Robison explained, "God has given me the role of pulling down and destroying anything that is raised above God or in place of God or that limits God's work in the nation, the church, or the world. That means the idolatry of excessive government or the idolatry of appetites and entertainment and pleasure, or anything else that gets between an individual and God" (Martin, 1981).

As the embodiment of morality in public life, Jimmy Carter became

---

[6] Figures supplied to the author by James Hunter.

a convenient target for these invectives. It was through Carter that the link between evangelicalism and politics, and between morality and politics, had been dramatized. The sense of entitlement that evangelicals had obtained created mutual obligations between themselves and their elected representative, whom they could argue had betrayed that sense of entitlement. Evangelicals had lent support to the Carter election, literally and figuratively, and could now argue that Carter had betrayed their sacred trust. In his book *The New Right: We're Ready to Lead* fundraiser Richard Viguerie commented, "Not only has the Carter administration ignored the born-again Christians, it has actively and aggressively sought to hurt the Christian movement in America" (1980, p. 156). Entitled to be heard, but betrayed, evangelicals should become actively involved, according to Viguerie, in the efforts of the New Right.

Whereas the secular Right, like Viguerie, relied on the imagery of political patronage to describe this sense of betrayal, leaders of the religious Right drew imagery from deep within the Protestant tradition. This imagery differentiated the political realm from the spiritual kingdom, granting it authority over all aspects of the temporal world, and pledging loyalty to it from Christian citizens—except for violations of divinely instituted moral principles. Hence, Jerry Falwell could admonish his viewers to "be subject to the higher powers" in all walks of life, from paying taxes to obeying the speed limits, and yet reserve the right to actively challenge any act of these powers deemed to be in violation of biblical morality. "Jimmy Carter," he remarked in 1976, "is now my President-elect and he will have my respect and support. I will pray for him daily. But I will oppose him when he violates moral codes which in my opinion are in opposition to Scripture" (Strober and Tomczak, 1979, p. 179).

Morality was the issue which gave unity to evangelicals and to which they felt they had something special to contribute. Their own definition of the moral domain was inclusive and by exploiting the full breadth of this definition, evangelical leaders who emerged as part of the New Right could address a broad range of political issues. In short, they could rely on biblical authority to validate their arguments to evangelicals.

THE STRUGGLE OVER SYMBOLIC BOUNDARIES

But as evangelical leaders began to participate in political discussions, the sheer act of participation affected the kinds of arguments that were made. It proved necessary, if moral claims were to be convincing to a larger audience, to build symbolic bridges between evangelicals' own understandings of morality and the secular norms defining the political sphere. Two symbolic boundaries deeply ingrained in thinking about political participation proved particularly vital, but also troublesome, to define. One was the boundary between morality and politics; the other, between religion and morality. Both had become blurred and now required redefinition. It was the struggle to define or redefine these boundaries that produced much of the ideological debate surrounding the rise of the religious right.

The religious right had been well served by the blending together of morality and politics during the 70's and now found it in its own interest to establish further symbolic connections between morality and the political sphere. In modern democracies, the principal means available for legitimating political claims are to associate them with images of *procedural rationality* or to link them symbolically with the *public interest.* Evangelicals relied on both of these tactics to legitimate their participation on behalf of traditional morality.

The connection between morality and procedural rationality had already been established in a general sense by the various Supreme Court decisions and Congressional committees that had dealt with questions of ethics and morality. These gave a precedent for assuming that moral positions could be legitimated by going through the motions of making judicial or legislative decisions. In addition, evangelicals began to dramatize their own adherence to the norms of procedural rationality through highly symbolic gestures. Activities such as the Washington for Jesus rally, the formation of lobbying groups, endorsement of bills such as the Family Protection Act, and public appearances with political candidates and officials served this purpose. The implicit function of these rituals was less to accomplish actual legislative victories as it was to establish a symbolic connection between evangelicals and the procedural norms of the polity.

Legitimation in terms of the public interest involves linking specific political claims to arguments about the society as a whole. Evangelicals connected their claims with a broad array of collective symbolism. The term "majority" was itself an image of this sort. Polls and petition campaigns were used to demonstrate the existence of this majority. Symbols of the nation-state were also particularly appropriate for this purpose. Broadcasts of Jerry Falwell's "Old Time Gospel Hour" routinely began with the American flag and closed with pictures of the Liberty Bell. Advertisements for the Moral Majority announced, "We care for America and for Americans." And headlines in publications such as the *Moral Majority Report* announced favorable legislation as "victories for America."

Critics of the religious Right, for their part, sought to disconnect the notion of morality from politics, reasserting that morality was indeed purely private and that the agendas of the new movements were strictly political after all. Liberal evangelical Mark Hatfield remarked, "What I react against is the equating of a political issue with one's morality or one's ethics or one's relationship to God."[7] Others were more extreme in their criticisms, raising the spectacle of political force to its extreme. "Their agenda," proclaimed an ACLU solicitation, "is clear and frightening: they mean to capture the power of government and use it to establish a nightmare of religious and political orthodoxy."

What both sides recognized, of course, was that the symbolic boundary between morality and politics was crucial. If the boundary was blurred, then evangelicals had a right to take political action and to do so with the authority of moral conviction. If the boundary was sharp, then evangelicals were merely meddling in issues that had better be left to those who knew more about politics.

The boundary between religion and morality took on similar ideological importance. While it remained valuable, as far as evangelicals were concerned, to maintain the link between morality and religion by invoking biblical injunctions, the constitutionality of involving religious groups in politics was sufficiently troublesome to necessitate some effort at differentiation. As a result, religion came to be divided into two parts: *morality*, on which there was apparent agreement among sectarian groups, thereby mitigating the accusation that sectarian religion was involved in politics; and *theology*, which was the focus of sectarian disagreement and therefore should not be involved in politics. Describing efforts to mobilize clergy against homosexuals in California, evangelical Tim LaHaye provided a particularly candid illustration of this distinction when he wrote, "Knowing pastors as we did, we all recognized that the only way to organize them was to make it clear that our basis of cooperation was moral, not theological . . ." (LaHaye, 1980, p. 199–200). The same distinction proved useful to the press, as the Moral Majority discovered in its repeated efforts to disavow being a religious organization.

On the other side, opposition tactics involved efforts to push the notion of morality as far into the religious corner as possible, thereby suggesting that religion was being illegitimately dragged into politics. People for the American Way, for example, ran broadcasts concluding "there's gotta be something wrong when anyone, even if it's a preacher, tells you that you're a good Christian or a bad Christian depending on your political point of view." The same broadcast linked religion and morality with privacy and individual diversity. Other critics relied on symbolism of

[7] Direct mail solicitation.

religious absolutism—the Ayatollah, Mullahs, Christian soldiers, holy wars, fundamentalist dictatorships—to suggest that any consensus about morality in politics was inconceivable except in the form of religious totalitarianism.

The war of ideology was a war of symbolism used to delineate the respective boundaries between religion, morality, and politics; for within each category, different standards of behavior and different styles of thought were appropriate. As evangelicals took up the claims of power, they did not abandon their primary concern for salvation and evangelism. But their religious symbolism was sufficiently adaptable to take advantage of the opportunities that their increased visibility and the growing concern about morality in the larger culture had provided. Biblical piety defined a moral domain that evangelicals could accept without reservation. As the boundaries between morality and politics were symbolically reconstructed, evangelicals found it only natural for their moral concerns to acquire a political dimension. Their conception of responsibility before God implied living as witnesses to moral conduct, and their new prominence gave added heart for this task. No longer were they speaking as a sectarian group, but as a representative of values that were in the interest of all.

CONCLUSION

What do we learn, in the end, from examining the symbolism that formed so vital a part of the political rebirth among American evangelicals? We learn, first, that religious systems are by no means reducible to a few simple beliefs with inevitable political consequences. Evangelicalism is a rich tradition of complex and varied symbolic themes. These themes are themselves sufficiently differentiated to permit highly specific responses to be undertaken in politics and in other arenas under varying conditions. The logic specifying that much will be required of those blessed with much, for example, functions as a "generative mechanism" within the language of evangelicalism, allowing behavior to be tailored to the availability of opportunities in different situations. Mechanisms such as these, to which almost no attention has been paid in the study of religion, are undoubtedly an important feature of all the world's enduring religions. Evangelicalism, as a single case in point, appears capable of adapting to highly varied circumstances, even in the face of modernity and secularity.

At the same time, religious systems do not permit the symbolism of which they are comprised to take on any shape the social environment may suggest. This is not because of some inherent rationality in the minds of individuals that must be obeyed. It is rather a result of the arrangements, the structure, that defines the character of religious symbolism itself. This symbolism creates categories of reality and defines connections among these categories. While these are by no means static, they exert their own force over social events because they define the very contexts in which thought takes place. It is, after all, impossible to think of religious groups involving themselves in politics without the categories ''religion'' and ''politics'' themselves affecting the kinds of thoughts that seem conceivable or meaningful.

We also learn that religious systems are not closed, but interact with the cultural climate in which they exist. The symbolic boundaries demarcating the sacred and the profane, the moral and the political, are subject to constant renegotiation in which symbols supplied both by religious tradition and by events in the larger culture play a role. This is especially the case in modern societies in which the availability of mass communications permits the negotiation process to take place on a highly visible society-wide scale.

As for the political rebirth of evangelicals, the major symbolic constructions that contributed to this development were the redefinition of evangelicals themselves through symbolic episodes, such as the Carter Presidency, and the reconstruction of morality to include more public or institutional meanings rather than a purely private connotation. These developments took place within the limitations of public discourse about religion and politics that had been set within the evangelical tradition itself and within the broader understandings associated with American democracy. The effects of unplanned events such as Watergate, on the one hand, and those of carefully planned activities such as the organized efforts of political action groups, on the other, were to rearrange the symbolic boundaries among religion, morality, and politics sufficiently to make it thinkable for participation in all of these spheres to occur simultaneously and to affect one another. The fundamental religious assumptions of evangelicalism were not denied or overturned in the process. Nor was it necessary for evangelicals to experience severe anxieties, as a ''status politics'' interpretation of these events would suggest, or to make use of vastly increased stores of political resources in order to mobilize themselves. The reconstruction of symbolic worlds created a domain in which participation simply became a sensible thing to do.

The political rebirth of evangelicals, contradicting what seemed to be the main patterns of several decades, is not testimony to the irrelevance or complete indeterminacy of religious convictions in the face of changing social circumstances. It is, instead, evidence of the capacity of religion to adapt to social conditions in ways yet little understood and to challenge not only the prevailing system of politics, but the prevailing views of academicians as well.

10 MORAL ISSUES AND STATUS POLITICS[1]

John H. Simpson

This chapter addresses three questions about the Moral Majority. First, how should support for the sociomoral platform of the Moral Majority be measured and, given a measurement method, what proportion of the American population is positively oriented toward the platform? Second, how is support for the platform distributed in terms of the social characteristics of the population and what is the meaning of the pattern of relationships? Finally, what stimulated some Fundamentalist Christians to take advantage of a public mood that is, apparently, supportive of their sociomoral platform and enter the American political arena in the late 1970's via organizations such as the Moral Majority?

[1] Portions and earlier versions of this chapter were read at the Annual Meeting of the American Association for the Advancement of Science, Toronto, Ontario, 1981; the Annual Meeting of the Western Association of Sociology and Anthropology, Winnipeg, Manitoba, 1981; the Annual Meeting of the Association for the Sociology of Religion, Toronto, Ontario, 1981; the Annual Meeting of the Society for the Scientific Study of Religion, Baltimore, Maryland, 1981; and, as a lecture, to the Institute for Christian Studies, Toronto, Ontario, 1982. The support of a Social Science and Humanities Research Council of Canada Leave Fellowship is gratefully acknowledged.

THE PLATFORM OF THE MORAL MAJORITY

A 1977 survey of the American population (General Social Survey, [GSS], see Davis, 1980) contains a number of items that bear directly upon Americans' attitudes towards prayer in the schools, abortion, homosexuality, and the woman's role.[2] Since the items appear in the same survey, it is possible to analyze the pattern of interitem relationships and to estimate the distribution of these patterns in the American population as a whole. This type of analysis is important because the Moral Majority has linked together a traditional view of the woman's role, opposition to abortion and homosexuality, and a positive view of school prayer, among other things, to form a sociomoral platform. Do these issues coalesce as a platform in the minds of Americans as a whole and, if they do, what proportion of the population endorses the platform of the Moral Majority? That question cannot be answered by simply reporting the marginal distributions of attitudes toward each of the separate platform items as is commonly done in the publication of public opinion polls, since a platform is, by definition, a *set* of positions (i.e., a joint frequency distribution) on a number of issues. To assess support for a platform, then, the analyst must determine the number of individuals in a population who endorse or oppose the set of issues comprising the platform.

The column labeled *Observed Frequency* in Table 10.1 contains a cross-classification of items from GSS 1977 measuring attitudes toward (A) homosexual relations between adults; (B) the United States Supreme Court ruling on prayer and Bible reading in the public schools; (C) the statement: "It is much better for everyone involved if the man is the achiever outside the home and the woman takes care of the home and family"; and (D) abortion for any reason.

[2] GSS 1977 is a full probability sample of all noninstitutionalized individuals of 18 years of age or older who live in the continental United States and speak English. For the items analyzed in this chapter, the GSS 1977 mnemonic variable names, questions, answer categories, and recodes, where applicable, are as follows: (A) Homosexual Relations—HOMOSEX, "What about sexual relations between two *adults* of the *same* sex—do you think that it is always wrong, almost always wrong, wrong only sometimes, or not wrong at all?" Favor = Almost always wrong, Wrong only sometimes, Not wrong at all; Oppose = Always wrong. (B) School Prayer Decision—PRAYER, "The United States Supreme Court has ruled that no state or local government may *require* the reading of the Lord's Prayer or Bible verses in public schools. What are your views on this—do you approve or disapprove of the court ruling? Favor = Approve; Oppose = Disapprove. (C) Woman's Role—FEFAM, "It is much better for everyone involved if the man is the achiever outside the home and the woman takes care of the home and family?" Modern = Disagree, Strongly disagree; Traditional = Strongly agree, Agree. (D) Abortion—ABANY, "Please tell me whether or not *you* think it should be possible for a pregnant woman to obtain a legal abortion if the woman wants it for any reason?" Favor = Yes; Oppose = No.

TABLE 10.1 Cross-Classification and Latent Structure Analysis of Attitudes[a]

Cell No.	(A) Homosexual relations	(B) School Prayer decision	(C) Woman's role	(D) Abortion	Observed frequency	Estimated frequency	Latent Class assignment
1	Favor	Favor	Modern	Favor	85 (6.2%)	82.0	1
2	Oppose	Favor	Modern	Favor	36 (2.6%)	35.4	1
3	Favor	Oppose	Modern	Favor	65 (4.7%)	66.0	1
4	Oppose	Oppose	Modern	Favor	47 (3.4%)	51.2	2
5	Favor	Favor	Traditional	Favor	37 (2.7%)	46.6	1
6	Oppose	Favor	Traditional	Favor	55 (4.0%)	52.7	2
7	Favor	Oppose	Traditional	Favor	53 (3.9%)	43.4	1
8	Oppose	Oppose	Traditional	Favor	130 (9.5%)	130.9	2
9	Favor	Favor	Modern	Oppose	43 (3.1%)	40.2	1
10	Oppose	Favor	Modern	Oppose	49 (3.6%)	46.1	2
11	Favor	Oppose	Modern	Oppose	32 (2.3%)	37.6	1
12	Oppose	Oppose	Modern	Oppose	116 (8.5%)	114.7	2
13	Favor	Favor	Traditional	Oppose	33 (2.4%)	30.3	1
14	Oppose	Favor	Traditional	Oppose	133 (9.7%)	137.8	2
15	Favor	Oppose	Traditional	Oppose	45 (3.3%)	47.0	2
16	Oppose	Oppose	Traditional	Oppose	411 (30%)	408.3	2

[a] See Text footnote 2 for details on the variables in this table.

Inspection of the percentages in Table 10.1 reveals that the single largest cell, by far (Cell 16 = 30.0%) contains those individuals who endorse the Moral Majority's position on the four issues. This cell is over three times as large as the next largest cell in the table, and about five times the size of the cell containing those who diametrically oppose the Moral Majority platform (Cell 1 = 6.2%). Furthermore, the remaining cell percentages exhibit remarkably little variation with a low of 2.3% and a high of 9.7%. Thus, the views of 30.0% of the respondents coincide with those of the Moral Majority; the remaining 70.0% of the sample is more or less evenly distributed among the various other combinations of attitudes toward the four items. According to the observed frequency counts in Table 10.1, then, there is a sizable plurality of respondents whose views are identical to those espoused by the Moral Majority, *but there is no absolute moral majority in the American population.*

While an inspection of Table 10.1 provides some useful and interesting information, the analysis can be carried further. If a researcher were interested in investigating the variable *support/nonsupport* for the sociomoral platform of the Moral Majority, she/he would have no difficulty defining respondents in Cell 16 of Table 10.1 as supporters. Likewise, those in Cell 1 are, clearly, nonsupporters. However, among the remaining fourteen cells in Table 10.1 there are many ambiguous cases. What, for instance, is to be done with respondents who favor homosexuality, abortion, school prayer, and a traditional role for women (Cell 7)? Should they be classified as *supporters, nonsupporters,* or in a third category of *in-between?* The researcher, then, who is interested in measuring *support* for the sociomoral platform of the Moral Majority is faced with the question of whether it is possible to partition Table 10.1 into *supporters* and *nonsupporters* in some non–*ad hoc* fashion.

The answer to the question of whether Table 10.1 can be partitioned as suggested, involves the detection of respondents who might be called *fellow travelers.* Cells 1 and 16 contain, respectively, the *pure* liberals and conservatives. Are there others in the table who do not hold exactly the same pattern of views as a *pure* liberal or conservative but who might be classified as having liberal or conservative tendencies? Indeed, can the table be partitioned into two groups, the *pure* liberals and their fellow travelers, on the one hand, and the *pure* conservatives and their fellow travelers, on the other hand?

While the table cannot be partitioned by inspection into liberals and conservatives, it is possible to test the hypothesis that the four-way cross-classification is accounted for or explained by an underlying or latent variable of two categories. If this hypothesis were sustained, we might then inquire whether the respondents in one category of the latent variable appear to be conservative and those in the other category liberal. If respondents do so appear, then the table will have been partitioned into conservative (supporters) and liberal (nonsupporters) groups of respondents.

The hypothesis can be tested by maximum likelihood latent structure analysis (MLLSA) (Goodman, 1974; Clogg, 1977).[3] Using this procedure it was found that Americans do tend to divide into two groups (and only two groups) in terms of their attitudes toward homosexuality, school prayer, abortion, and the woman's role.[4] In other words, we have empirical evidence that Americans' attitudes toward these items are interrelated and can be simply classified into two camps.[5]

How many respondents are conservative or liberal according to Table 10.1?[6] Twenty-eight percent of the cases are classified by the MLLSA procedure as falling into the first latent class (liberal). Seventy-two percent are, therefore, in the conservative category: 30% are *pure conservatives* (Cell 16) and 42% are *fellow traveling conservatives*. While there is no absolute moral majority of pure conservatives in the United States that supports the entire platform of the Moral Majority, a substantial majority

[3] The estimated frequencies in Table 10.1 were generated by the computer program MLLSA (Clogg, 1977). The minimum amount of information which the researcher must supply in order to use the program (in addition to the cross-classification being analyzed) is the number of latent variables and the number of categories for each variable which the researcher hypothesizes as necessary in order to account for the observed cross-classification. Beyond that, restrictions can be imposed on the latent class probabilities and on the conditional probabilities that an individual is in a category of an observed variable given that she/he is in a particular category of a latent variable. Models with restrictions are known as restricted latent structure models, while those without any restrictions are classified as unrestricted latent structure models. The model used to generate the expected frequencies in Table 10.1 is an unrestricted single variable two-class latent structure model.

[4] X^2/n is an index of the fit of a model where n is degrees of freedom. A model provides a good fit to observed data when X^2/n is approximately 1.00 (Clogg, 1977). With 6 degrees of freedom and a X^2 of 6.401, a two-class model fits the data very well.

[5] By way of clarification, it should be understood that the assignment of respondents in the cells of Table 10.1 to one of the two latent classes is purely formal. That is, the MLLSA Procedure does not "know" that respondents in Cell 1 favor homosexual relations, the Supreme Court prayer ruling, a modern view of the woman's role, and abortion. The assignment to latent classes follows from the mathematics of the MLLSA procedure, which takes as input the assumptions of the researcher. The assumptions of the researcher are, themselves, formal. For unrestricted latent structure models, these assumptions are limited to the number of latent variables and the number of classes per variable. The only assumption, then, that is built into the latent class assignments in Table 10.1 by the researcher is the assumption that a single two-class latent variable explains the observed cross-classification in Table 10.1.

[6] Unlike assignments to latent classes, the labeling of the latent classes is a matter of the researcher's judgment. One should attempt, of course, to choose labels that make sense in terms of the variable categories that define cells in the table. Furthermore, labels should conform to the reasonable constraint that whatever label is attached to a latent class, that label can be sensibly attached to all cells that are assigned to the latent class.

of the population either wholly subscribes to the Moral Majority platform or is sufficiently similar to those who do to be labeled *conservative*.[7]

It should be kept in mind that these conclusions are not based on respondents' replies to questions that specifically mention the Moral Majority's platform as a singular object for judgement. What the analysis does indicate, is that in 1977 a substantial proportion of Americans held a combination of attitudes toward social and moral issues that two years later was successfully articulated as a national public platform by the Moral Majority.

CORRELATES OF ORIENTATION TO THE MORAL PLATFORM

What are the social correlates of a conservative or liberal orientation to the Moral Majority's platform? While sex has no effect upon conservative orientation (males 71.4%; females 72.5%), there are decided age and marital status effects. The older a respondent is, the more likely it is that she/he will be conservative (Table 10.2). The strong effect of age may explain some of the figures in the marital status table (Table 10.3). Thus, the marked degree of conservatism among the widowed and the relative liberality of the never-marrieds may be due to skewed age distributions within each of these categories. The differences in platform support between the married, the separated, and the divorced suggests that family stability is a salient factor in determining attitudes toward the Moral Majority.

Tables 10.4 and 10.5 show the effects of region and urbanization upon platform orientation. As can be seen, the Southern regions are considerably more conservative than most of the other regions in the continental United States. The contrast between the conservatism of the

---

[7] Researchers should be aware that the assignment of respondents to the latent classes by the MLLSA procedure provides an opportunity to create a new variable for further investigation that is based upon the observed cell in which a respondent falls and the latent class assignment of respondents in that cell. Thus, researchers who use GSS 1977 can create a variable *nonsupporter/supporter* or *liberal/conservative* with respect to the platform of the Moral Majority directly from the results reported in Table 10.1 by assigning respondents who fall into Cells 1, 2, 3, 5, 7, 9, 11, or 13 to one category (nonsupport or liberal) of the new variable. Respondents who fall into Cells 4, 6, 8, 10, 12, 14, 15, or 16 would be assigned to the other category (supporter or conservative) of the new variable. Researchers using data sets other than GSS 1977 will want to employ the MLLSA procedure, themselves, in order to analyze the cross-classification of items measuring attitudes toward Moral Majority issues, and then use the results obtained to create a new variable for further analysis.

TABLE 10.2. Age and Orientation to the Sociomoral Platform of the Moral Majority

Age	Percent conservative
10–19	60.7 (28)
20–29	55.9 (311)
30–39	66.5 (275)
40–49	75.4 (228)
50–59	79.9 (239)
60–69	82.4 (165)
70–79	91.9 (99)
80 or over	94.7 (19)

South as a whole and the relative liberality of the New England and the Pacific regions is quite striking.

The degree of conservatism among rural dwellers contrasts with the relative liberality of those who inhabit the twelve largest Standard Metropolitan Statistical Areas (SMSAs). The suburbs of the largest SMSAs are somewhat less liberal than their central cities, while the suburbs of the smaller SMSAs are more liberal than their associated metropolises. The smaller cities and the smaller SMSAs are more conservative than either the suburbs or the large SMSAs, but less conservative than the rural hinterland.

Turning next to the effects of religion, Protestants are somewhat more conservative (76.7%) than Roman Catholics (70.4%), although the difference is not large. Both Protestants and Roman Catholics are decidedly more conservative than either Jews (36.7%) or those who indicate no religious preference (40.3%). Among the major Protestant traditions, there is a modest decline in platform support from the Baptists (north and south combined) of whom 82.3% are conservative to the Presbyterians (71.7%),

TABLE 10.3. Marital Status and Orientation to the Sociomoral Platform of the Moral Majority

Marital status	Percent conservative
Widowed	87.9 (141)
Married	76.0 (878)
Separated	66.0 (53)
Divorced	61.7 (94)
Never married	50.0 (204)

TABLE 10.4. Region and Orientation to
the Sociomoral Platform of
the Moral Majority

Region	Percent conservative
New England	48.3 (58)
Middle Atlantic	68.1 (213)
East-North Central	72.7 (319)
West-North Central	71.6 (102)
South Atlantic	81.6 (277)
East-South Central	86.9 (61)
West-South Central	85.2 (108)
Mountain	71.9 (57)
Pacific	54.9 (175)

with the Methodists (76.6%) and the Lutherans (74.8%) falling between. Episcopalians are considerably more liberal than any of the other major Protestant traditions; only 48.3% of those identified with the tradition are conservative. When Protestants are classified according to whether they indicate a preference for a mainline denomination or tradition or for some other Protestant orientation, those identified with the mainline are less conservative (70.7%) than non-main-liners (87.7%). Finally, the frequency of attendance at religious services has a marked effect upon conservative orientation. Of those who attend religious services at least once a week,

TABLE 10.5. Size of Place and Orientation to
the Sociomoral Platform of the
Moral Majority

Size	Percent conservative
Central city of 12 largest SMSAs	55.3 (114)
Central city of the remainder of the 100 largest SMSAs	71.0 (193)
Suburbs of 12 largest SMSAs	61.1 (95)
Suburbs of the remaining 100 largest SMSAs	63.6 (176)
Other urban	74.0 (572)
Other rural	87.7 (220)

85.9% are conservative in their orientation to the Moral Majority's platform while only 64.4% of those who attend less frequently are conservative.

As reported in Table 10.6, educational advancement is associated with a decrease in the proportion of respondents who are conservative in their orientation to the Moral Majority's platform. The enormous difference between the lowest education category (less than high school— 87.1% conservative) and the highest education category (graduate— 35.9% conservative) is particularly dramatic. While some of the effects of education upon orientation may be explained by age, it is unlikely that cohort effects would cause the relationship between education attainment and attitudes toward the platform of the Moral Majority to be seriously attenuated.

Further analysis, examining the effects of several of these variables, indicates that support for the Moral Majority is not simply a Bible-Belt phenomenon. Non-mainline Protestants throughout the land champion the platform of the Moral Majority. High levels of support are found among the aged, rural dwellers, the working and lower classes, and the poorly educated. On the other hand, the young, city dwellers, self-identified members of the upper class, and those with graduate degrees are the least likely to support the platform. These results suggest that the farther one is from the dominant center of American society and the less one possesses of the desiderata of the society (education, youth, prestige), the more conservative one is in orientation to the sociomoral platform of the Moral Majority. The more ardent supporters of the Moral Majority, then, appear to be drawn disproportionately from the periphery of the society and not from the dominant center (cf. Hagan, Silva, and Simpson, 1977; Simpson and Hagan, 1981).

As Thomas Luckmann (1967) has pointed out, there is a tendency in modern societies to push religion away from the dominant center and into institutional backwaters and the private realm. The analysis presented here clearly indicates that support for the Moral Majority has a firm base

TABLE 10.6. Degree and Orientation to the Sociomoral Platform of the Moral Majority

Degree	Percent conservative
Less than High School	87.1 (473)
High School	69.8 (675)
College, 2-year	53.3 (30)
College, 4-year	48.0 (123)
Graduate School	35.9 (64)

among the religiously involved, and especially among non-mainline Protestants. It is also clear that the Moral Majority finds favor among downscale
Americans. Perhaps, this conclusion will not surprise many. However,
the dramatic entry into national politics in the late seventies of those
opposed to homosexuality, the Equal Rights Amendment, the Supreme
Court school prayer decision, and abortion, among other things, did
surprise some observers. What social currents pulled the religious under-
dogs of American society with their platform of personal morality into
the center of the arena of national politics in 1980?

THE MORAL MAJORITY: A SOCIOLOGICAL INTERPRETATION

Among sociologists and historians it has become commonplace to view
right-wing movements in American public life as instances of "status politics" (Hofstadter, 1962; Gusfield, 1963; Bell, 1963). Movements such
as Temperance, Coughlinism, McCarthyism, and the John Birch Society,
according to the status politics argument cannot be primarily understood
in terms of economic or class-based protest. This conclusion is based
on the observation that such movements either cut across class lines,
appeal to one segment of a class and are opposed by another segment,
seek goals that are exceedingly difficult to interpret as expressions of
economic life, or occur in times of economic prosperity rather than depression. According to the status politics hypothesis, these movements are
political responses by groups whose values, traditions, life styles, status,
and security have been threatened in some way.

There can be no doubt that the founders of the Moral Majority are
concerned with promoting and invigorating what they consider to be
traditional American moral values and practices. But, in the present situation, do aspects of modernity so threaten the evangelical/fundamentalist
sector with loss of status and security that they are driven to express
themselves politically in vindictive moral outrage?

There are three flaws in this explanation of current fundamentalist activity in the political arena. First, modernity and modernism have posed a
constant threat to Fundamentalism for years (Marsden, 1980). Given the
unchanging threat, something in addition to the threat must have stimulated the rise of the Moral Majority. Second, about 50 years ago Fundamentalists were subjected to a process of radical status degradation and
have occupied a marginal niche in American politics and culture ever
since. Fundamentalists, therefore, are at present not so much concerned
with the loss of status and security as they are with the problem of how
to improve their status and security. In the third place, the status-loss/

moral-outrage hypothesis fails to take into account what some observers would interpret as the recent weakening, decline, and, perhaps, even failure of modernity in America; a circumstance which, it can be argued, the Fundamentalists are taking advantage of to enhance their position in the American public arena, a position attributable to a series of events beginning with the imposition of Prohibition in 1920.

The ratification of the Eighteenth Amendment to the Constitution of the United States in 1919 created the legal basis for Prohibition. This act represented the symbolic apogee of middle-class Protestantism as the source of a normative model for American public morals and behavior. The fact that the ethic of abstinence became the legal norm for Protestant and non-Protestant alike was, at the same time, a status triumph for the Evangelical/Fundamentalist Protestant life style and a status degradation of non-Protestants, especially immigrants and others whose cultural practices included the consumption of alcoholic beverages (Gusfield, 1963).

While middle-class Evangelical/Fundamentalist Protestantism triumphed with the imposition of Prohibition and swept into the 1920's as a powerful force in the public arena, it was not invulnerable to attack and eventual degradation. There was, to begin with, a counterculture of urban sophistication which stood in opposition to American Gothic morality. Its most visible spokesman was the journalist and critic H. L. Mencken who, with his acidic humor, spent a lifetime skewering the unsophisticated, teetotaling, Bible-thumping "boobus Americanus." Against the "booboisie," Mencken counterposed the "smart set"—those urbane, slightly naughty Americans who were knowledgable about European High Culture and such matters as where to find malt liquor: "The telltale sign, 'Sea Food,' [was] the universal euphemism for beerhouse in Maryland and Pennsylvania throughout the thirteen awful years" (Mencken, 1963, p. 206).

While members of a diffuse counterculture mocked the Eighteenth Amendment, and its perpetrators, by their desire and ability to find and consume illegal potable alcohol, other events contributed more dramatically to the public denigration of militant Fundamentalist Protestantism during the 1920's. Within the Protestant denominations, controversy flared over modernism and the theory of evolution. Conservative and Fundamentalist churchmen fought bitter battles against their more liberal brethren in church conventions, assemblies, and councils. While some skirmishes were won by the Fundamentalists, in general they were not successful in pressing their demands in any of the large, main-line denominations which included a significant liberal voice such as the Episcopalian, Methodist, and northern Baptist and Presbyterian churches. Fundamentalists, then, failed to become ascendent in those mainline denominations where they posed a challenge to moderates and liberals (Furniss, 1954).

Fundamentalists and their fellow travellers can still be found within all of the mainline Protestant denominations. But by the end of the 1920's, the edge was off the cause in these denominations. The last major upheaval involving Fundamentalists within a mainline denomination was the self-separation in 1935 of the followers of J. Grescham Machen from the Presbyterian Church in the United States of America to form the Presbyterian Church of America.

Although Fundamentalists did not succeed in capturing the mainline Protestant denominations, it was not the lost intra-church battles that would be remembered as heaping aspersion upon their heads. Rather, it was the denouement of the so-called "monkey trial" in 1925 that fixed an image of fundamentalism as unbending, irrational, and uncivil in doctrine and practice, a movement fit only to be cast aside in the name of science, progress, and civilization.

John T. Scopes, a high school instructor, was tried in Dayton, Tennessee in 1925 for contravening a state statute forbidding the teaching in public schools of anything which denied the Biblical account of the Divine creation of man and which suggested that man is descended from a lower order of animals. While Scopes was convicted and fined $100.00, the trial is remembered for the cross-examination by Clarence Darrow of William Jennings Bryan who, though acting as a lawyer for the prosecution, was called to the witness stand by Darrow, the lawyer for the defense. Because the judge would not allow the defense to call expert witnesses, Darrow, in desperation, summoned Bryan to testify (Furniss, 1954).

At the time, Bryan was the most important public figure identified with the Fundamentalist cause; Bryan is, arguably, the most important public figure in American history to have been associated with Fundamentalism. Three times the candidate of the Democratic Party for President (1896, 1900, and 1908) and Secretary of State during Woodrow Wilson's first term as President (1912–1916), he was an active supporter of Prohibition; after its imposition, he took up the cudgels for the Fundamentalist cause in the churches and the political arena as a proponent of such anti-evolution laws as the Tennessee statute Scopes was charged with violating.

On the witness stand, Bryan was decimated by Darrow who, carrying the battle into the enemy's own camp, showed Bryan to be less than a Biblical expert and, therefore, something less than what he claimed to be. Darrow extracted testimony from Bryan that man was not a mammal, a position recognized even by Bryan's ardent supporters as indefensible. Darrow clearly made a fool of Bryan, as was his intention, in order to arouse opposition to Fundamentalism (Darrow, 1932). Five days after the trial ended, the "Great Commoner" died, "the result, some said, of mental assassination at the hands of the atheist Darrow, but perhaps more accurately the consequence of diabetes and an excessively large chicken dinner on a hot summer's day" in the small country town of Winchester, Tennessee (Furniss, 1954, p. 91).

Fundamentalism did not die with Bryan. It never again, however, had a national leader with his oratorical powers and political stature. The rejection of Fundamentalism by the mainline Protestant denominations and Bryan's degradation at the hands of Darrow marked the decline of right-wing Protestantism as a force to be taken seriously in the public arena of American life. With the repeal of Prohibition in 1933, right-wing Protestantism was removed from the arena of national politics. It lingered as a cultural side show until the 1980 election.

If the passing of the Eighteenth Amendment symbolized a status triumph of rural Protestant Americans over the Eastern upper classes, the Catholic and Jewish immigrants, and the urbanized middle classes, then Repeal "meant the repudiation of old middle-class virtues and the end of Protestant domination" (Gusfield, 1963, p. 126). Within a span of 13 years, the Protestant right went from the dizzy height of having its culture legally recognized to the degradation and rejection of Repeal. Since Fundamentalism, Temperance, and Prohibition were inextricably intertwined as a cultural complex, the repeal of Prohibition not only struck a blow at the wide spectrum of rural American Protestant mores, values, and customs—it added to the devaluation of Fundamentalism as a respectable set of beliefs and practices. The sense of status decline that was experienced by members of the Women's Christian Temperance Union applies, as well, to the movement of Fundamentalism into the nation's cultural backwaters: "We were once an accepted group. The leading people would be members. Not exactly the leading people, but upper-middle class people and sometimes leaders. Today they'd be ashamed to belong. . . . Today it's kind of lower-bourgeois. It's not fashionable any longer . . ." (Gusfield, 1963, p. 138).

Clearly, Roman Catholics, Jews, and the urban middle classes made cultural and political gains at the expense of the native Protestant right as a result of events in the 1920's and early 1930's. However, those sociologists and historians who interpret right-wing movements among Protestants since the early 1930's as primarily responses to threats posed by non-WASPs to WASP values and culture, overlook something of far greater importance to the social position of the Protestant religious Right than the portent of non-WASP ascendance—the solidification of a division among Protestants into two great camps, one disdainful of the other. On the one hand, there emerged from the events of the 1920's and 1930's a mainline Protestantism that, purged for the most part of Fundamentalism, tended to move with the dominant mode of American culture and society and its foundation in managerial capitalism (cf. Simpson and Hagan, 1981). On the other hand, there stood the vast array of elements, including Fundamentalism, that make up the underside of American Protestantism. Some of these elements were large denominations that carried on the Fundamentalist tradition, e.g., the Southern Baptists. Also included were the seemingly endless number of sectlike bodies spun out in the nineteenth and early twentieth centuries—churches with Arminian or Wesleyan ancestry. Finally, there were the genuine products of the "great American religion machine," itself, for example, Jehovah's Witnesses, Seventh Day Adventists, and the Mormons.

While differences in doctrine, polity, mores, and practice existed among the denominations and groups on both sides of the Protestant divide, what the mainline denominations had in common and, therefore, what the underside of American Protestantism suffered from was the self-assured air of cultural superiority of mainline Protestants who defined their religious expressions as civil, rational, tolerant, and inoffensive. To those in the other camp, they imputed oddness, incivility, intolerance, strange beliefs, excess emotion, peculiar practices; they were not in keeping with how the "right" or "best" people do things.

How, then, do the "right" or "best" people in America do things when it comes to religion? John Murray Cuddihy (1978) has persuasively argued that under the constraint of church-state separation and in the presence of a public culture dominated by a secularized Puritanism stressing individualism, propriety, modernist simplicity, and the unostentatious display of the self—in short, aesthetic and communal restraint, "a decorum of imperfection"—there has been a development of a "religion of civility." The central feature of the religion of civility is the relinquishment of monopolistic claims to superiority. The Roman Catholic claim to uniqueness (the "one true church"); the Jewish claim to uniqueness ("the chosen people"); the Protestant Fundamentalist claim to uniqueness ("Jesus only saves") are all at variance with the decorum of a dominant secularized Puritanism that defines any claim to superiority (except, possibly, its own) to be in bad taste. In each case—Protestant, Catholic, Jewish—a civil nontriumphal version of the tradition has been worked out. This adaptation began in the late 1930's, but flowered only after the end of World War II in the works of Reinhold Niebuhr (for the Protestants), John Courtney Murray (for the Roman Catholics), and Arthur Hertzberg (for the Jews) (Cuddihy, 1978).

As America moved into the post–World War II period, Fundamentalists not bore only the wounds of degradation acquired in the 1920's and 1930's, but also found themselves increasingly marginalized in terms of the developing religion of civility. Both accommodation within Protestantism (the ecumenical movement) and the cultural importance attached to religious practice shorn of ghetto, parochial or evangelical excesses (cf. Herberg, 1960) reinforced the image of the incivility of intransigent right-wing Protestantism that continued to insist "you must be born again." Increasingly, Fundamentalist, Evangelical, and Conservative Christians realized that the real enemy was not the Roman Catholic or Jew but the smiling, flexible, civil Protestant modernist who wrote them off as "religious fanatics" unwilling to take the rough edges off their beliefs and practices and glide along smoothly with others in the prosperity of post-war America.

As civil, mainline Protestantism flowered with the "return to religion" in the fifties, the Evangelical/Fundamentalist/Conservative Protestant right wing quietly held on. It maintained its institutional infrastructure and even added to it, the most notable accretions being, perhaps, the influential journal *Christianity Today* (the evangelical answer to *The Christian Century*) and the founding of Fuller Theological Seminary. Not to be forgotten in this period are the revival crusades of Billy Graham which, arguably, served to maintain and reproduce the Protestant religious right rather than expand it through the conversion of the unchurched.

In the post-war period, the focus of the Protestant religious Right was, until recently, almost exclusively turned inward and centered upon purely religious matters. In this regard it is worth noting that even the issue of domestic communist influence did not spark sustained, organized, national action among evangelical and conservative Protestants. To be sure, evangelical Protestants, like many other Americans, held and voiced anticommunist sentiments and, more often than not, lent support to the likes of McCarthy and Robert Welch of the John Birch Society; but McCarthyism and the John Birch Society did not arise from within the organizational domain of the Protestant religious Right. Not even the Christian Anti-Communism Crusade of the Australian, Dr. Fred C. Schwarz, found active, national, organized sponsorship among the Protestant religious Right. The business and the military/naval establishment, in comparison, were more supportive (Buckley and Bozell, 1954).

What finally brought the Protestant religious Right back into the national political arena in force after an effective absence of fifty years? Lipset and Raab (1981) attribute its resurgence to a sense of loss of security and status induced by "aspects of modernity" and transformed into moral outrage. As I have argued, it is difficult to endorse this view as an adequate account of the Protestant right wing's renaissance, since the underside of American Protestantism, in general, and its Conservative/Evangelical/Fundamentalist segment, in particular, have had little status and public repute to lose. Furthermore, what aspects of modernity pose a clear and present danger that specifically threaten the Protestant religious Right? The most obvious candidates would appear to be the gay and women's liberation movements. Yet, the empirical findings presented earlier in this chapter clearly suggest that opposition to the goals of these movements reaches far beyond the confines of the evangelical sector of the American population.

Rather than the threat of modernity, it was the perceived mistakes and failures of modernity in its guise as establishment America that provided the Protestant religious Right with the opportunity to go public once more. As America came "unglued" (Mann, 1979) in the late 1960's and the 1970's, evangelical Christians held firm. Long accustomed to maintaining their beliefs and rituals in the midst of the established, hostile culture of liberal civility, "outside" disturbances posed no threat to them. As it became increasingly evident that the established powers were not entirely in control of things, the "old-time religion" looked better and better. Surrounded by a flood of puzzling and disturbing events—assassinations, riots, campus discontent, Vietnam, liberation movements (Chicano, Native American, women and gay)—and, finally, the hostage incident in Iran, the Evangelical/Fundamentalist persuasion was something that survived, relatively unchanged, from the less puzzling past. As such, it provided a strong source for a sense of cultural continuity.

Of all the events and movements that stimulated the Fundamentalists the most important, perhaps, were Watergate and the gay and women's liberation movements. Watergate and its aftermath conveyed a pervasive sense of moral decay eminating from the symbolic center of the nation—the Office of the President. The gay and women's movements provided an opportunity to concretize, through opposition, the diffuse sense of moral decline in terms of attitudes and behaviors that were available in the local community and over which the ordinary citizen could exert some control.

As the custodians of a tradition of personal moral purity, the Evangelical/Fundamentalists grasped the opportunity to go on the offensive in the wake of Watergate and the gay and women's movements. The Reverend Adrian Rodgers, the head of the Southern Baptist Convention, put the case rather colorfully in an address to a crowd of 200,000 evangelical Christians gathered at the "Washington for Jesus" rally in April 1980: "The scream of the great American eagle has become the twitter of a frightened sparrow. America must be born again or join the graveyard of nations." In terms of specific issues, the Reverend John Gimenez, a cochairman of the rally, acknowledged that most of its planners "favor school prayer and oppose abortion, homosexuality, and the Equal Rights

Amendment" (*New York Times,* April 30, 1980, p. A20). Forty-six years after the disgrace of Repeal, the spiritual heirs of the folks who brought Prohibition had a new public moral agenda and were back in business.

CONCLUSION

In concluding this chapter, the relationship between secularization in American society and the meaning of the Moral Majority as a status politics phenomena will be briefly discussed. Before discussing that topic, how-ever, a question that may have occurred to some readers should be answered. Is there an inconsistency between my critique of Lipset and Raab (1981) and the use in the chapter title of the term "status politics" thereby suggesting that the Moral Majority is, after all, a status politics phenomenon?

In fact, the point of view expressed in this chapter is not an alternative to a status politics explanation but, rather, an attempt to enlarge that hypothesis. Thus, I am proposing that the "classic" status politics perspec-tive be broadened to embrace not only the anxiety induced protests of declining groups attempting to cut their losses but also the collective efforts of devalued groups striving to enhance their sociopolitical posi-tions. This view is based on the assumption that culture and power are separate elements in modern democratic social systems and that the cul-tural threat which one group may pose for another is distinct from the capacity of a group to impose its mores and lifestyle on others through politics. Clearly, the culture of modernism has historically posed a threat to the Evangelical/Fundamentalist complex. It is also true that Fundamen-talism poses a threat to the modern temper. This mutual cultural threat has been a constant feature of American life for many years. What has changed from time to time is the relative power positions of the carrier groups in the public arena, power being roughly measured by the extent a group can politically impose its cultural rules on others. Thus, while politics has been an arena for the expression of the anxieties of groups on the decline, it can also serve as a point of focus for new-found legiti-macy, efficacy, and entitlement in the never-ending race for power and prestige in American society.

Finally, what is the meaning of the Moral Majority as a status politics phenomenon in secular America? The modern secular attitude of disdain and contempt for religion has firm philosophic roots in the thought of Friedrich Nietzsche, to whom the status politics tradition owes its inspiration (cf. Gusfield, 1963). What is the origin, Nietzsche asks, of the ethic of concern and love for the poor and weak of this world? Nietzsche's answer is "resentment," a slave class' (the Hebrews in Egypt, the early Christians in the Roman Empire) resentment of the inaccessible power, freedom, and beauty of their aristocratic masters. From a position of weakness, fear, and anxiety, the slave class transvalues that which they are—poor, suffering and bereft of power—into virtue and goodness, "the poor shall inherit the earth," etc.

The ethic of care for the stricken of this world according to Nietzsche, springs from the malice and vindictiveness of those who lack aristocratic power, freedom, and beauty. This ethic, however, has been transcended by modern man (Nietzsche's Superman), in whom, no longer constrained by the gods, power, freedom and beauty find their apotheosis. For those not of the new order, the Superman has only detached disdain. Even the man of resentment is not his enemy. "He tolerates no other enemy but a man in whose character there is nothing to despise and much to honour!" (Nietzsche, 1954, p. 650).

Nietzsche, I believe, in a powerful metaphorical vision, has captured the essence and inner meaning of the secularized European order in which, as an ideal, everyone becomes, in effect, an aristocrat unhampered by the gods in the pursuit of freedom, power, and beauty. Secularization, then, in a milieu informed by an aristocratic tradition (even though it may long ago have ceased to wield power) involves the democratization, if you will, of the aristocratic ideal. Everyone becomes a psychological aristocrat possessed by an air of detached disdain toward the slave-class religious ethical mentality.

It is a commonplace sociological observation that there is no aristocratic tradition in American society. As the forces of secularization have progressively engulfed the society, I would argue there has been no effective replacement of a religious horizon as the inner meaning of existence by a cultural vector of aristocratic disdain for religion. What, then, is the inner essence of the stance toward religion in a secular, mobility-conscious America? It is, I submit, ambivalence tinged with slight embarrassment.

In Mark Twain's novel, *Huckleberry Finn*, the title character provides a portrait of the prototypical American on the move. Huck, the son of an untamed, illiterate, river-bottom woodsman, finds himself caught up in the civilizing influences of town life on the Mississippi River. As Huck observes:

> Living in a house and sleeping in a bed pulled on me pretty tight mostly, but before the cold weather I used to slide out and sleep in the woods sometimes, and so that was a rest to me. I liked the old ways best but I was getting so I liked the new ones, too, a little bit. The widow said I was

coming along slow but sure and doing very satisfactory. *She said she warn't ashamed of me.* [Twain, p. 210, emphasis added.]

Was the widow, herself, only one generation out of the woods? Twain does not tell us, but the point is there, nevertheless. In the turbulent movement of Americans away from the rudeness of their humble origins, there has been no displacement of those origins with an air of aristocratic disdain for them. Rather, a line of involvement has always been maintained, if only barely and tenuously, in the possibility of being embarrassed by the past and one's origins. Behind the culture of civil secularity, then, stands the shadow of uncivil "born-again" America. Secular America may appear to be haughty and disdainful toward its uncivil past but it honors it with ambivalent uneasiness. Thus, it is remembered where "the flambeaux of chautauqua smoked and guttered, and the bilge of idealism ran in the veins, and Baptist pastors damned the brooks with the sanctified, and men gathered who were weary and heavy laden" (Mencken, 1962, p. 243). In that remembrance, uncivil Protestant America persists.

11 | ANOTHER GREAT AWAKENING?

Phillip E. Hammond

Insofar as the 1970's and 1980's in America exhibit an evangelical fervor reminiscent of the Second Great Awakening in the nineteenth century, one is tempted to ask if we are experiencing another Great Awakening. Polls tell us that perhaps as many as 40% of adult Americans claim to have had a born-again experience, and 20% are judged, by rather stringent criteria, to be solidly evangelical.[1] While buckboard and tent revivalists have not reappeared, the electronic church—TV and radio preachers with massive budgets and significant audiences—more than compensates as a measure of popularity. Bumper stickers and book sales are yet other indications, as are Bible study groups in college dormitories and, of course, the growth of conservative denominations in the face of decline by so-called mainline denominations.

---

[1] The evidence to which we refer is widely reported and generally uniform. The data utilized here come chiefly from the survey by Gallup for *Christianity Today* and published in that journal periodically during 1980, in Gallup's Princeton Religious Research Center's *Emerging Trends* newsletter, or in the secondary analysis of James D. Hunter, "Contemporary American Evangelicalism," Ph.D. Dissertation, Rutgers University, 1980.

207

The question, then, is what to make of all this. Are we in the midst of another cultural reform period, developing a new set of understandings for decades to come, as happened in the nineteenth century, or is the religious emotionalism of today more a fad destined to fade away leaving little impact on social institutions?

This chapter will offer a mixed, and tentative, judgment: On the one hand, the current evangelical movement in America is not an awakening comparable to the Second Great Awakening; its political effects and consequences for democracy are not analogous. On the other hand, the current evangelical movement probably does represent an important phase of a cultural transformation that future historians may well regard as an awakening. In short, the current religious fervor is not itself an awakening, but it very likely is an element of a larger movement destined to become an awakening.

The correctness of this thesis, however, is of less importance than developing appropriate means for framing the thesis. Data can be marshalled on both sides of any issue, meaning that theories are needed to make sense of the data. Our chief concern here, then, is with the development of theory, a task we try to accomplish by bringing together two lines of intellectual inquiry not often combined.

TOCQUEVILLE REVISITED

Alexis de Tocqueville visited America in 1831, toward the end of a wave of religious fervor known now as the Second Great Awakening. A dominant feature of his *Democracy in America* (1835–1840) was the religious factor and its relation to politics. Once alerted to the fact that Tocqueville was observing an America experiencing a religious revival, we can—as I propose to do here—use his work to help determine whether some other period of religious revival is another "awakening."

Where Tocqueville revealed his special insight was in noting the consequences of religion for democracy. "Religion," he wrote, "should . . . be considered as the first of their *political* institutions . . ." (292, emphasis added). As the son of a once-aristocratic family, he saw much to fear in "democracy," by which he meant "equality" of individuals, or as we might say in modern jargon, the declining importance of ascribed characteristics. Believing the *ancien régime* was doomed to disappear, and its replacement by democracy (in the above sense) inevitable, Tocqueville visited the American democratic experiment just decades after its founding, curious to understand its dynamics.

The prognosis, in his mind, was not good. "One must admit that equality

. . . opens the door . . . to very dangerous instincts. It tends to isolate men from each other so that each thinks only of himself" (444). Such egocentricity thus weakens the institutional structure:

> Among democratic peoples new families continually rise from nothing while others fall, and nobody's position is quite stable. The woof of time is ever being broken and the track of past generations lost. Those who have gone before are easily forgotten, and no one gives a thought to those who will follow. . . . Aristocracy links everybody, from peasant to king, in one long chain. Democracy breaks the chain and frees each link. [Pp. 507–508]

The consequence is despotism—unrestrained rule by those who seek office for private gain at public expense. Operating under the myth of "the will of the people," politicians in fact maintain power by discouraging that will from ever taking human shape, a goal not difficult to achieve inasmuch as citizens—each now a freed link—devote their energies to economic striving, status anxiety, and protection of their own rights at the expense of the collectivity. With a prescience remarkable for a contemporary of Karl Marx, Tocqueville noted that in a democracy, everyone would be uncooperative, disinclined toward political participation, and concerned chiefly about law and order, insofar as they were politically involved at all. If everybody in a democracy is equal, then nobody knows limits on his own aspirations, but neither does he have concerns beyond his own aspirations.[2]

Thus, the great counterforce to despotic democracy is religion:

> Every religion places the object of man's desires outside and beyond worldly goods and naturally lifts the soul into regions far above the realm of the senses. Every religion also imposes on each man some obligations toward mankind, to be performed in common with the rest of mankind, and so draws him away, from time to time, from thinking about himself. [Tocqueville, 1969, pp. 444–445]

It is understandable, then, that Tocqueville, finding not despotic democracy in America but what he called republican democracy, would rely heavily on the religiousness of Americans to explain the absence of despotism in their society.

Actually, Tocqueville identified several countervailing forces to the despotism inherent in democracy. One of these—the geographic vastness of America and therefore the ability of Americans, when restless, literally to "move on"—is of no particular theoretical interest here, though of

---

[2] Because of the unusual outline of *Democracy in America,* these claims by Tocqueville appear as nuggets throughout the two-volume work; but perhaps Vol. II, Part 2, exhibits the greatest density. A secondary source of considerable value in this regard is Poggi (1972).

course as a kind of statement of "the frontier hypothesis" it preceded Frederick Jackson Turner's thesis by more than half a century.[3]

A second source of republican democracy was found in the laws, that is, the self-conscious ways the framers of American government designed a separation of powers, a federated system, an independent judiciary, and a Bill of Rights immune to legislative tinkering. This system, Tocqueville believed, enabled Americans to conceive of their laws as God-given and thus significantly beyond quibbling over.

The third source Tocqueville called the "habits and mores" of Americans, and it is here especially where religion plays its role in helping maintain a democratic republic. The phrase "habits and mores," the French analyst said, refers to "the whole moral and intellectual state of a people" (p. 287), and of the three sources, it is most important (pp. 305–308). Religion, moreover, is the center of this moral and intellectual state, and indeed fourteen of the eighteen pages devoted to habits and mores are focused on religion. In these pages, for example, one encounters Tocqueville's assertion, quoted above, that religion is America's "first political institution." It would be hard to overestimate the importance the Frenchman attached to the role played by religion in maintaining political democracy.

Tocqueville's stature as a theorist rests on more than the mere identification of sources of republican democracy, however. In addition, and more importantly for social theory, he identified the channels through which these sources exercise their influence. Not just the ideas important to democracy, in other words, but the social structures through which those ideas operate captured Tocqueville's attention; it was his awareness of these channels that allowed him fully to appreciate how important religion was in American life in the 1830's, and it is the same awareness that allows us today to assess—in the manner of Tocqueville—the social meaning of the current evangelical movement.

In tracing just how religion serves to counteract the despotic tendency of democracy, Tocqueville discovered the feature of American life by which his analysis is best remembered—the voluntary association:

> Americans of all ages, all stations in life, and all types of disposition are forever forming associations. There are not only commercial and industrial associations in which all take part, but others of a thousand different types— religious, moral, serious, futile, very general and very limited, immensely large and very minute. Americans combine to give fetes, found seminaries,

---

[3] Not expressed with Turner's sophistication, to be sure, Tocqueville's discussion is nonetheless more than a simple "escape valve" mechanism for dissidents; he points to the consequences for those remaining in the eastern cities of the availability of evermore western land to those who migrate.

build churches, distribute books, and send missionaries to the antipodes. Hospitals, prisons, and schools take shape in that way. Finally, if they want to proclaim a truth or propagate some feeling by the encouragement of a great example, they form an association. [p. 513]

It is easy to infer from this paragraph just how paramount a motive for forming associations religion was. Not only are seminaries, missionaries, and churches mentioned directly, but so were the books being distributed probably Bibles, and we know that the founding of hospitals, schools (and even prisons) was an activity primarily of churches in the 1830's. Thus, Tocqueville's generalization that Americans form voluntary associations was based significantly on his observations of churches and the activities of their members.

Religion, then, counteracted despotism in part by bringing people together for causes transcending their selfish interests. In doing so, it created not only channels of political influence that restrained civil (would-be despotic) government, but it provided also a mantle of legitimacy— perhaps parallel with, but external to, government—which no individual alone could provide. Remarkably, this connection was seen clearly by Tocqueville:

I have known Americans to form associations to send priests out into the new states of the West and establish schools and churches there; *they fear that religion might be lost in the depths of the forest and that the people growing up there might be less fitted for freedom* than those from whom they sprang. [p. 293; emphasis added.]

A first channel, then, exemplified by the voluntary association, was whatever encouraged and enabled people to participate *together,* to identify and pursue their *mutual* goals. Religion, via the church, was obviously a major instance of this channel in the 1830's, a point we shall return to presently.

The second channel is somewhat more difficult to comprehend but is nonetheless frequently noted in Tocqueville's work, no doubt because of the curious rendering into English its expression takes—"self-interest properly understood." By this phrase, Tocqueville referred to the transmutation of the democratic impulse toward selfish concern into a self-interest more nearly coinciding with the general welfare. It was, so to speak, the democratic equivalent of *noblesse oblige.* [4]

---

[4] "When the world was under the control of a few rich and powerful men, they liked to entertain a sublime conception of the duties of man. It gratified them to make out that it is a glorious thing to forget oneself and that one should do good without self-interest, as God himself does. . . . American moralists do not pretend that one must sacrifice himself for his fellows because it is a fine thing to do so. But they boldly assert that such sacrifice is as necessary for the man who makes it as for the beneficiaries" (Tocqueville, 1969, p. 525).

The currents flowing through this second channel were, as in the voluntary association channel, many and varied, and Tocqueville found occasion to sprinkle his discussion of them throughout his two volumes. One current, for example, was tantamount to the modern-day notion of "delayed gratification"—the capacity to perceive one's long-range interest as coinciding with the community's interest, even at the expense of immediate personal payoff (p. 529). Another current was American chauvinism—"Nothing is more annoying in the ordinary intercourse of life than this irritable patriotism of the "American" (p. 237)—the ready assumption that one's government has decided wisely. Still another channel was the American respect for law and for others' rights protected by law (pp. 237–241).

These various currents shared—i.e., they flowed together through the channel of "self-interest properly understood"—the characteristic of converting self-interest into republican virtue. "The idea of rights," wrote Tocqueville, "is nothing but the conception of virtue applied to the world of politics" (pp. 237–238). And here, of course, was where religion once again intervened in American democracy because the church was the fount of such sentiment.

> In the United States, when the seventh day comes . . . every citizen, accompanied by his children, goes to a church. . . . He is told of the countless evils brought on by pride and covetousness. He is reminded of the need to check his desires and told of the finer delights which go with virtue alone, and the true happiness they bring. . . . Elsewhere in the book I have pointed to the causes helping to maintain American political institutions, among which religion seemed one of the most important. Now, when speaking of individuals, religion again comes into the picture. [p. 542]

> Not only do the Americans practice their religion out of self-interest, but they often even place in this world the interest which they have in practicing it. Priests in the Middle Ages spoke of nothing but the other life. . . . But preachers in America are continually coming down to earth. Indeed they find it difficult to take their eyes off it. [p. 530]

Perhaps what Tocqueville strove to convey with his notion of "self-interest properly understood" is what we would today call the "civil religion"—the tendency to view political or community activity as ordained not by self-interest, or even denominational interest, but by an ideology transcending all divisions of a society. Certainly *Democracy in America* makes frequent reference to Americans' moral homogeneity in the midst of doctrinal diversity. "Each sect worships God in its own fashion," Tocqueville noted, "but all preach the same morality" (p. 290). Moreover, despite the multitude of theological formulations, "not a single religious doctrine in the United States is hostile to democratic and republican institutions" (p. 289; see also pp. 291; 295–296; 298–299; 432; 436;

447–449). That is to say, from every quarter of American religious life came the message that the interests of every citizen are bound up in spiritual issues; the pursuit of self-interest must be guided by transcendental considerations.

> If you give democratic peoples education and freedom and leave them alone, they will easily extract from this world all the good things it has to offer. . . . Since their social condition by its nature urges them this way, there is no need to fear that they will stop. But while man takes delight in this proper and legitimate quest for prosperity, there is a danger . . . he may lose the use of his sublimest faculties and that, bent on improving everything around him, he may at length degrade himself. . . . In a democracy therefore it is ever the duty of lawgivers and of all upright educated men to raise up the souls of their fellow citizens and turn their attention toward heaven . . . to propagate throughout society a taste for the infinite, an appreciation of greatness, and a love of spiritual pleasures. [p. 543]

As we have already noted, in 1831 Tocqueville seemed chiefly to find this second channel for the civil religious message also in churches.

Tocqueville's analysis of republican democracy in America—his identification of the forces countering despotism—thus relied heavily on churches and religion. One can ask, correlatively, what American church historians have to say about the period of Tocqueville's visit, and what are the implications for his analysis of their findings. The answer is that historians verify Tocqueville's observations of religion and confirm his theoretical insights by their descriptions of the period of the Frenchman's visit and the decades following.

For example, Tocqueville observed, "In every state of the Union, but especially in the half-peopled lands of the West, there are preachers hawking the word of God from place to place (p. 534). Church historian William G. McLoughlin (who makes no reference to Tocqueville, incidentally) says of the same period:

> Camp meetings were communal in nature; churches became the centers of community life; and, above all, although a conversion was an individual confrontation of the soul with God, the sustaining fellowship of Christian brethren provided the continuity that routinized and canalized the fervor of the awakening into orderly social institutions. [McLoughlin, 1978, p. 132]

This "organizing process," as Donald G. Mathews calls it (1969, pp. 23–43) took different shape in New England, the South, and the "half-peopled lands of the West," but organization occurred, and largely through the church:

> They organized missionary activities to New England's northern frontier . . . ; they worked for temperance, against dueling, to improve Sabbath observance. They urged the legislature to enforce the blue laws and local constables to arrest prostitutes and gamblers. Among the most important of the

new benevolent associations were the Home and Foreign Mission Society (1812), the American Bible Society (1816), the American Education Society (to educate ministers) (1816), the African Colonization Society (1817), the American Tract Society (1825), and the American Temperance Society (1826). [McLoughlin, 1978, p. 112]

Harper's Monthly, Harper's Weekly, and *The Ladies Repository* were only some of the "strongly religious" journals published during this period, and were under Methodist aegis, according to Timothy L. Smith. But a "vast river of Bibles, books, magazines and pamphlets flowed from the presses of the American Bible and Tract society" as well (Smith, 1957, pp. 36, 39).[5] In fact:

> By 1850 nine separate societies were employing 2,675 Home missionaries to establish churches and Sunday schools in "destitute" communities at a total annual expenditure of $500,000. Most of these organizations were denominational offshoots of the nonsectarian American Home Missionary Society, which supported 40 percent of the workers. [p. 39]

Reminiscent of Tocqueville's priests sent west to keep religion and freedom alive, Smith speaks of these home mission crusaders who "considered themselves as much civilizing and Americanizing agents as soul winners" (p. 40).

In other words, church historians confirm the role played by religion in the creation and operation of voluntary associations, but they also concur that the message spread was neither individualistic nor sectarian but community-oriented and civil religious; it was self-interest properly understood.

The upshot of the Second Great Awakening, as Tocqueville could not have observed but as he did anticipate, was a common culture in America, religious at its core. It was a culture that, by redefining the Colonial-Revolutionary ideal, stirred Americans of all kinds, those who peopled the frontier, as well as those remaining in the urban east, allowing all to "be" a single nation. Surviving even the Civil War, this core culture defined America and Americanism from about the time of Tocqueville's visit until nearly the end of the nineteenth century. The very year Tocqueville arrived, in fact, the Reverend Herman Humphrey, president of Amherst College, was announcing the new consensus as just that. The nation, he said, had at last achieved a sense of "the true American union, that sort of union which makes every patriot a Christian and every Christian a patriot" (in McLoughlin, 1978, p. 106).

---

[5] Smith is another oft-cited historian of the Second Great Awakening who makes no mention of Tocqueville.

This is the quality that made the Second Great Awakening an "awakening." Not only were hearts stirred and passions inflamed but, as a consequence, the very definition of society underwent a change, a change in this case lasting nearly a century. Tocqueville somehow perceived this religious spirit of America at the time of his visit, but—via his notions of voluntary association and "self-interest properly understood"—he also perceived the subtle reverberations for civil life this spirit brought; democracy in America was significantly a function of the religious fervor of the first few decades of the nineteenth century.[6] Indeed, not until the waning years of that century did urbanization and industrialization, evolution and cultural relativity, and, of course, massive immigration, bring about yet another awakening or redefinition onto the American people. Until then, the analysis Tocqueville made in 1831 remained pretty much in force.[7]

ARE WE EXPERIENCING ANOTHER GREAT AWAKENING?

Awakenings, it is fair to say, are not merely religious events but, as Tocqueville helped us to see, events, religious at the core, with broad social consequence. Thus, as phrased at the outset of this essay, are we in the midst of another cultural reform movement with evangelical Christianity at its core, or is the current religious scene more nearly a fad? To be sure, no certain answer can be given at this time, but with Tocqueville's model (especially as buttressed by the nineteenth century historical record) as a guide, we can at least frame the question properly.

That question would seem to be double-barreled. First, does current evangelicalism promote voluntary association and thus social participation? Are people, by being drawn into the evangelical movement thereby encouraged to enact more broadly the roles of citizens? Tocqueville observed this cause-effect link in 1831; we can ask about it in the present day.

---

[6] Amazingly, Tocqueville also anticipated the conflicts that would arise over slavery and over Indian territory because the American consensus called for contradictory courses of action.

[7] That is not to say there was no religious change in the nineteenth century. But the changes that took place did not force a reshaping of the "national faith" just discussed until late in the century, giving rise to a new consensus, dissent from which is symbolized by the Modernist-Fundamentalist split of the 1920's. See George M. Marsden (1980), for a detailed account of the nineteenth century events leading up to the reshaping of the national faith in the twentieth.

Second, does the "enthusiastic spirituality" exhibited today get trans-muted into "self-interest properly understood"? Are persons, inspired by the emotional message of salvation through Jesus Christ, led to an ideology of pluralistic tolerance, to community-oriented activity, to a more universalistic moral code? Tocqueville observed this cause-effect link, and we can look for it, too.

Obviously, what is happening religiously can be significant without being an awakening, in the sense that word is used here. Historians have designated "awakening" in the cases of the First Great Awakening (1730–1760) and the Second (1800–1830), however, because they were more than religious events and their forces spilled out into social and political life to change the entire culture. We are asking, therefore, with the aid of two key insights by Tocqueville, about the "awakening" poten-tial of the current religious scene.

Evangelicals in present-day America report church attendance at twice the rate of other Christians, i.e., Catholics and nonevangelical Protestants. Moreover, they engage in voluntary work through the church at compa-rably higher rates. Since by definition evangelicals believe that the gospel message should be spread, it is not surprising to find, too, these people are much more likely than other Christians to declare their beliefs to others, distribute literature, or otherwise evangelize (Hunter, 1980, Chapt. 5).

In the 1980 election, evangelicals were found to be registered to vote at higher rates than were nonevangelicals of similar demographic charac-teristics (PRRC September 1980). Because of the media attention to Jerry Falwell's Moral Majority and certain other agencies of the evangelical movement, the public is probably led to exaggerate the political impact of evangelicalism, but it appears nonetheless that evangelicalism can evoke a kind of citizenship not unlike the voluntary associational behavior Tocqueville noted.

Does it? Outside of ecclesiastical activity, evangelicals tend to lag be-hind others in community participation. The reason is simple: Among people with the same demographic characteristics, evangelicals are more likely to be registered to vote, but those demographic characteristics themselves are associated with low rates of political participation. Indeed, the major social dimensions known to diminish voluntary associational activity—low occupational prestige, low income and educational levels, and rural or small town residence—are the same dimensions associated with having an evangelical outlook. If one adds being female, Southern, older, and Black to the list of characteristics predisposing persons to evangelicalism, then the tendency toward social participation among evangelicals is seen to be even more muted. Table 11.1 contains illustra-

TABLE 11.1. Relationship of Family Income, Involvement in One or More Voluntary Associations (Other Than a Church), and Being "Born Again" (Christians only)

	Total family annual income		
	Less than $10,000	$10,000–20,000	More than $20,000
Percentage Belonging to 1+ voluntary associations (other than a church)	28	34	49
Percentage "Born Again"	48	40	34
	$N =$ (632)	(251)	(356)
Percentage Belonging to 1+ voluntary associations among the:			
"Born Again"	29 (299)	33 (99)	49 (121)
Others	27 (333)	34 (152)	48 (235)

tive data.[8] It shows, in the top half, the proportion at each income level of those who: (1) belong to one or more voluntary associations other than a church; and (2) describe themselves as "Born Again." As is clear, increases in income lead to social participation but away from "Born Again" identity. Increases in educational attainment or occupational prestige reveal the same pattern.

The bottom half of Table 11.1 then shows that, with income held constant, being "Born Again" has absolutely no effect on social participation outside the church, at least as measured by membership in voluntary associations. (Once again, other measures of socioeconomic status reveal the same pattern.) Evangelicalism appears *not* to induce greater civic participation.[9]

Reasons for this state of affairs are not hard to come by. George M.

[8] These findings were made available to me by Professors Dean Hoge and Douglas Sloane of the Boys Town Center, Catholic University. My gratitude is great. The data are from the "Unchurched American" survey, done by the Gallup Organization in 1978 for the National Council of Churches.

[9] The Connecticut Mutual Life Insurance Company's 1981 *Report on American Values in the '80's,* especially pp. 72–76, seem to contradict this generalization. But in fact their "most religious" category—which undoubtedly is comprised chiefly of "evangelicals" because of the measuring device—is shown simply to be more involved locally—by visiting neighbors, discussing "local" issues, or being involved in "community" affairs, all of which could (and probably do) include church activities.

Marsden, speaking at least of Fundamentalists among Evangelicals, says they:

> reveal almost no systematic political thought except perhaps some inherited
> wisdom from the days of the nineteenth-century evangelical establishment.
> . . . [R]evivalists, premillenialists, holiness teachers, and Baptist and Presbyte-
> rian conservatives had concerned themselves relatively little with such sub-
> jects since the Civil War. Certainly they had developed no clear consensus
> on them except that the church should not be involved in political affairs.
> [Marsden, 1980, p. 208]

Thus, it is not surprising to find, as James Hunter did in his reanalysis of Gallup's *Christianity Today* poll data, that, while evangelicals are far more likely than others to agree the church should speak out on ethical, political, and economic issues, they also assign lower priority to such matters than to matters of individual salvation and happiness (Hunter, 1980, Chapt. 5). Hunter finds, correlatively, that evangelical publishing houses eschew social issues. In addition to narrowly theological books, they publish almost exclusively books focused on such subjective issues as "knowing oneself," gaining confidence, or how to be happy (1980, Chapt. 6).

In summary, then, evangelicalism in present-day America appears to encourage greater participation in church activities but does little or noth-ing to increase other voluntary associational activity, or at least voluntary activity with broad political ramifications. There is little evidence via this channel, therefore, that an awakening is in the making.

How about the other channel? Does evangelicalism in our day seem to promote a moral outlook by which personal aims are also seen as socially constructive, an outlook inclusive of all?

On the face of it, evangelical doctrine would appear to be singularly intolerant because of the centrality given to belief in Christ as the only means of salvation, a theological assertion agreed to by nine of ten evan-gelicals, compared with only one-third of nonevangelicals.[10] Formal assen-ters to the doctrine know they live in a religiously plural society, however, so the issue becomes one of how they maintain their unique Christian claims while according civil privileges to others. The answer, as Hunter makes clear, is by "domesticating" God, making the message of salvation into one of "sociability and gentility." The result is "a civility which pro-claims loudly 'No offense, I am an Evangelical' " (Hunter, 1980, p. 195).

---

[10] In 1924 in Middletown, the Lynds found 94% of the high school students affirming that "Christianity is the one true religion and all peoples should be converted to it." A half-century later the figure dropped to 38% (see Caplow and Bahr, 1979).

In other words, evangelicals are only formally intolerant; informally and in behavior, they adjust to the fact of pluralism.

Such a strategy for getting along in a modern world while holding formally to a deviant doctrine is not conducive to generating the *next* orthodoxy, however. Individually, evangelicals may be able to absorb whatever new cultural understandings come into existence, but *their* religious movement is unlikely to be the source of those new understandings.

Consider an agency like Moral Majority, admittedly on the conservative political fringe but nevertheless a part of evangelicalism. Certainly it offers its ideology as a civil religion for Americans. But Gallup finds an inverse relationship between knowledge about Moral Majority and approval of it; the more people know about the outfit, the less they like it (PRRC, January, 1981)! Moral Majority seems unlikely to do more than make headlines and create possible mischief in certain election campaigns. Similarly with TV evangelism; its audience is considerably smaller than generally implied in the press, and, despite enormous publicity in 1980, actually declined during that year (Martin, 1981). When their spokesmen say, therefore, that conservative moral values will dominate American politics for the rest of this century, they are at best only partly correct. Certainly no evidence suggests the triumph of their style of biblical moralism now or in the future.

Three reasons, already implied, can be offered. First is the demographic makeup of those attracted to evangelicalism. It is a population not noted for sustained political skill, participation, or even interest. Second, insofar as evangelicalism promotes upward mobility or develops increased attraction for the middle classes, it must itself become "respectably mainstream" and therefore tolerant of moral styles other than its own. Third, the moral platform of evangelicals contains some planks severely at odds with historical currents. Everyone can "affirm" family values, of course, but divorce rates are not likely to decrease, birth rates are not likely to increase, women's participation in more and more arenas outside of the house is not likely to be reversed, and children are not likely to find home an adequate substitute for the technical training required to live in this modern world. Traditional family values can be affirmed, therefore, but they are doomed to be elusive in reality.

All in all, then, the social and political interests of evangelicals seem destined to remain pretty much self-interests alone. They appear on the private agendas of some Americans and some religious organizations, but, not being "properly understood," they are unlikely to become the nation's agenda. This assessment, combined with the previous assessment that evangelicalism seems to enhance social participation only narrowly in ecclesiastical ways, suggests the judgment that the current evangelical movement is not a repeat Great Awakening. Individuals may be being "Born Again," but the movement is not giving birth to a new cultural understanding we all may come to share.

ANOTHER PERSPECTIVE ON EVANGELICALISM AND AWAKENINGS

But if the current evangelical movement is not itself an awakening in the tradition of the Second Great Awakening Tocqueville observed, nevertheless the religious emotionalism of our day may be linked to a kind of cultural reformation some would call an awakening. Most notably this is the position of William G. McLoughlin, whose *Revivals, Awakenings, and Reform* is, despite its brevity, a masterpiece of historical synthesis. Human institutions and the worldviews making sense of them, says McLoughlin, assume:

> a fixed or normative relationship of one man or a group to another, of one generation to another. They prepare men for continuity, not change; they are means by which men try to insure stability, order, regularity, and predictability in their lives. . . . But times change; the world changes; people change; therefore institutions, world view, and cultural systems must change. [McLoughlin, 1978, p. 9]

Furthermore, he proposes:

> to view . . . great awakenings that have shaped and reshaped our culture since 1607 as periods of fundamental ideological transformation necessary to the dynamic growth of the nation in adapting to basic social, ecological, psychological, and economic changes. The conversion of great numbers of people from an old to a new world view . . . is a natural and necessary aspect of social change [McLoughlin, 1978, p. 8]

Following Anthony F. C. Wallace (1956), McLoughlin conceives of awakenings as occurring in stages. First is a crisis in legitimacy, felt as individual stress, wherein the once-dominant worldview is found wanting. Second is a stage during which this sense of personal distress comes to be seen as institutional failure, with disagreement about why this is so, and what is to be done about it. Third is the creation of a new worldview, generally symbolized by symbols of cultural death and rebirth. The fourth stage involves the restructuring of old institutions, a process usually undertaken initially by younger members of society. Fifth, and finally, is the absorption of nearly everybody into the new world view and the new institutional patterns it upholds (McLoughlin 1978, pp. 9–23).

What makes this Wallace-McLoughlin scheme pertinent here is that during the second stage, when widespread crisis is felt as institutional disarray, there almost always

> arises a nativist or traditionalist movement within the culture, that is, an attempt
> . . . to argue that the danger comes from the failure of the populace to
> adhere more strictly to the old beliefs, values, and behavior patterns. . . .
> [The nativists'] solution is double-edged. First they call for a return to the
> "old-time religion," "the ways of our fathers," and "respect for the flag"
> (or other symbols of the old order). Second, they tend to find scapegoats
> in their midst . . . upon whom they can project their fear; then, by punishing
> these "outsiders," they can set an example of revived authority. [McLoughlin,
> 1978, p. 14]

The evidence we have just reviewed suggests that the current evangelical movement, while not a presage of the next worldview, is perhaps a nativist cry of alarm about the loss of legitimacy for the worldview just past. It is a reassertion of this dying worldview and a call to resuscitate the institutions—especially of marriage, family, and child care—once believed to operate reasonably well.

What complicates the perception of contemporary evangelicalism as a nativist response to a cultural crisis is the inclusion in the nativist movement in the 1970's and 1980's of a number of ideological elements carried over from the nativist response in the previous awakening. While we will not take the space here to go into detail, a few words are necessary to establish the historical context for this last assertion.

The theological and sociopolitical worldview arising out of the Second Great Awakening held firm, as we saw, throughout most of the nineteenth century, but its legitimacy was, by early twentieth century, brought into doubt by such forces as immigration, industrialization, and—especially for theology—evolution and cultural relativity. A new worldview thus came into being. Just when the new worldview came into being is arguable, of course, but certainly by World War II most Americans agreed politically on government involvement, both domestically and overseas, in regulating the economy, policing behavior, and upholding people's welfare. They agreed socially that urbanism and secular education represented paths to success. And they agreed theologically on some brand of Social Gospel and of "higher criticism" of the Bible.

But the consensus was not complete. Several factions held out, opposed to government interference perhaps, or to the disappearance of rural life, or to the teaching of Darwinism. By the 1920's, persons with some or all of these objections had developed into the Fundamentalist movement, a force felt chiefly but by no means exclusively in church life. The target of ridicule, as at the time of the 1925 Scopes trial, this dissent nonetheless persisted through all the decades of this century. In the 1920's its enemies were Darwinism, Modernism, Bolshevism, and Spiritism, while today those enemies carry such labels as "evolutionism as fact," "Godless communism," or "secular humanism."

Followers of this dissent, in other words, are still around, nourished through Bible Institutes, evangelical colleges, Christian day schools, Campus Crusade for Christ, Carl McIntire's American Council of Christian Churches, Billy James Hargis' Christian Crusade, the Inter-Varsity Christian Fellowship, and of course Billy Graham. If somehow Graham's premillennialist message never became the new orthodoxy, still it helped keep alive such elaborate evangelical infrastructures as these. With the addition of radio preaching, and then TV, there is little wonder that dissent from the dominant worldview of the middle decades of this century stayed alive. H. L. Mencken would see William Jennings Bryan buried just days after the Scopes trial, but Fundamentalism in its various forms survived not only Mencken's ridicule, but the cynic himself.

Of course, the current crisis of legitimacy is not the same as gave rise to Fundamentalism in the 1920's. Not for decades have most Americans believed Protestantism would prevail worldwide, that increased capitalism would solve all societal problems, or that all ethnic differences would melt in the metropolis. Today what we despair over is different. We have lost faith in Keynesian economics, in the United States as world policeman, and in the good faith of government legislators. City life has brought not utopia but the jungle again, and secular education proves hollow for many. The Social Gospel proved no more adequate a guide to the Kingdom than did the New Deal, and, while biblical scholarship has kept apace, it has been of interest to only a few of the intellectual elite, not a path to new understanding by the faithful.

There seems little doubt, then, a crisis exists in the American worldview emerging out of (though not just because of) the passing of the Depression and the successful execution of World War II. The quiet years of the Eisenhower Administration symbolized not just the complacency of most citizens (especially the "silent generation" of youth) but indicated as well a fairly high degree of agreement on what was true, on what was important, on what was real. Daniel Bell (1960) even suggested that ideological debate on such matters had ended.

But for whatever reasons—the failure of the civil rights movement, the Vietnam incursion, the seemingly ineradicable poverty in a nation of plenty, or the inability to forge a workable foreign policy recognizing the existence of Third World and socialist nations—the 1950's consensus eroded. By the 1960's, the erosion was apparent, and by the 1970's, it is fair to say, the Wallace-McLoughlin second stage (where personal distress is translated into more institutional failure) was abroad in the land.

As James Q. Wilson (1980) points out, the signs of this second stage were almost classical: an expanded cohort of young people, unconventionality in morality, alienation from extant institutions, public disorder and high crime rates, and declining party loyalties. Clearly, Americans had moved beyond the stage of personal malaise to the stage of doubting their institutions and disagreeing over both diagnosis and remedy.

In such a context, therefore, it is hardly surprising to see also a vigorous nativist or traditionalist movement, a movement promising to revitalize the culture by returning to the old ways, even as internal enemies (liberals or secular humanists in this case) are identified and blamed for the crisis.

The current evangelical movement, especially in its political expressions, quite readily fits this description. More accurately, nativists and traditionalists grabbed hold of the evangelicalism already there and gave it new vigor. Responding now to institutional crises different from those of 1890–1920, evangelicalism nevertheless borrowed heavily from its ideological predecessor, fundamentalism. The similarity is seen in the biblical inerrancy doctrine, for example, or in the appeals to family virtue and the simple life of small town America, uncomplicated by new-fangled education which, anyway, only teaches secular humanism. The similarity is seen too, especially in the right wing of evangelicalism, in the potential for virulent and paranoid politics. Righteousness without the patina of education—or, as Tocqueville would say, self-interest *not* properly understood—tends toward despotism.

Despotism, at least from evangelicalism, is unlikely in our day, however, for the same reasons evangelicalism is unlikely to provide the next worldview. Soul-winning served in the nineteenth century, as Tocqueville acutely observed, as the power behind institution building and belief in a common, civil oriented religion. By contrast, its twentieth century expression is, as McLoughlin notes, "a divisive, not a unifying, force in a pluralistic world" (1978, p. 214).

It must be repeated, however, that these observations are tentative. Major cultural shifts go notoriously unnoticed by the persons living through them, leaving to the next generation not just the new worldview but its recognition as well. Our purpose here, therefore, has been to identify the proper question more than the correct answer. More than the issue of whether we are experiencing a religious revival in America is involved, we have also been asking how the religious fervor of our day can be understood. Tocqueville had a marvelous grasp of these matters a century and a half ago; we have tried shining some of his light on the shadows of today.

VI | Conclusion

12 | THE MAKING OF THE NEW CHRISTIAN RIGHT

Robert C. Liebman

For more than five decades, the vast majority of American evangelicals kept their distance from politics. The duties of personal piety and a commitment to proselytizing took priority over political involvement. In towns and cities, evangelicals devoted considerable energies to building churches and winning souls for Christ. At the national level, they developed religious broadcasting and publishing empires and nurtured a variety of organizations dedicated to educating clergymen, supporting missionary work, and servicing the increasing number of Christian schools. They took pride in the steady growth of their ranks and seemed content to leave political questions to their counterparts in the Protestant mainstream.

The 1970's brought a decisive turn of events. Against the background of pro-abortion legislation, movements for gay and women's rights, and the national trauma of Watergate, the sharp line between the kingdom of God and the kingdom of Caesar began to blur. Unwilling to turn their backs on what appeared to be a deepening moral crisis in America, evangelicals shifted their attention to the sphere of public life. Some connected moral decline with the widely perceived failure of public education. Others argued that the call for gay and women's rights threatened the eventual demise of the family. Still others argued that a lack of moral leadership was responsible for America's diminished international prestige.

The evangelical response to these events took two paths. The first involved separatism, a familiar strategy in evangelical life. As they came to deplore trends in the wider society, evangelicals strengthened their own institutions. Thousands of parents withdrew their children from public schools and sent them to newly formed Christian academies. Evangelical colleges expanded their offerings and saw their enrollments soar. Religious broadcasters developed Christian alternatives to secular programming and built their audience share. But the separatist strategy satisfied only a portion of the evangelical community. Evangelicals were an inextricable part of American society. They could not insulate themselves from events in their local communities and from the implications of national policy.

Partly as a consequence of the strengthening of evangelical institutions, many evangelicals took the road of confrontation. Some sought to defend their local communities against the onslaught of cultural styles which appeared to threaten family life and standards of decency. Their anger culminated in the creation of hundreds of local groups to stem the tide of pornography, to challenge gay rights legislation, or to keep sex education out of public schools. Provoked by attempts to impose federal and state regulations, other groups formed to defend cherished institutions such as Christian schools threatened by the removal of their tax-exempt status or by the imposition of state certification requirements for teachers. Still other groups courted national power to protect religious broadcasting empires from the actions of the Federal Communications Commission or church organizations which found themselves under the scrutiny of the Securities and Exchange Commission. They organized massive letter-writing campaigns, engaged expensive legal talent, and packed hearing rooms with fervent supporters.

Some of these local and national organizations won notable successes. But the great majority were single-issue groups that faded away quietly at the end of their campaigns. There was little coordination among their efforts and no centralized organization to weld the voices of protest into a national political force.

By the end of the decade, the situation was changed by the appearance of a small number of evangelical groups which promised to mold these disparate activities into a powerful national movement. Moral Majority, Christian Voice, Religious Roundtable, and other organizations issued a call for evangelicals to take their rightful place in American political life.

Evangelicals, they claimed, were the conscience of the nation. It was their God-given duty to make their voices heard or to suffer in silence as America fell from greatness. Through meetings, mailings, media campaigns, and massive voter registration drives, they sought to mobilize evangelicals and other morally conservative Americans into a strong political bloc. Only through political action, they claimed, could the righteous emerge triumphant.

A NEW CHRISTIAN RIGHT?

The appearance of the New Christian Right took most political observers by surprise. Led by such firey figures as Carl McIntyre and Billy James Hargis, an older Christian Right had its heyday during the anticommunist crusades of the 1950's. While its remnants endured, its leadership was locked into battles long past and found few listeners for its list of charges against liberal churches and its claims of treason on the part of national officials.

The New Christian Right had little in common with its predecessors. What was new about the movement was its scope, its scale, and its size. In all three of its features, the New Christian Right represented a significant departure from the traditions of evangelical involvement in politics.

Through most of the twentieth century, the great majority of evangelical crusades were single-issue campaigns. The calls for prohibition, for school prayer, and for the teaching of creationism were typical of the limited goals which characterized evangelical politics. Most local campaigns also shared narrow targets. In towns and cities, hundreds of pastors led their congregations against objects of scorn: saloons, pornographic bookstores, adult theatres, and abortion clinics. The campaign for community standards extended to local school boards where fundamentalists protested the introduction of sex education programs and proclaimed the rights of parents to review textbooks and library purchases. As evangelicals created alternatives to public schools, they defended their right to set standards of discipline and to hire teachers of their choosing.

What was new about the New Christian Right was its insistence on joining a variety of issues into a broad sociomoral program. Organizations like Moral Majority and Christian Voice set out a Christian position on a range of issues from abortion to Zimbabwe. Many of these issues were longstanding, but their advocates represented disparate groups within the evangelical community which rarely made common cause for political action.

The New Christian Right did not merely enlarge the battles for single issues. It embarked on a war of ideologies. Secular humanists became the chief objects of attack. Secular humanism became a screen on which the New Christian Right projected all that was hostile to its own beliefs. Secular humanists stood accused of deifying human reason and denying God's word, of encouraging permissiveness through moral relativism, and of separating God from government and society. Through their alleged control of the federal bureaucracy, of public education, and of the media, secular humanists were held responsible for the nation's moral decline. New Christian Right leaders levied similar charges against the liberal National Council of Churches, which it held to be closer to secular humanism than to historic Christianity. By setting forth a broad ideological program, the movement's leadership courted a vast constituency of morally concerned Americans.

In addition to the scope of its program, the New Christian Right was distinguished by the national scale of its constituency and activities. In the opinion of many analysts, evangelical crusades were largely Southern phenomena or at best, were confined to the larger boundaries of the nation's Bible belt. The New Christian Right was neither. Its roots lay in California, where groups of evangelical clergy organized to oppose gay rights legislation; in Indiana, where evangelicals mobilized on behalf of the Church Freedom Legislative Package; and in North Carolina, where evangelical parents rallied in defense of Christian schools. Its major organizations planted chapters throughout the nation. Moral Majority established state affiliates in all fifty states by the end of 1980. In fact, its largest chapter was in Washington state, far distant from the Bible Belt. The national scale of the New Christian Right bespoke the broad representation of evangelicals and fundamentalists throughout the nation. To be sure, the dispersion of its primary constituency produced an uneven pattern of recruitment and activities. But it is clear that the New Christian Right drew adherents from a broad geographic base.

Finally, the New Christian Right represented a movement of considerable size. How large is impossible to determine. Memberships in its major national organizations like Moral Majority and Christian Voice number in the hundreds of thousands. But memberships provide an uncertain estimate of the following of social movements. When reliable estimates are not available from surveys or other sources, the volume of movement actions offers a surer guide.

In press accounts, the activities of national organizations—lobbying, media campaigns, etc.—received the bulk of attention. These accounts overlooked the millions of small events that gave shape to the movement. Some of these events were carried out by individuals who registered to vote or wrote their Congressmen. Others were carried out by groups who distributed literature at churches or rallied on the steps of state capitols. These events, along with thousands of meetings and marches, signalled the mobilization of the New Christian Right.

For some, participation in these local events represented their first experience with politics. For others, their actions represented their first political experience outside the polling place. These experiences were shared by much of the leadership of the New Christian Right. Theirs was a movement of fusion which sought to cement hundreds of local, regional, and national groups, including many which they had a hand in forming. The membership rolls of their organizations belied the actual size of the movement. Its dimensions were clearer in the extraordinary number of political activities carried out by ordinary people at the grassroots.

In the broad scope of its program, the national scale of its activities, and the large size of its following, the New Christian Right represented a new turn in politics. For the first time in many decades, evangelicals found a political voice which they could claim as their own. Moreover, by invoking the imagery of evangelicals as the conscience of the nation, its leadership claimed to speak for a majority of moral Americans of all faiths. In the breadth of its purposes, the New Christian Right was a movement with which to be reckoned.

STRATEGY AND CIRCUMSTANCE

One of the most important insights in the literature on social movements concerns the distinction between social movement organizations and the broader cultural environment in which movements emerge. The cultural environment includes the reservoir of sentiment and the repertoire of activities which compose the larger social movement. Movement organizations act to provide a common focus for diffuse bodies of sentiment and a common program for disparate activities. The correspondence between the larger social movement and the organizations which claim to speak in its name is always problematic. Movements and movement organizations are rarely the same.

The distinction was missed in most popular accounts of the New Christian Right. Journalists treated the New Christian Right like an iceberg, shining their lights on its most visible groups and its most prominent personalities. With few exceptions, they rarely broke beneath the surface to probe the larger body of activities which brought these features into view or the underlying tensions which brought the larger social movement into being. Instead, they let the appearance of national organizations and movement celebrities tell the story of the making of the New Christian Right.

The preoccupation with organizations and individuals marked many interpretations. Some observers portrayed the movement as a creature of the secular New Right. Others saw the New Christian Right as the creation of televangelists. Still others described it as the invention of emboldened religious leaders bent on establishing a Christian nation.

The essays in this volume provide little support for these interpretations. Take the link with the secular New Right. Several of the essays make it clear that New Right political entrepreneurs like Paul Weyrich and Howard Phillips played important roles in the birth of such conservative Christian groups as the Religious Roundtable and Moral Majority. Ready and willing to provide assistance to these groups, their contributions were considerable. But it is doubtful that they were crucial to the making of the New Christian Right. Experienced in building local churches and, in many cases, organizing national religious groups, the organizational talents of clergymen like Jerry Falwell were equal to the task of establishing social movement organizations. Their ties with national networks of evangelicals were the decisive factors in the mobilization of the New Christian Right.

Or take the role of televangelists. The 1970's saw extensive growth in the reach of the electronic church. The message of evangelism was flashed to the most distant corners of the nation. The varied enterprises of televangelists—colleges, hospitals, and foreign missions—grew in step with the steadily increasing stream of contributions. Some saw in televangelism the religious equivalent of a political machine. They suggested that televangelists were a united force and that they could turn the attention of their audiences from prayer to politics. The chapters in this book cast doubt on both these claims. The nation's televangelists were not a monolith and more than half of the "Big 8," including Oral Roberts, Rex Humbard, Jimmy Swaggart, and Robert Schuller, kept politics off the screen. Others, like Falwell, watched their audience share decline as they increased the political content of their programming. In addition, there is no firm evidence to suggest that the more political televangelists orchestrated a national movement at the grassroots. If televangelists planted the seeds of political concern, it was up to local clergy to reap the harvest of political activism.

Or take the claim that the New Christian Right represented a religious crusade. In an atmosphere charged by the Iranian crisis, some went so far as to compare Jerry Falwell with the Ayatollah Khomeni and to predict that America would soon be held hostage by the New Christian Right. While it is true that its leaders clothed the movement in religious imagery and called for a return to God, the essays presented here suggest that they were more concerned with practical politics than with making God's kingdom on earth. Like the secular New Right, the New Christian Right was not a proselytizing movement. Its major organizations seemed more willing to organize discontent than to tend to lost souls. None of the main-stream Protestant churches aligned with the New Christian Right, and its apparent departure from the Great Commission disquieted the nation's major evangelical denominations. Essentially a "parachurch" movement, the New Christian Right gained a firm hold only among independent churches, minor denominations, and the ranks of dissidents within main-stream Protestant churches.

Common to all three of these explanations is the tendency to interpret the New Christian Right in the image of its leadership. By focusing on the national organizations at the movement's summit, they lost sight of its base of support in local churches and its base of activities in local communities. While these interpretations attribute the appearance of the movement to the machinations of its leadership, our research suggests the importance of looking at local and national evangelical campaigns which preceded the emergence of political organizations like Christian Voice and Moral Majority. Often ignored in popular accounts, these ac-tions not only provided the political baptism for many who would become leaders of national organizations, they readied the troops who would carry out the political campaign at the grassroots. It was the existence of evangelical organizations and the experience of previously politicized groups that made possible the mobilization of political organizations like Moral Majority. The structure of these political organizations, the tactics they employed, and the character of their personnel reflected the legacy of preexisting groups and prior activities.

Strategy alone cannot explain the making of the New Christian Right. A social movement is more than the set of its political organizations. Social movements are large episodes of collective action of which the workings of formal organizations are only a part. The underlying cultural tensions and political opportunities that define the cultural environment give shape to social movements. If the focus on strategy emphasizes the role of formal organizations and leadership, attention to the cultural environment calls for examination of the role of circumstance.

The appearance of the New Christian Right surprised many observers who held that religious beliefs were an anachronism in modern America. Their pronouncements were contradicted by a wealth of social science data which showed that the vast majority of Americans held fast to a belief in God and believed religion to be an important part of their lives. Surveys of religious practice demonstrated that despite occasional fluctuations the proportion of Americans who report regular attendance at churches and synagogues remained unchanged since the Second World War. In addition, cross-national surveys revealed that among all advanced industrial nations Americans had the highest proportion of church attendance.

However, over time the proportions of Americans who claimed membership in the major denominations changed considerably. The explanations for the shifts were numerous, including differences in fertility rates, the effects of age-distributions, and the changing residential patterns within American cities. But the figures were clear. Among Protestants, who compose the majority of Americans, liberal denominations lost members, while conservative denominations grew.

Contributing to the shift was one of the most striking religious developments of the 1970's: the growth in the number of evangelicals. Several national polls reported increases in the number of Americans who subscribed to the defining features of evangelism, including the claim of being born again, a commitment to spreading the Gospel, and a belief in the literal interpretation of the Bible. Conservative estimates stated that at the end of the decade evangelicals accounted for a fifth of the nation's electorate.

The 1970's also brought changes in the character of evangelical institutions. The number of Christian schools increased sharply. Enrollments in evangelical colleges climbed. Evangelical outreach was strengthened by an efflorescence of religious media. The circulation of evangelical magazines grew, as did the number of radio and television stations sponsored by evangelicals. Probably the most notable development was the arrival of televangelists on prime-time.

Apart from the spread of the electronic church, most of the developments within the evangelical community went unnoticed. However, a number of events in the late seventies brought a new awareness of the place of evangelicals in American life. Most significant was the election of Jimmy Carter, a born-again Southern Baptist, to the White House. After his inauguration, magazines like *Time* and *Newsweek* carried feature stories about evangelicals and the national networks produced documentaries about born-again Americans.

While new-found national attention contributed to the legitimation of evangelicals, it does not explain their turn to politics. The events which were crucial to the politicization of evangelicals came from changes in the larger cultural environment. Two sets of circumstances were important: changes in the relationship between church and state and shifts in the symbolic boundaries among religion, morality, and politics.

The First Amendment imposes an ambiguous boundary between the affairs of church and state. Throughout American history, clergy and laity have resisted the attempts of government to regulate the affairs of religious institutions. In this regard, the 1970's were little different. IRS attempts to remove the tax exemptions of racially imbalanced Christian schools and colleges set off major debates in Congress and the Federal bureaucracy and a storm of protest at the grassroots. Although it was quickly dismissed by the Federal Communications Commission, a 1974 petition calling for strict limits on the licensing of nonprofit religious stations brought over eleven million pieces of mail by the middle of 1982. Investigations of the financial practices of church organizations by federal and state authorities and the attempt to tax ministries like the Unification Church, which owned commercial enterprises brought outcries from churchmen. These threats of government intervention came at the very moment when many evangelicals were developing a comprehensive program of religious alternatives to secular institutions. In their fear of encroachment by public officials on what was deemed to be sacred terrain, evangelicals made common cause with clergy from mainstream Protestant denominations.

A second set of symbolic events blurred the distinction between private morality and public institutions. The most significant was the national trauma of Watergate. The event dramatized the connection between private morality and the public good and demonstrated that personal immorality could threaten the whole of society. The legacy of Watergate was an intensified concern with the conduct of public officials and the ethics of private leaders. In addition, major Supreme Court decisions altered the boundaries between private morality and public policy. The most notable was the 1973 decision on abortion, which awakened profound questions about the responsibilities of government in the protection of human life. To those who believed in the existence of human life at the moment of conception, the decision appeared to give sanction to a national policy of infanticide. With strong support from evangelicals and Catholics, the right-to-life movement became a major political force. In the aftermath of Watergate and the abortion decision, morality came increasingly to be viewed as a public issue, rather than a matter of private concern.

Both sets of circumstances encouraged evangelicals and other religious Americans to enter political life. Government interventions in the affairs of churches led them to defend cherished institutions. Government intrusions into the sphere of morality led them to affirm revered values. The perception that these moral and institutional concerns were widely shared by religious Americans led the leadership of the New Christian Right to invoke the imagery of a moral majority.

On the one hand, their perception was not unrealistic. The politicization of religious concerns was not a process unique to evangelicals. Moral issues crossed denominational lines and made strange bedfellows of worshippers split by deep theological divides. For example, Roman Catholics, Baptists, and Orthodox Jews lined up against abortion and homosexuality. Members of feuding Protestant denominations found unity in the campaign for prayer in schools. Common moral concerns provided the basis for cooperation among evangelicals and members of other denominations.

On the other hand, the leaders of the New Christian Right were wrong in suggesting that evangelicals spoke in a single voice. Some, like Bob Jones III, proclaimed that practicing Christians had no place in politics. Their sharp attack on Jerry Falwell and Moral Majority made it clear that the strategy of separation and the priorities of personal piety had not been forgotten in some quarters. Others on the evangelical left condemned the leadership of the New Christian Right for forgetting the Social Gospel and for favoring militarism above world peace. Stern opposition to abortion, firm support for school prayer, and a sense that the nation is spiritually adrift united most evangelicals. Beyond that, their internal differences on other social issues bespoke the great diversity within the evangelical house.

While they may have sympathized with many of their principles, most evangelicals disagreed with the purposes of political organizations like Moral Majority. Their voting record in the 1980 Presidential election demonstrated that evangelicals were not a unified political bloc. The fact that the vast majority of evangelicals stayed aloof from groups like Majority and Christian Voice speaks for itself. Like their leadership, supporters of these groups came disproportionately from the ranks of independent fundamentalists and from those at the margins of mainstream denominations.

Whatever the size or the character of its constituency, the New Christian Right is significant because of what it says about America. The circumstances which brought about the politicization of evangelicals suggest that the boundaries among religion, morality, and politics are never sharp and are ever changing. The combination of strategy and circumstance that produced the New Christian Right had echoes in earlier movements for abolition and for civil rights. If the New Christian Right is not an aberration, but rather one in a long line of movements which express deep moral concerns, then we must ask what its making tells us about social movements in America.

RETHINKING SOCIAL MOVEMENTS

The chapters in this volume represent a variety of perspectives, but they share common ground in making two suggestions for the study of social movements like the New Christian Right. The first concerns the importance of the cultural environment in the emergence of social movements. The second speaks to the contributions of leadership and strategy to the making of social movements.

Some of the most venerable theories in the social sciences connect the rise of social movements with broad shifts in values. In these theories, what goes on in the minds of individuals takes precedence over what happens in the larger society. In so doing, these theories cast ideologies as closed systems. In our terms, they diminish or deny the importance of the cultural environment.

The politicization of evangelicals took those who held these theories by surprise. For it was not the changing values of evangelicals which urged them into politics. The biblical prescripts which evangelicals invoked were longstanding. Rather, these values took on new meaning as evangelicals experienced a sense of political entitlement that came from the symbolic link between their own identity and that of the larger society. Their sense of political entitlement led them to express familiar values through new forms of action. That evangelicals would emerge as a political force could not have been ascertained by theories which held that evangelical ideology was a world unto itself. Theories which acknowledge the effects of the cultural environment of which they were part provide a more convincing explanation for the restructuring of evangelical ideology.

A second strand of social movement theory credits movement leadership with the appearance of social movements. These theories suggest that movements come about through a mixture of intention and ingenuity. In contemporary America, the power of the media to portray movement leaders as national celebrities often gives the argument added weight.

The making of the New Christian Right suggests some important contributions of movement leadership. Movement leaders give voice to widely held discontents and give shape to calls for change. They identify friends and target enemies. They frequently marshall resources and devise strategies. In all these ways, they make movements visible. But movement leaders do not make social movements. Most often, they steer organizations that claim to speak for the movement as a whole.

Social movements are more than sets of social movement organizations and the leaders that guide them. They are large episodes of political action involving thousands of events of varying types and sizes. Meetings, marches, mailings, and so on are the stuff of which movements are made.

Our suggestions about the importance of the cultural environment and the limited role of movement leadership draw a different picture of social movements from that which was used to explain the making of the New

Christian Right. They cast social movements as sets of events rather than aggregates of individuals. They emphasize activities rather than attitudes. They suggest that it is not the unity of purpose, but the simultaneity of action which is the distinguishing feature of social movements. More than the strategies and intentions of leaders and participants, the making of social movements depends on the character of the underlying tensions within the cultural environment, on the opportunities for political action within a population, and on the relations between competing social movements within a society.

These considerations make it difficult to assess either the impact or the implications of the New Christian Right. In the long run, social movements are often recognized as indicators of once current concerns, rather than as important instruments of change. It is well known that social movements in religion and politics flourish only when they provide their adherents with explanations for the problems of everyday life and with the possibilities for their resolution. The New Christian Right has many contenders who seek to provide such explanations and to promote their own programs of change. It is clear that the New Christian Right has set forth a number of questions of great concern to many Americans. It is less clear that the New Christian Right will be able to provide them with the answers they seek.

BIBLIOGRAPHY

Armstrong, Ben (1979). "The Electric Church." Thomas Nelson, New York.

Asimov, Isaac (1981). The blind who would lead. *Macleans* **94,** Febr., No. 6.

Associated Press (1980). Evangelist denies Joneses' charges. *Greenville (S.C.) News,* July 18, p. E3.

Associated Press (1981). Moral majority doubles revenue. *New York Times,* Dec. 10, p. A21.

Avery, William O., and Gobbel, A. Roger (1980). The word of God and the words of the preacher. *Rev. Religious Res.* **22,** 41–43.

Baker, Robert A. (1974). "The Southern Baptist Convention and Its People, 1607–1972." Broadman, Nashville, Tennessee.

Baptist Bible College (1981). "Baptist Bible College 1981–1983." Baptist Bible College, Springfield, Missouri.

Baptist Bible Fellowship (1981). "Directory: Pastors and Churches." Baptist Bible Fellowship, Springfield, Missouri.

Baptist Press (1980). Rogers joins group to push for prayers in public schools. *Baptist Courier* 112, Febr. 7, p. 2.

Barnhart, Joe E. (1981). Humanism as a new scapegoat. Paper presented at the annual meetings of Society for the Scientific Study of Religion, Baltimore, Maryland.

Barringer, Felicity (1980). Born again clout. *Washington Post* July 15, B1.

239

Beach, David (1981). Keepin' an eye on Satan. *Cleveland Plain Dealer Sunday Magazine,* June 21.

Bell, Daniel (1960). "The End of Ideology." The Free Press, Glencoe, Illinois.

Bell, Daniel (ed.). (1963). "The Radical Right." Doubleday, Garden City, New York.

Bellah, Robert N. (1978). Commentary and proposed agenda: The normative framework for pluralism in America. *Soundings* **LXI,** Fall, p. 3.

Bellah, Robert N. (1981). Cultural Pluralism and Religious Particularism. An address delivered at the conference on "Freedom of Religion in America." Annenberg School of Communications, University of Southern California: April 29.

Bennett, William J. and Eastland, Terry (1980). The "new right" Christians. *Wall Street J.,* Sept. 17.

Berger, P. L. (1969). "The Sacred Canopy." Anchor Press, Garden City, New York.

Berger, P. L. (1977). "Facing Up to Modernity." Basic Books, New York.

Berger, P. L. (1979). The worldview of the new class. In "The New Class?" (B. Bruce-Briggs, ed.). Transaction Books, New Brunswick, New Jersey.

Bible Broadcasting Network (1980). Morning Sunshine, July 7.

Briggs, Kenneth A. (1980a). Evangelical preachers gather to polish their politics. *New York Times,* Aug. 21, p. B9.

Briggs, Kenneth A. (1980b). Bishops, on social policy, seem to shun hard line. *New York Times,* Nov. 14, p. 8.

Briggs, Kenneth A. (1980c). Evangelical colleges reborn. *New York Times Magazine,* Dec. 14, pp. 140–154.

Briggs, Kenneth A. (1981a). Graham warns on arms and "dangers" in TV evangelism. *New York Times,* Jan. 29, p. 7.

Briggs, Kenneth A. (1981b). Church leaders at parley, assert government restricts their freedom. *New York Times,* Feb. 15, p. 14.

Broughton, Walter (1978). Religiosity and opposition to church social action: A test of a Weberian hypothesis. *Rev. Religious Res.* **19,** Winter, pp. 154–166.

Brown, Harold O. J. (1977). "Reconstruction of the Republic." Arlington House, New Rochelle, New York.

Bruce-Briggs, B. (ed.) (1979). "The New Class?" Transaction Books, New Brunswick.

Bryant, G. (1979). Entanglement by the New Right, Part I. Pamphlet distributed by the National Education Association.

Buchanan, Patrick (1975). "Conservative Votes, Liberal Victories." Quadrangle, New York Times, New York.

Buckley, William F., Jr. (1970). "Did You Ever See a Dream Walking?" Bobbs-Merrill, Indianapolis, Indiana.

Buckley, William F., Jr., and Bozell, L. Brent (1954). "McCarthy and His Enemies: The Record and Its Meaning." Henry Regnery, Chicago, Illinois.

Burnet, Thomas M. (1981). Evangelist says politics not his crusade. *United Press Intern.,* Apr. 12.

Caplow, Theodore and Bahr, Howard M. (1979). Half a century of change in adolescent attitudes. *Public Opinion Quart.* **43,** Winter, pp. 1–17.

Carpenter, Teresa (1980). The Moral Majority targets New York. *The Village Voice,* Nov. 19–25.

Clendinen, Dudley (1980). "Christian new right's" rush to power. *New York Times,* Aug. 18, p. B7.

Clogg, Clifford C. (1977). Unrestricted and Restricted Maximum Likelihood Latent

Structure Analysis: A Manual for Users. Working Paper 1977–09, Population Issues Research Office, The Pennsylvania State University.

Clymer, Adam (1980). Reagan presses in speech on coast for "Born Again" Protestant vote. *New York Times,* May 27, p. B8.

Clymer, Adam (1981). Religious oriented right-wing group plans drive. *New York Times,* April 12, p. 13.

Clymer, Adam (1981a). Conservatives gather in umbrella council for a national policy. *New York Times,* May 20.

Clymer, Adam (1981b). Conservative political committee evokes both fear and adoration. *New York Times,* May 31, p. 1.

Clymer, Adam (1981c). Independents spent $10 million on Reagan in '80. *New York Times,* Nov. 29, p. 15.

Congressional Quarterly, Inc. (1980). Domestic violence. *Congressional Quart. Weekly Rept.* **38,** 3662.

Connecticut Mutual Life Insurance Company (1981). *Rept. on American Values in the '80's.*

Connors, Kenneth (1980). Public issues and private morality. *Christian Century* **97,** Oct. 22.

Conservative Digest (1981). Roundtable's President Ed McAteer is music man of religious right. *Conservative Dig.,* Jan.

Cousins, Norman (1981). The threat of intolerance. *Saturday Rev.* Jan. 8.

Covert, Harry (1981a). Moral Majority observes 2nd birthday. *Moral Majority Rept.* **2,** May 18, p. 11.

Covert, Harry (1981b). Southern Baptists support Moral Majority. *Moral Majority Rept.* **2,** July 20, p. 3.

Crawford, Alan (1980). "Thunder on the Right." Pantheon, New York.

Crippen, Timothy (1981). Religion, Politics, and the American Family: Some Observations and Comments. Unpublished paper, University of Texas.

Cuddihy, John Murray (1978). "No Offense: Civil Religion and Protestant Taste." Seabury, New York.

Darrow, Clarence S. (1932). "The Story of My Life." Scribner's, New York.

Dart, John (1981). Behold, the birth of the condensed bible is near. *Greenville (S.C.) News,* Dec. 26, 11A.

Data Center (1981). "The New Right: Readings and Commentary." Data Center, Oakland.

Davidson, James D. (1972). Religious belief as an independent variable. *J. Sci. Study Religion* **11,** March, pp. 65–75.

Davis, James A. (1980). "General Social Surveys, 1972–1980, Cumulative Codebook." National Opinion Research Center, Chicago, Illinois.

Dionne, E. J., Jr. (1980a). The mail order campaigners. *New York Times,* Sept. 7, Sect. 3, p. 9.

Dionne, E. J., Jr. (1980b). Fund-raising data worry Democrats. *New York Times,* Sept. 25, p. 8.

Drew, Elizabeth (1981). Jesse Helms. *The New Yorker* **57**(22), 78–95.

Durkheim, Emile (1965). "The Elementary Forms of the Religious Life." Free Press, New York.

Ebersole, Luke Eugene (1951). "Church Lobbying in the Nation's Capital." Macmillan, New York.

Edwards, Lee (1981). Paul Weyrich: Conscience of the New Right. *Conserv. Dig.* **7**(7), 2–8.

Elder, William H., III (1981). Politics and the New Right—toward 1984. *Baptist Joint Committee's Rept. from the Capital* **36,** March, pp. 10–11.

Falwell, Jerry (1980). "Listen America!" Doubleday, New York.

Falwell, Jerry (1981). Christians in Government: What the Bible says. Pamphlet distributed by Moral Majority, Lynchburg, Virginia.

Falwell, Jerry (1981a). My turn: the maligned majority. *Newsweek,* Sept. 21, p. 17.

Falwell, Jerry (1981b). Interview with Rev. Jerry Falwell KERA television, Sept. 6.

Falwell, Jerry (ed.). (1981). "The Fundamentalist Phenomenon." Doubleday-Gallilee, Garden City, New York.

Fitzgerald, Frances (1981). A disciplined, charging army. *New Yorker* **57,** May 18, 53–144.

Fore, William (1980). Forms of self-deception and hypocrisy. *Christian Century* **97,** Oct. 22.

Furniss, Norman E. (1954). "The Fundamentalist Controversy, 1918–1931." Archon Books, Hamden, Connecticut.

Gabriel, Ralph H. (1956). "The Course of American Democratic Thought," 2nd ed. Ronald Press, New York.

Gallup, George (1980). The Gallup Poll: Attitudes Toward the Moral Majority Explored in Survey, Dec. 14. Field Newspaper Syndicate.

Gantz, Walter and Kowalewski, Paul (1979). Religious Broadcasting as an Alternative to TV: An Initial Assessment of Potential Utilization of the Christian Broadcasting Network Alternative. Unpublished Paper Presented to the Theory and Methodology Division, Association for Education in Journalism Convention, Houston, 1979.

Gasper, Louis (1963). "The Fundamentalist Movement." Mouton, The Hague.

Gelarden, R. Joseph (1980). Moral Majority seeks to infiltrate GOP. *Indianapolis Star,* Mar. 23, 8.

Gibbs, David R., Mueller, Samuel A., and Wood, James R. (1973). Doctrinal orthodoxy, salience, and the consequential dimension. *J. Sci. Study Religion* **12,** March, pp. 33–52.

Gilder, George (1981). "Wealth and Poverty." Basic Books, New York.

Glen, Maxwell (1979). The Electronic Ministers Listen to the Gospel According to the Candidates. *Nat. J.* **11,** 2142–2145.

The Globe and Mail. April 30, 1980. Repentance Rally Draws 175,000 in Washington, p. 18.

Goodman, Leo A. (1972). A modified multiple regression approach to the analysis of dichotomous variables." *Amer. Soc. Rev.* **37,** 28–46.

Goodman, Leo A. (1974). The analysis of qualitative variables when some of the variables are unobservable: Part I. A modified latent structure approach. *Amer. J. Soc.* **79,** 1179–1259.

Gouldner, Alvin (1979). The New Class Project I & II. *Theory and Society,* Fall.

Graham, Billy (1980). An agenda for the 1980's. *Christianity Today,* Jan. 4, pp. 23–27.

Gusfield, Joseph R. (1963). "Symbolic Crusade: Status Politics and the American Temperence Movement." University of Illinois Press, Urbana, Illinois.

Guth, James L. (1980). The New Christian Right: An Interpretive Essay. Paper presented at the National Endowment for the Humanities Summer Seminar on Southern Culture in Continuity and Change. University of North Carolina, Chapel Hill.

Bibliography **243**

Guth, James L. (1981a). The Politics of the Evangelical Right. Paper presented at the Annual Meetings of the American Political Science Association, New York.

Guth, James L. (1981b). The Southern Baptist Clergy: Vanguard of the Evangelical Right? Paper presented at the Annual Meetings of the Southern Political Association, Memphis.

Guttmann, Allen (1967). "The Conservative Tradition in America." Oxford, New York.

Hadden, Jeffrey K. (1969). "The Gathering Storm in the Churches." Anchor, Garden City, New York.

Hadden, Jeffrey K. and Swann, Charles E. (1981). "Prime Time Preachers: The Rising Power of Televangelism." Addison-Wesley, Reading, Massachusetts.

Hagan, John, Silva, Edward T., and Simpson, John H. (1977). Conflict and consensus in the designation of deviance. *Social Forces* **56,** 320–340.

Harnack, W. (1981). Editorial. *The Humanist* **41,** Mar./Apr.

Harris, Louis (1980). Pollster gives conservative groups credit for Reagan win. *Greenville (S.C.) News,* Nov. 15, 3A.

Harrison, Paul (1959). "Authority and Power in the Free Church Tradition." Princeton University Press, Princeton, N.J.

Hart, Jeffrey (1966). "The American Dissent: A Decade of American Conservatism." Doubleday, Garden City, New York.

Hartz, Louis (1955). "The Liberal Tradition in America." Harcourt, Brace, and World, New York.

Henderson, Robert T. (1980). Ministering to the Poor: Our Embarrassment of Riches. *Christianity Today* **24,** Aug. 8, 16–18.

Hendricks, John Stephen (1977). Religious and Political Fundamentalism. Unpublished doctoral dissertation, University of Michigan.

Henry, Carl F. (1980). Evangelicals: out of the closet but going nowhere?" *Christianity Today* **24,** Jan. 4, 16–22.

Herberg, Will (1960). "Protestant-Catholic-Jew," Rev. Ed. Doubleday, Garden City, New York.

Herbers, John *et al.* (1980). Series of articles on evangelical Christians in politics. *New York Times,* Aug., pp. 17–20.

Hodgson, Richard S. (1976). "Direct Mail in the Political Process." Direct Mail/Marketing Association, Inc., New York.

Hofstadter, Richard (1955). "The Age of Reform." Random House, New York.

Hofstadter, Richard (1963). The pseudo-conservative revolt. *In* "The Radical Right: The New American Right Expanded and Updated," (Daniel Bell, ed.), pp. 76–95. Doubleday, Garden City, New York.

Hofstadter, Richard (1962). "Anti-Intellectualism in American Life." Random House, New York.

Hoge, Dean R. (1976). "Division in the Protestant House." Westminster Press, Philadelphia, Pennsylvania.

Hoge, Dean R. (1979). A test of theories of denominational growth and decline." *In* "Understanding Church Growth and Decline, 1950–1978" (Dean Hoge and James Roozen, eds.), pp. 179–197. Pilgrim Press, New York.

Hunter, James Davison (1980). The new class and the young evangelicals. *Rev. Religious Res.* **22,** Dec. pp. 155–169.

Hunter, James Davidson (1981). The new religions: demodernization and the protest against modernity. *In* "The Social Impact of New Religious Movements" (Bryan Wilson, ed.). Rose of Sharon Press, New York.

Hunter, James Davidson (1983). "American Evangelicalism: Conservative Religion and the Quandary of Modernity." Rutgers University Press, New Brunswick.

Hunter, Marjorie (1980a). Evangelist calls for restoration of prayer. *New York Times,* July 31, p. A14.

Hunter, Marjorie (1980b). The churches are at odds over yet another school prayer bill. *New York Times,* Aug. 3, Section 4, p. 20.

Huntington, Deborah and Kaplan, Ruth (1980). Whose Gold is Behind the Altar? Corporate Ties to Evangelicals. California Student Christian Movement, Berkeley, California.

Huntington, Samuel P. (1957). Conservatism as an ideology. *Amer. Political Sci. Rev.* **51,** 454–473.

Ingram, Larry C. (1981). Role ambiguity among Southern Baptist pastors. *J. Sci. Study Religion* **20,** 119–129.

Jeffries, Vincent, and Tygart, Clarence E. (1974). The influence of theology, denomination, and values upon the positions of clergy on social issues. *J. Sci. Study Religion* **13,** 309–324.

Jenkins, John (1981). Toward the anti-humanist new Christian nation. *The Humanist* **41,** July/Aug.

Johnson, Stephen D. and Tamney, Joseph B. (1982). The Christian right and the 1980 presidential election. *J. Sci. Study of Religion* **21,** June.

Jorstad, Erling (1981). "The Politics of Moralism." Augsburg, Minneapolis, Minnesota.

Kelley, Dean M. (1972). "Why Conservative Churches are Growing." Harper and Row, New York.

Kennedy, D. James (1980). Letter of invitation to the August, 1980 Dallas National Affairs Briefing, July.

Kirk, Russell (1953). "The Conservative Mind." Henry Regnery. Chicago, Illinois. Reprinted 1978.

Koller, Norman B. and Retzer, Joseph D. (1980). The sound of silence revisited. *Soc. Anal.* **41,** Summer, pp. 155–161.

Kotz, Nick (1978). King Midas of the new right. *The Atlantic* **242**(5), 52–61.

Ladd, Everett C., Jr. (1979). New divisions in U.S. politics. *Fortune* **99,** March 26, pp. 88–92+.

LaHaye, Tim (1980). "The Battle for the Mind." Fleming H. Revell, Old Tappan, New Jersey.

Lamont, Corliss (1981). Answering the moral majority. *The Humanist* **41,** July/Aug.

Lasch, Christopher (1975). The family and history. *The New York Review of Books,* Nov. 13.

Lemann, Nicholas (1981). The evolution of the conservative mind. *The Washington Monthly* **13**(3), 34–41.

Lindsey, Hal (1970). "The Late Great Planet Earth." Zondervan, Grand Rapids, Michigan.

Lindsey, Robert (1979). Fundamentalist political unity in politics sought. *New York Times,* Sept. 20, A13.

Lipset, Seymour M. and Raab, Earl (1978). "The Politics of Unreason." University of Chicago Press, Chicago, Illinois.

Lipset, Seymour M. and Raab, Earl (1981). The election and the evangelicals. *Commentary* **71,** March, 25–32.

Lora, Ronald (1971). "Conservative Minds in America." Rand McNally, Chicago, Illinois.

Lorentzen, Louise J. (1980). Evangelical life style concerns expressed in political action. *Soc. Anal.* **41,** 144–154.

Luckmann, Thomas (1967). "The Invisible Religion." New York: Random House, New York.

McCarthy, John D. and Zald, Mayer N. (1973). "The Trend of Social Movements in America: Professionalization and Resource Mobilization." General Learning Press, Morristown, New Jersey.

McCarthy, John D. and Zald, Mayer N. (1977). Resource mobilization and social movements: a partial theory. *Amer. J. Soc.* **82,** May, pp. 1212–1239.

McFadden, Joe (1980). Moral majority forces help fell representative Buchanan. *Washington Post,* Sept. 4, A4.

McGovern, George (1981). Interviews. *SNEA Impact* **13,** No. 4, Feb., 2.

McIntyre, Thomas J. and Obert, John C. (1979). "The Fear Brokers." Pilgrim Press, New York.

McLoughlin, William G. (1978). "Revivals, Awakenings, and Reform." University of Chicago Press, Chicago, Illinois.

McPherson, William (ed.) (1973). "Ideology and Change: Radicalism and Fundamentalism in America." National Press Books, Palo Alto, California.

Maeroff, Gene I. (1981). Protestant day schools open at rate of 3 a day. *New York Times,* Feb. 10, p. 13.

Mann, Arthur (1979). "The One and the Many: Reflections on the American Identity." University of Chicago Press, Chicago, Illinois.

Marsden, George M. (1980). "Fundamentalism and American Culture: The Shaping of Twentieth Century Evangelicalism, 1870–1925." Oxford, New York.

Martin, William (1981). God's angry man. *Texas Monthly,* April, pp. 152–156, 223–233.

Martin, William (1981). The birth of a media myth. *Atlantic* **247,** June, pp. 7–16.

Marty, Martin E. (1976). "A Nation of Behavers." University of Chicago Press, Chicago, Illinois.

Marty, Martin E. (1980). Sizing up the armies of the Moral Majority. *Miami Herald,* Dec. 21.

Marx, Leo (1964). "The Machine in the Garden." Oxford, New York.

Mathews, Donald G. (1969). The Second Great Awakening as an organizing process, 1780–1830. *Amer. Quart.* **21,** 23–43.

Maust, John (1978). The growing pains of overexposure. *United Evangelical Action,* Summer, pp. 8–10.

Maust, John (1979). Preaching the gospel and the Bill of Rights. *Christianity Today* **23,** Apr. 6, pp. 44–45.

May, A. L. (1980). Fundamentalists' effects on politics questioned. *(Raleigh, N.C.) News and Observer* Aug. 31, pp. 8–VI.

Mayer, Allan J. (1980). A tide of born-again politics. *Newsweek* Sept. 15, pp. 28–36.

Mead, Frank S. (1980). "Handbook of Denominations in the United States." Abingdon, Nashville, Tennessee.

Mencken, H. L. (1962). "A Mencken Chrestomathy." Knopf, New York.

Mencken, H. L. (1963). "Heathen Days: 1890–1936." Knopf, New York.

Menendez, Albert (1977). "Religion at the Polls." Westminster, Philadelphia, Pennsylvania.

Meyer, Frank (1970). The recrudescent American conservatism. *In* "Did You Ever See a Dream Walking?" (William F. Buckley, Jr., ed.), pp. 75–92. Bobbs-Merrill, Indianapolis, Indiana.

Meyer, John W. (1970). The charter: conditions of diffuse socialization in schools. *In* "Social Processes and Social Structures" (W. Richard Scott, ed). Holt, Rinehart and Winston, New York.

Meyers, Marvin (1957). "The Jacksonian Persuasion." Random House, New York.

Michalsky, Walt (1981). The masquerade of fundamentalism. *The Humanist* **41,** July/Aug., pp. 15–51.

Milavsky, J. Ronald (1981). Survey on Sex, Religion, and Television: Preliminary Results. Slide Presentation, NBC Department of Social and News Research, June.

Miles, Michael W. (1980). "The Odyssey of the American Right." Oxford University Press, New York.

Miller, Judith (1981). Goldwater vows to fight tactics of "new right." *New York Times,* Sept. 16, p. 1.

Mintz, Morton (1980). Evangelical groups plan November 2 political appeal at churches. *Washington Post* Oct. 5, p. A6.

Moberg, David (1972). "The Great Reversal: Evangelicals Versus Social Concern." Lippincott, Philadelphia, Pennsylvania.

Morgan, Edward (1980). What They're Saying About the New Right . . . . *NEA Advocate* **14,** Jan./Feb., p. 7.

Morgan, Richard (1968). "The Politics of Religious Conflict." Pegasus, New York.

Moser, Ted (1980). If Jesus were a congressman. *Christian Century* **97,** Apr. 16, pp. 444–446.

Myers, Lisa (1980a). Evangelicals flexing new found muscle. *Washington Star,* June 30.

Myers, Lisa (1980b). Evangelicals making plans for coming battles at polls. *Washington Star,* July 1.

Nash, George H. (1979). "The Conservative Intellectual Movement in America Since 1945." Basic Books, New York.

The New York Times. (1980). 200,000 March and Pray at Rally in Capital, Apr. 30, p. A1.

The New York Times. (1980). Dispute on Religion Raised by Campaign," Nov. 9, p. 31.

Newman, William M., and Wright, Stuart A. (1980). The effects of sermons among lay catholics. *Rev. Religious Res.* **22,** 54–59.

Nickerson, Colin (1981). Great reawakening in New England—fundamentalist religion grows. *Boston Sunday Globe,* July 26, p. 2.

Nietzsche, Friedrich (1954). "The Philosophy of Nietzsche." The Modern Library (Random House), New York.

Nisbet, Robert (1980). "History of the Idea of Progress." Basic Books, New York.

North, Gary (1981). Christian Reconstruction. Pamphlet published by the Institute for Christian Economics.

Nygren, Malcolm (1969). The church and political action. *Christianity Today* **13,** Mar. 14, pp. 9–12.

Oakeshott, Michael (1962). "Rationalism in Politics." Methuen, London.

Oberschall, Anthony (1973). "Social Conflict and Social Movements." Prentice-Hall, Englewood Cliffs, N.J.

Page, Ann L. and Clelland, Donald A. (1978). The Kanawha county textbook controversy: a study of the politics of lifestyle concern. *Social Forces* **57,** 265–281.

Park, J. C. (1980). The new right network. *Rept. 17th Annu. Conf. on Human Civil Rights in Education.* National Education Association, Washington, D.C.

Peek, Mary (1980). What every teacher should know about the new right. Pamphlet distributed by the *NEA Task Force on Academic Freedom.*

Penfield, H. Irvin and Davis, Natalie M. (1981). The Moral Majority and Politics: Religious Attitudes as Correlates of Voting Behavior. Paper presented at the annual meetings of the Mid-West Political Science Association, Cincinnati.

Perry, James M. (1981). Moral majority finds its own units may need guidance. *Wall Street J.,* Feb. 12, p. 1.

Peterson, Bill and Sussman, Barry (1981). Moral majority is growing in recognition, but it remains unknown to half the public. *Washington Post,* June 13, p. A2.

Pew, J. Howard (1966). Should the church "meddle" in civil affairs? *Readers Dig.* **88,** May, p. 53.

Phillips, Kevin (1969). "The Emerging Republican Majority." Arlington House, New Rochelle, New York.

Pierard, Richard V. (1981). An innocent in babylon. *Christian Century* **98,** Feb. 25, pp. 190–191.

Plowman, Edward (1979). Is morality all right? *Christianity Today* **23,** Nov. 2, pp. 76–85.

Poggi, Gianfranco (1972). "Images of Society." Stanford University Press, Palo Alto, California.

Quebedeaux, Richard (1974). "The Young Evangelicals." Harper & Row, New York.

Quebedeaux, Richard (1978). "The Worldly Evangelicals." Harper and Row, New York.

Quinley, Harold (1974). "The Prophetic Clergy." Wiley, New York.

Raines, Howell (1980). Reagan backs evangelicals in their political activities. *New York Times,* Aug. 23, p. 8.

Range, Peter Ross (1981a). Thunder from the right. *New York Times Magazine,* Feb. 8, pp. 23–54+.

Range, Peter Ross (1981b). Inside the new right war machine. *Playboy* **28,** Aug., pp. 99–102, 116, 216–219.

Ravenel, Ruth (1980). The thee decade: how the press tripped over one of 1980's biggest stories. *Washington Journalism Rev.,* Dec.

Reuther, Rosemary (1980). Politics and the family: recapturing a lost issue. *Christianity and Crisis,* Sept. 29.

Ribuffo, Leo (1980). Liberals and that old-time religion. *The Nation,* Nov., pp. 570–573.

Ringer, Benjamin B. and Glock, Charles Y. (1954/1955). The political role of the church as defined by its parishioners. *Public Opinion Quart.* **18,** Winter, pp. 337–347.

Rossiter, Clinton (1962). "Conservatism in America." Random House, New York.

Rothenberg, Stuart (1981). "Campaign Regulation and Public Policy: PACs, Ideology, and the FEC." Free Congress and Education Foundation, Inc., Washington, D.C.

Rothmyer, Karen (1981). Citizen Scaife. *Columbia Journalism Rev.* **20** (2), 41–50.

Rusher, William A. (1975). "The Making of a New Majority Party." Sheed and Ward, New York.

Sabato, Larry J. (1981). "The Rise of Political Consultants: New Ways of Winning Elections." Basic Books, New York.

Sandeen, Ernest R. (1970). "The Roots of Fundamentalism: British and American Millenarianism 1800–1930." University of Chicago Press, Chicago, Illinois.

Sapp, William D. (1975). Factors in the Involvement of Southern Baptist Pastors in Governmental Decision Making. Unpublished doctoral dissertation, Southern Baptist Theological Seminary.

Sawyer, Kathy (1980). Linking politics and religion. *Washington Post,* Aug. 24, p. H1.

Sawyer, Kathy and Kaiser, Robert (1980). Evangelicals flock to GOP standards. *Washington Post,* July 16, p. B1.

Scanzoni, John (1980). Resurgent fundamentalism: marching backward into the '80's? *Christian Century,* Sept. 10–17, 847–849.

Schuller, David S., Strommen, Merton P., and Brekke, Milo L. (1980). "Ministry in America." Harper & Row, New York.

Seattle Post-Intelligencer. (1980). Moral Majority: A New Political Force Here, Aug. 31, p. A12.

Selvin, Hanan, and Hagstrom, Warren D. (1960). Determinants of support for civil liberties. *Brit. J. Soc.* **11,** 51–73.

Shapiro, Margaret (1981). A moral majority split. *Washington Post,* June 26, p. A1.

Shriver, Peggy L. (1981). "The Bible Vote: Religion and the New Right." Pilgrim Press, New York.

Shupe, Anson and Stacey, William (1982). "Born Again Politics and the Moral Majority: What Social Surveys Really Show." The Edwin Mellen Press, New York.

Shurden, Walter B. (1981). The Christian Life Commission. *Quart. Rev.* **42,** Oct.–Nov.–Dec., 63–75.

Siegel, Paul S. (1971). Prestige in the American Occupational Structure. Unpublished doctoral dissertation, Department of Sociology, University of Chicago, Chicago, Illinois.

Silverman, Steve (1981). The Religious Majority. Unpublished paper, Department of Politics, Princeton University, Princeton, NJ.

Simpson, John H. and Hagan, John (1981). Conventional religiosity, attitudes toward conflict, crime, and income stratification in the United States. *Rev. Religious Res.,* Dec. 23, 167–179.

Skerry, Peter (1980). Christian schools versus the I.R.S. *The Public Interest* **61,** Fall, pp. 18–41.

Smith, Timothy L. (1957). "Revivalism and Social Reform." Abingdon, New York.

Snow, David A., Zurcher, Louis A., Jr., and Ekland-Olson, Sheldon (1980). Social networks and social movements: a microstructural approach to differential recruitment. *Amer. Soc. Rev.* **45,** Oct., pp. 787–801.

Solod, Lisa (1981/82). The Nutshell interview: Jerry Falwell. *Nutshell,* pp. 34–41.

Sorauf, Frank (1976). "The Wall of Separation." Princeton University Press, Princeton, NJ.

Sorauf, Frank (1980). Political parties and political action committees: two life cycles. *Arizona Law Rev.* **22,** 445–463.

Stacey, William A. and Shupe, Anson D., Jr. (1982). Civil Religion, The Electronic Church, and Support for the Moral Majority: Demographic and Social Correlates. Monogr. No. 20, Center for Social Research Monograph Series, The University of Texas at Arlington, Arlington, Texas.

Stark, Rodney, Foster, Bruce, Glock, Charles Y., and Quinley, Harold C. (1971). "Wayward Shepherds: Prejudice and the Protestant Clergy." Harper & Row, New York.

Stein, Ben (1981). Norman Lear vs. the Moral Majority: the war to clean up TV. *Saturday Rev.,* Feb., pp. 23–27.

Steinfels, Peter (1980). "The Neo-conservatives." Simon and Schuster, New York.

Stone, Allan, and Bagamery, Anne (1980). The electronic pulpit. *Forbes* **126,** July 7, pp. 116–118.

Streng, Frederick J. (1976). "Understanding Religious Life." Dickenson, Belmont, California.

Strober, Gerald and Tomczak, Ruth (1979). "Jerry Falwell: Aflame for God." Thomas Nelson, Nashville, Tennessee.

Swomley, John M., Jr. (1981). The decade ahead in church-state issues. *Christian Century* **98,** Feb. 25, pp. 199–203.

Tilly, Charles (1978). "From Mobilization to Revolution." Addison-Wesley, Reading, Massachusetts.

de Tocqueville, Alexis (1969). "Democracy in America." Translated by George Lawrence. Anchor, Garden City, New York.

Tonsor, Stephen J. (1977). The second spring of American conservatism. *National Rev.* **29,** 1103–1107.

Towns, Elmer (1972). "America's Fastest Growing Churches." Impact Books, Nashville, Tennessee.

Towns, Elmer, Vaughan, John N., and Seifert, David J. (1981). "The Complete Book of Church Growth." Tyndale House, Wheaton, Illinois.

Turner, Wallace (1980). Group of evangelical protestants takes over the G.O.P. in Alaska. *New York Times,* June 6.

Twain, Mark (1946). *"The Portable Mark Twain."* Viking Press, New York.

Tygart, Clarence E. (1977). The role of theology among other "belief" variables for clergy civil rights activism. *Rev. Religious Res.* **18,** Spring, pp. 271–278.

U.S. News and World Report (1979). Preachers in politics, Sept. 24, pp. 37–41.

United Press International (1980). Evangelical group disagrees with 276 in congress. *New York Times,* Nov. 2, p. 34.

Valentine, Foy (1970). How to preach on political issues. *In* "Politics: A Guidebook for Christians." (James D. Dunn, ed.), pp. 70–85. The General Life Commission of the Baptist General Convention of Texas, Dallas, Texas.

Vecsey, George (1980). Militant television preachers try to weld fundamentalist Christians' political power. *New York Times,* Jan. 21, p. A21.

Viereck, Peter (1962). *"Conservatism Revisited."* Free Press, New York.

Viguerie, Richard A. (1980). "The New Right: We're Ready to Lead." The Viguerie Company, Falls Church, Virginia.

Wallace, Anthony F. C. (1956). Revitalization movements. *Amer. Anthropol.* **58,** 264–81.

Wallis, Jim, and Michaelson, Wes (1976). The plan to save America. *Sojourners* **5**, April, pp. 4–12.

Wallis, Roy and Bland, Richard (1979). Purity in danger: a survey of participants in a moral-crusade rally. *Brit. J. Soc.* **30**, June, p. 2.

Washington Department Township, New Jersey *News Report.* 1980. November 26.

Weber, Max (1905). "The Protestant Ethic and the Spirit of Capitalism." Scribners, New York. Reprinted 1958.

Weinraub, Bernard (1980). Independent panels press campaign to aid Reagan. *New York Times,* Oct. 5, p. 11.

Weinraub, Bernard (1981). Foundations support conservatism by financing scholars and groups. *New York Times,* Jan. 20, p. 17.

Wells, David F., and Woodbridge, John D. (eds.) (1977). "The Evangelicals." Abingdon, Nashville, Tennessee.

Whalen, Richard J. (1974). "Taking Sides." Houghton-Mifflin, Boston.

Wicker, Tom (1980). The elections: why the system has failed. *New York Review of Books* **27**(13), p. 11–15.

Wills, Garry (1976). What religious revival? *Psych. Today,* April, 74 ff.

Wills, Garry (1979). "Confessions of a Conservative." Penguin, New York.

Wilson, James Q. (1973). "Political Organizations." New York, Basic Books, New York.

Wilson, James Q. (1980). Reagan and the Republican revival. *Commentary* **70,** 25–32.

Wimberley, Ronald C. (1976). Testing the civil religion hypothesis. *Soc. Anal.* **37,** 341–52.

Wimberley, Ronald C. (1978). Dimensions of commitment: generalizing from religion to politics. *J. Sci. Study of Religion* **17,** Sept., 225–240.

Wimberley, Ronald C. (1979). Continuity in the measurement of civil religion. *Soc. Anal.* **49,** Spring, 59–62.

Wimberley, Ronald C., Clelland, Donald A., Hood, Thomas C., and Lipsey, C. M. (1976). The civil religious dimension: is it there?" *Social Forces* **54,** June, pp. 890–900.

Winter, J. Alan (1973). Political activism among the clergy: sources of a deviant role. *Rev. of Religious Res.* **14,** Spring, pp. 178–186.

Wolfe, Tom (1976). The me decade and the third great awakening. *New West,* Aug. 30, pp. 27–48.

Yankelovich, Daniel (1981). "New Rules in American Life." Random House, New York.

Yinger, J. Milton and Cutler, Stephen J. (1981). The Moral Majority Viewed Sociologically. Unpublished paper, Department of Sociology and Anthropology, Oberlin College.

Zwier, Robert (1981). The Moral Majority in the 1980 Elections: The Cases of Iowa and South Dakota. Paper presented at the annual meetings of the American Political Science Association, New York.

INDEX